IMAGES
of America

EARLY NATIONAL CITY

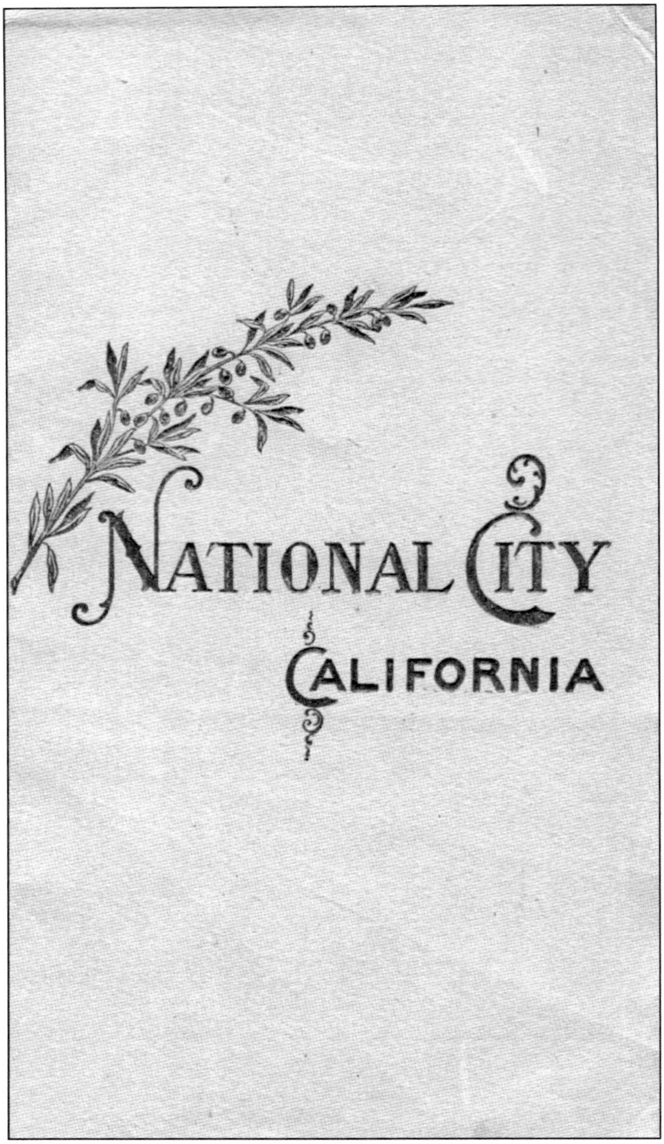

CHAMBER OF COMMERCE BROCHURE, C. 1906. When the city incorporated on September 10, 1887, the olive branch was placed on the city seal. This symbol of peace was a natural choice with which to represent National City, as so many acres were planted in olive trees. National City father Frank Kimball owned the National City Olive Oil Works, which produced oil that was shipped all over the country.

ON THE COVER: The first free kindergarten in San Diego County was begun in National City in April 1889, under the sponsorship of Sarah Kimball. The local newspaper reported, "This week is a great success. There are at present 17 little ones in daily attendance, the smallest being two and a half years old and the oldest seven." (Courtesy of the National City Public Library's Kile Morgan Local History Room.)

IMAGES
of America

EARLY NATIONAL CITY

Marilyn Carnes and Matthew Nye

ARCADIA
PUBLISHING

ISBN 978-0-7385-5910-0

Published by Arcadia Publishing
Charleston SC, Chicago IL, Portsmouth NH, San Francisco CA

Printed in the United States of America

Library of Congress Catalog Card Number: 2008926275

For all general information contact Arcadia Publishing at:
Telephone 843-853-2070
Fax 843-853-0044
E-mail sales@arcadiapublishing.com
For customer service and orders:
Toll-Free 1-888-313-2665

Visit us on the Internet at www.arcadiapublishing.com

This book is dedicated to Francis Augustus Kimball (1832–1913), who through great generosity and vision, adversity, and humor dreamed of a city rising from the barren lands of the National Ranch and gave everything he had to make it a reality.

Contents

ACKNOWLEDGMENTS

It is the snapshots from family albums and treasured professional photographs commemorating special events that bring any narrative of National City alive. Throughout the years, many folks with ties to National City have thoughtfully donated their photographic memories to the National City Public Library's Kile Morgan Local History Room. Except where otherwise credited, the images in this book were drawn from their significant collection. Anne Campbell, city librarian at the conception of this endeavor, believed in the project of making the history of National City more accessible to the public and lent her valuable support in this effort. Minh Duong, the library's current city librarian, was an enthusiastic supporter of this project. Mary Allely and Philip Price, both librarians in the National City Public Library local history room, gave their help and encouragement. The Sweetwater Authority graciously gave their permission to use several photographs, from their collection, of the Sweetwater Dam shown on pages 100 and 101. We thank David Rumsey Map Collection (www.davidrumsey.com) for permission to use their image "Bird's Eye View of National City," reproduced on pages 12 and 13. We deeply appreciate Thomas J. Tenoever's expertise on the computer, which was graciously shared with us, and Thomas Carnes's many hours of tedious editing. A project such as this cannot be accomplished without the support and encouragement of family and friends—and to each of these dear people, we say a big thank-you.

INTRODUCTION

The story of National City is closely tied to that of Francis "Frank" Augustus Kimball, a small man (5 feet, 3 inches) with a large heart and a never-ending abundance of energy with which to promote his city. While Frank, Warren, and Levi Kimball purchased the National Ranch together, Frank led in all endeavors and so deserves the largest share of credit for the city's success, for he paid the biggest personal price.

The Kimballs of Hopkinton, Contoocook Village, New Hampshire, were a close-knit family of five brothers and two sisters. The boys worked with their father, Asa, on the family farm as well as in the construction trade. In 1861, Frank and his older brothers, Warren and Levi, sailed to California, where they became active in the construction trade in Oakland, eventually owning their own business. By 1868, the brothers had decided to invest in acreage in Southern California, and the National Ranch, below San Diego, was chosen as the ideal spot. In June 1868, Frank wrote in his diary that he had agreed to buy 26,632 acres from Francois Pioche for $30,000, one-third in cash, with the balance in three annual payments at eight percent per annum.

The Kimball brothers purchased a former Mexican land grant known as Rancho de la Nacion. This name, anglicized to National Ranch as California became a state, denoted what are now National City, Chula Vista, and Bonita. In the early years, National City referred to the more densely populated area bounded roughly by the bay to the west and Highland Avenue to the east, and from north to south by Division Street to Thirtieth Street. What was referred to as the National Ranch, or more simply "the Ranch," lay east and south of this area and contained larger tracts of land.

Frank was representative of the many New Englanders who migrated to National City in response to his persistent entreaties. He was a hard worker, doing much physical labor, but he also enjoyed literary and cultural pursuits; Frank was well read and enjoyed music. In his diary of February 1, 1874, he notes, "Herding sheep in town plat all day. Singing in the evening." From his diaries, it seems that he had a weekly evening sing at his home, with Elijah Valentine on the organ. Kimball faithfully kept a diary for over 50 years; it is through these invaluable records that one is able to glimpse the lives of the early residents.

As promoters of a new community, the Kimballs were quick to provide for the needs of new settlers. They established a lumberyard, a wood planing mill, and brick kilns, all to supply the demand for material with which to construct new homes and barns. When Almira Wincapaw died in February 1870, they immediately set aside land for a cemetery, and then graded a road up the hill and dug the first grave, in what we know today as La Vista. As children arrived, the need for a school was apparent. Frank Kimball sent to San Francisco for Elizabeth Starr, giving her land in payment for teaching duties, and then built the schoolhouse out of his own funds. As new churches formed, the Kimballs could be counted on to lend financial support.

The county of San Diego is most indebted to Frank Kimball for his major part in bringing the railroad to the area, establishing National City as the terminus of a transcontinental line. After over a decade of unsuccessful attempts to negotiate a deal, Kimball took out a mortgage on his home to finance once again a trip east, representing the interests of National City and San Diego. This time, he was successful, and in October 1880, the agreement was signed, with the Kimball Brothers donating 10,000 acres of land to the railroad syndicate and also one half of the unsold lots in National City, in contrast to San Diego's contribution of 4,500 acres.

Frank became a very wealthy man but was never willing to sit back and enjoy the fruits of his labors—rather he continually furthered the growth of his new city by advertising its attributes to Easterners, by serving as a state agricultural commissioner and as an elected member of the school board, and by promoting local business enterprises. These activities all were at a cost to his personal fortune. In 1888, at the height of the land boom, Frank reported a net worth of $1.4 million. Ten years later, after several of his commercial interests failed and a dishonest employee had signed his name (without his knowledge) on several bank notes that Kimball couldn't cover, Frank and Sarah were forced to sell their orchards and property and finally their house. In 1897, they moved out of their beloved home of almost 30 years into a nephew's drafty upstairs apartment over a restaurant. He begged several businessmen to repay what he had formerly loaned them but to no avail. At the age of 70, Frank was doing manual labor, anything he could get, to put food on the table. Slowly he was able to acquire a home of his own. At the end of his life, he was able to say (in his diary), "I spent the best years of my life trying to make those around me happier, and the result is unsatisfactory. I am confronted at every step by ungrateful people, but I look back and thank God I have lived. As far as I know, I have done my best." And he did.

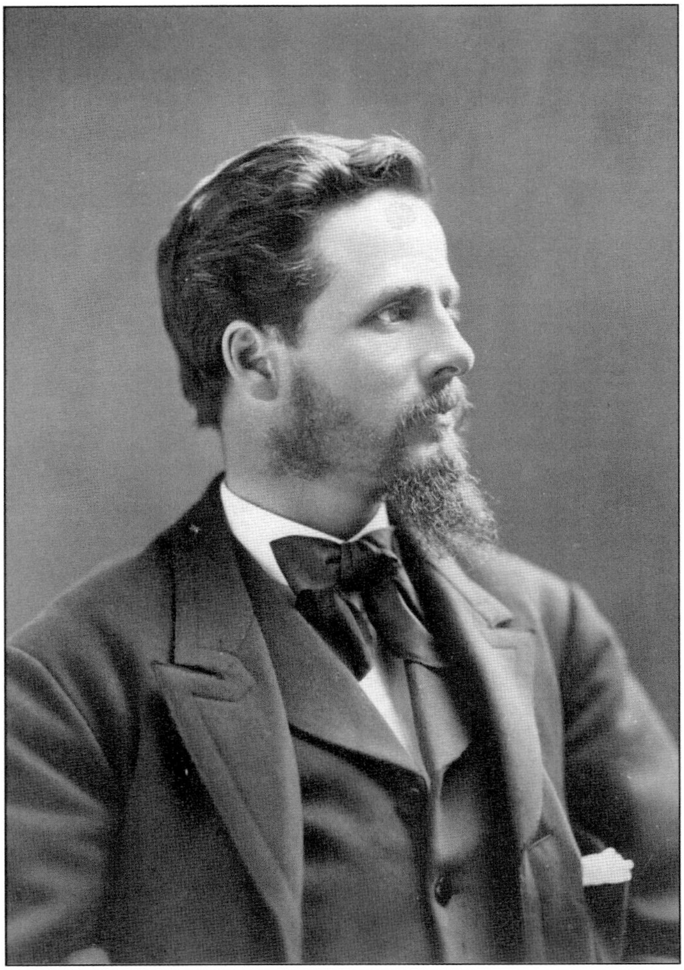

FRANCIS AUGUSTUS KIMBALL. Known to all as Frank, Kimball was born on the family farm in Hopkinton, Contoocook Village, New Hampshire, in 1832. After purchasing Rancho de la Nacion in June 1868, he spent the rest of his life promoting his city. He was a man of integrity and foresight who made great contributions in the areas of rail transportation and agriculture.

One

Maps and Vistas

Sage Scrub to City

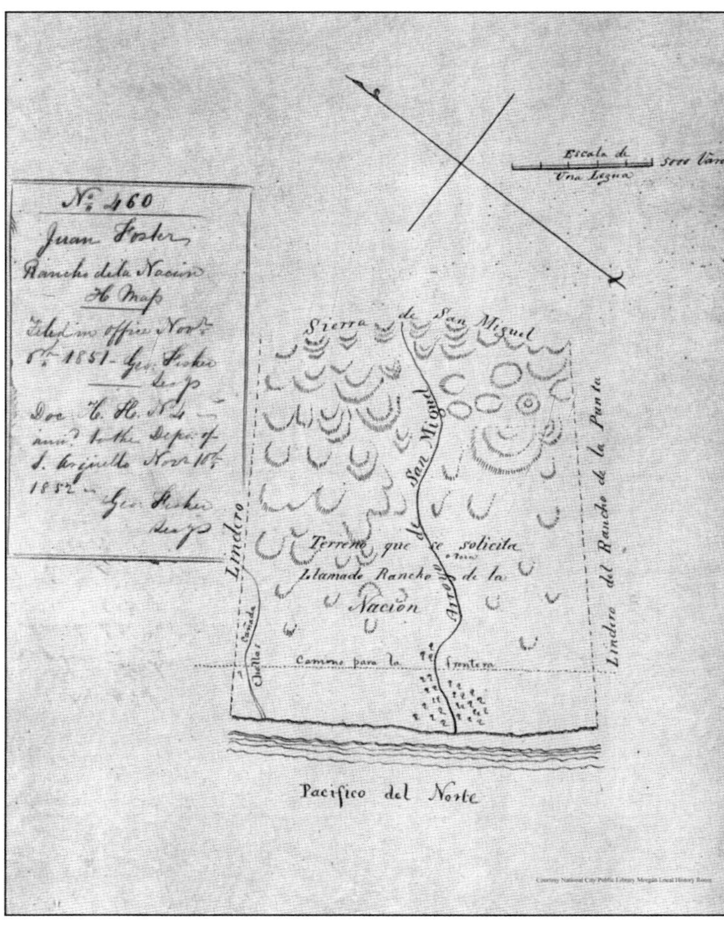

Rancho de la Nacion, 1851. John Forster, an Englishman, married Ysadora, the sister of Pio Pico, governor of Alta California. It was Pico who gave his brother-in-law the property of Rancho del Rey in 1845, with the stipulation that he build a house, occupy it for a year, and cultivate a piece of land. Forster renamed the tract Rancho de la Nacion, building an adobe in the Sweetwater River valley, near where Rohr Park is today. When California became a state, this map, showing the boundaries of Rancho de la Nacion, was presented to the U.S. government upon application for a land patent.

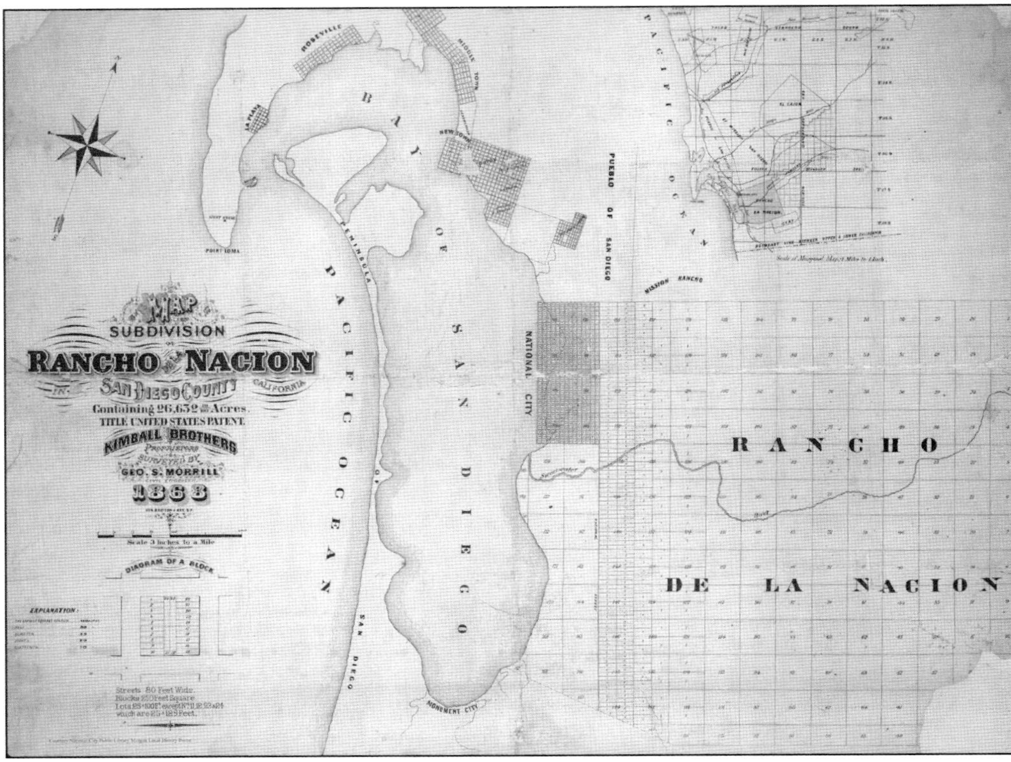

MORRILL MAP, 1868. Civil engineer George S. Morrill plotted out the 26,632 acres of Rancho de la Nacion for the Kimball brothers in 1868. The majority of the land was divided into quarter sections, while the property at the northwest corner (what was to become National City) was further plotted into blocks and lots. Streets were designed to be 80 feet wide and blocks 250 feet square. Lots were 25 feet by 100 feet.

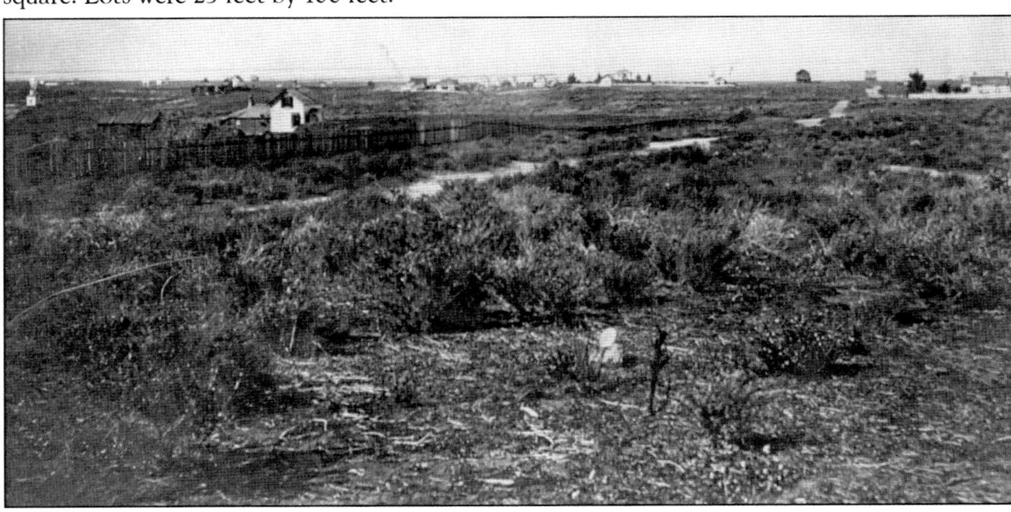

VIEW TOWARD BAY, 1874. On March 23, 1874, Frank Kimball hired photographer J. C. Parker to capture the view of the new wharf and bay on a tower he had constructed. Taken at Tenth Street and National City Boulevard, this was for a chamber of commerce publication he was working on. Kimball's two-story home can be seen, right of center, surrounded by trees. The Kimball Wharf, built in 1871, can just be viewed in the distance (on the left).

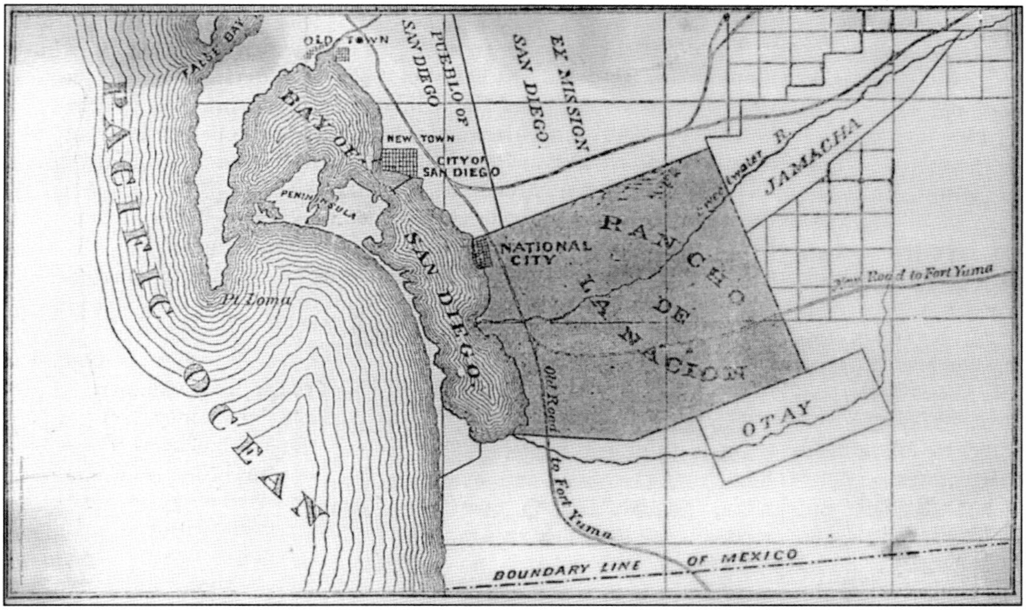

MORRILL MAP DETAIL, 1868. This detail shows Rancho de la Nacion in relationship to the surrounding area of southwestern San Diego County. Another Mexican land grant, Rancho Otay, is shown at the southeast corner of Rancho de la Nacion and is present-day Eastlake. Rancho de la Nacion covered an area of 42 square miles and originally included what is today National City, Chula Vista, Bonita, and Sunnyside.

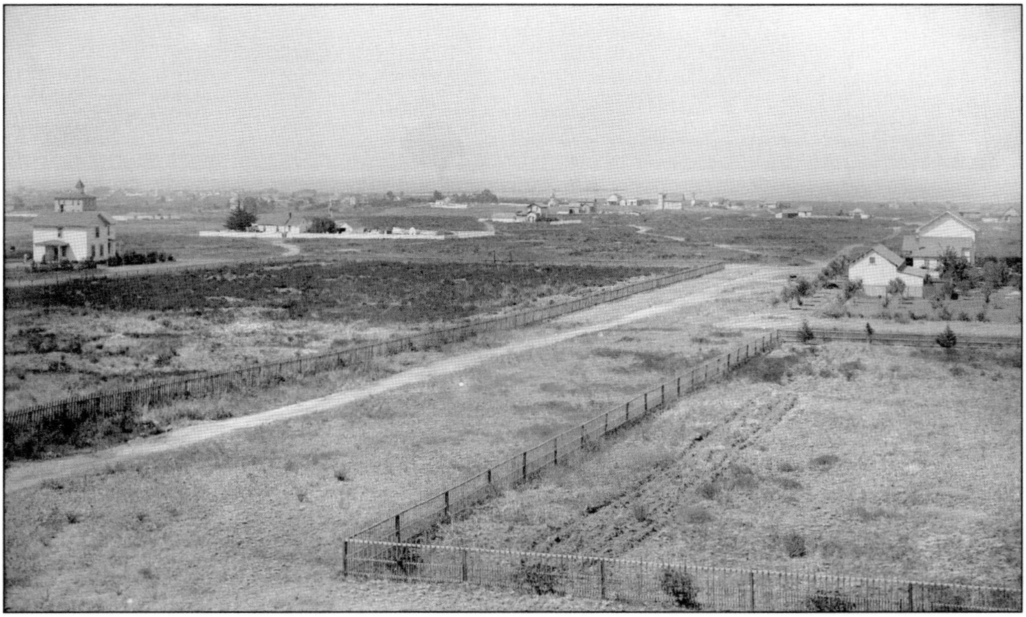

VIEW WEST, C. 1882. The photographer was standing at approximately Sixth Street and J Avenue when this image was taken. The schoolhouse, known as Academy Hall, with its distinctive cupola, stands on the left (behind the white house). Frank Kimball's home, surrounded by trees, can be seen in the center distance, as well as the Kimball Wharf at Seventeenth Street, with a ship docked alongside it.

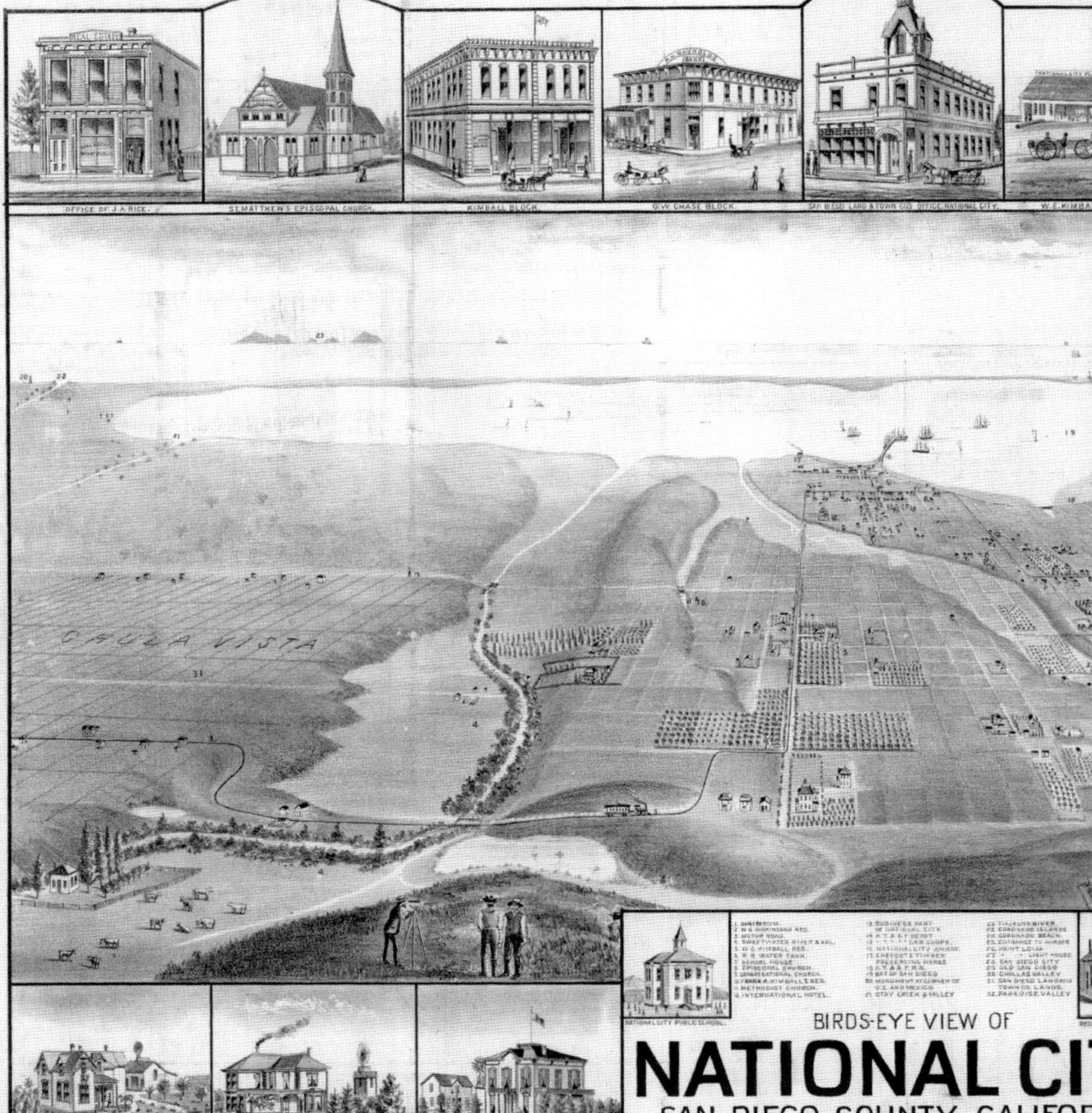

NATIONAL CITY, CAL.

NATIONAL CITY is the terminus of the Atchison, Topeka & Santa Fe transcontinental system, located on San Diego Bay, about the center of the harbor. The site is a beautiful one for a large city, the residence portion being sufficiently elevated to command a fine view of the harbor and ocean beyond. Here are located the shops of the California Southern railroad, branch of the Atchison system, which continually employ a large force of men; the railroad company's wharf, a substantial structure of creosoted piles, where a number of vessels are always discharging cargoes—at present, principally supplies for the railroad company, consisting of coal, lumber, ties, etc.; the headquarter offices of the California Southern Railroad Company, commodious depot building, coupon-ticket office, Wells, Fargo & Company's expre etc.; the headquarter office of the Sa Land and Town Company, who have 40,0 consisting of city lots and suburban 5-acr choice fruit ranches, etc.. for disposal. located the headquarter office of the Natio

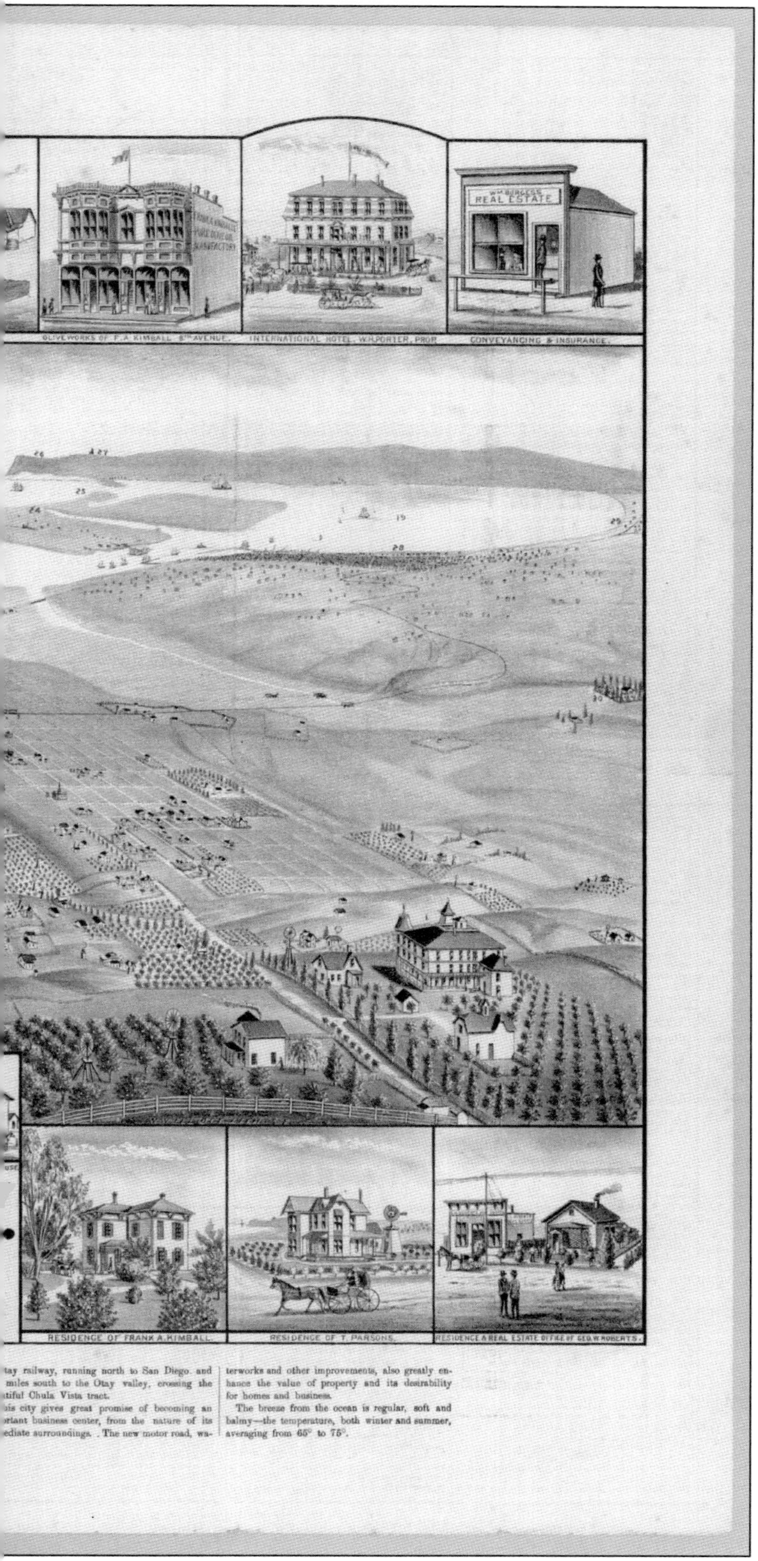

BIRD'S-EYE VIEW OF NATIONAL CITY. This rendering provided the viewer with a charming interpretation of the rural National City community. Bird's-eye views were a very popular genre in the late 19th century, and Wallace W. Elliot produced many such lithographs throughout the state. Published by the proprietors of the *National City Record*, precursor to the *Star-News*, this image served as an advertising vehicle for the city, promoting its growth. The local newspaper announced on March 4, 1887, that W. W. Elliot's lithographed copies would sell for 25¢ and that they were "selling like hotcakes." (Courtesy of the David Rumsey Map Collection.)

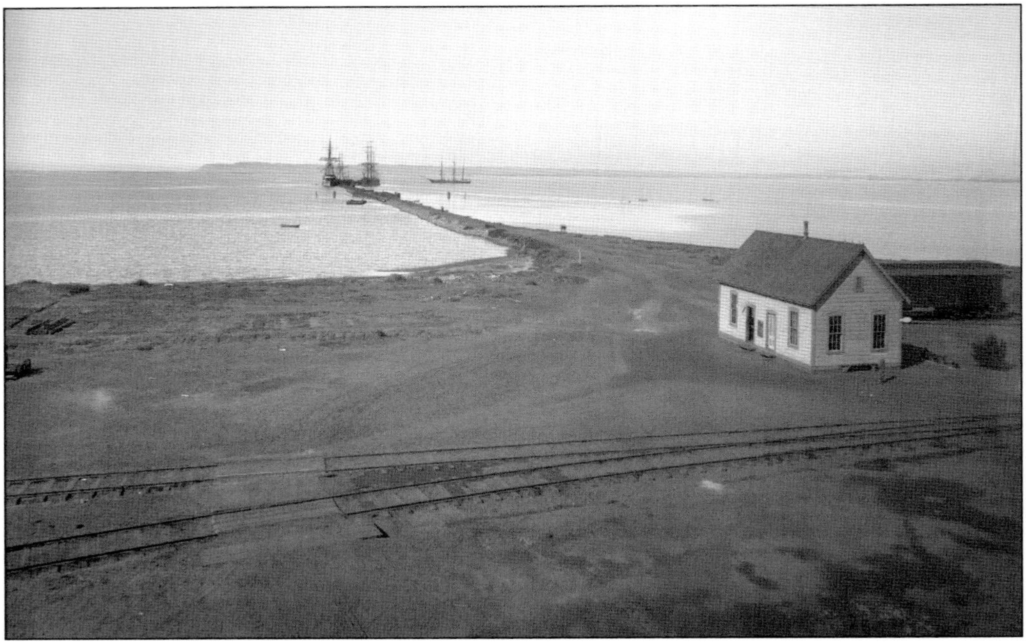

California Southern Railroad Wharf, c. 1882. Located at the foot of Seventeenth Street, this wharf replaced the original one built in 1871 by the Kimball Brothers. Civil engineer Fred Copeland, brother-in-law to the Kimballs, was hired to build both wharves. The 1871 Kimball Wharf had extended 1,800 feet into the bay and was 24 feet wide. Unfortunately it was made of untreated wood, deteriorated rapidly, and collapsed on March 26, 1877.

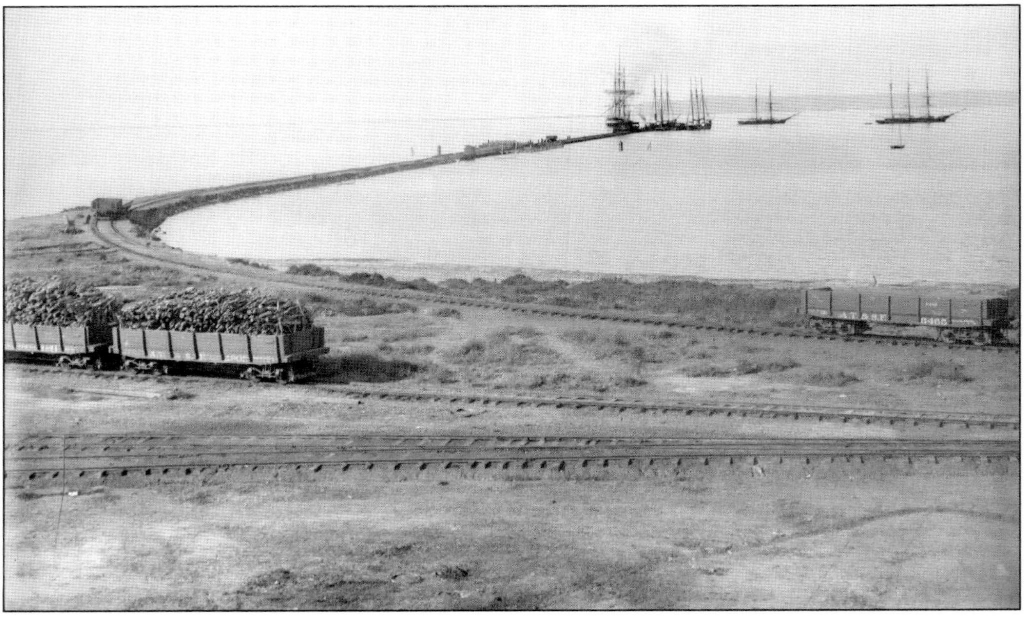

Rail Line by the Wharf. The new wharf built by the California Southern Railroad extended only 500 feet into the bay and could only unload heavier cargos at high tide or by lighter (a flat-bottom boat). On July 11, 1881, when the first locomotive was off-loaded onto the wharf, it was cause for great excitement. The engineer invited Frank Kimball to take the throttle and drive it all the way to the engine shed.

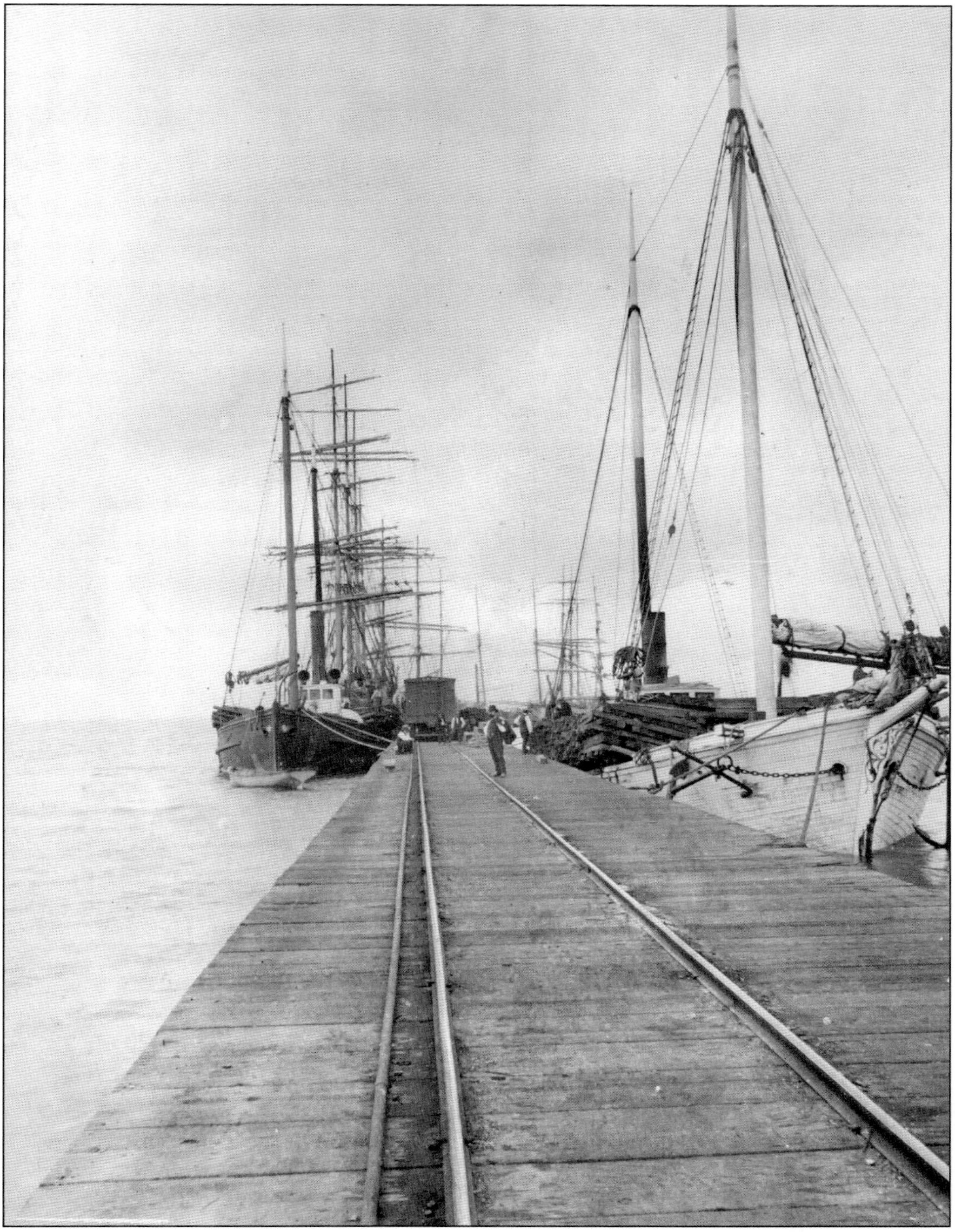

OFF-LOADING CARGO AND PASSENGERS. Ships in the bay were a frequent and noteworthy sight, bringing supplies and passengers from San Francisco. The *Orizaba* was one of the first ships to regularly provide transportation from National City to other ports along the coast. It was said that her captain, Henry J. Johnston, favored National City because of the hospitality of the Kimballs, who frequently hosted the officers in their home. During the boom period of 1886–1888, the *San Diego Sun* noted the arrival of ships, stating that eight vessels were in their city's port, bringing 1,260,128 feet of lumber. National City's own local paper, the *National City Record*, replied in print, "Yes, but 1,111,340 feet of it is for National!"

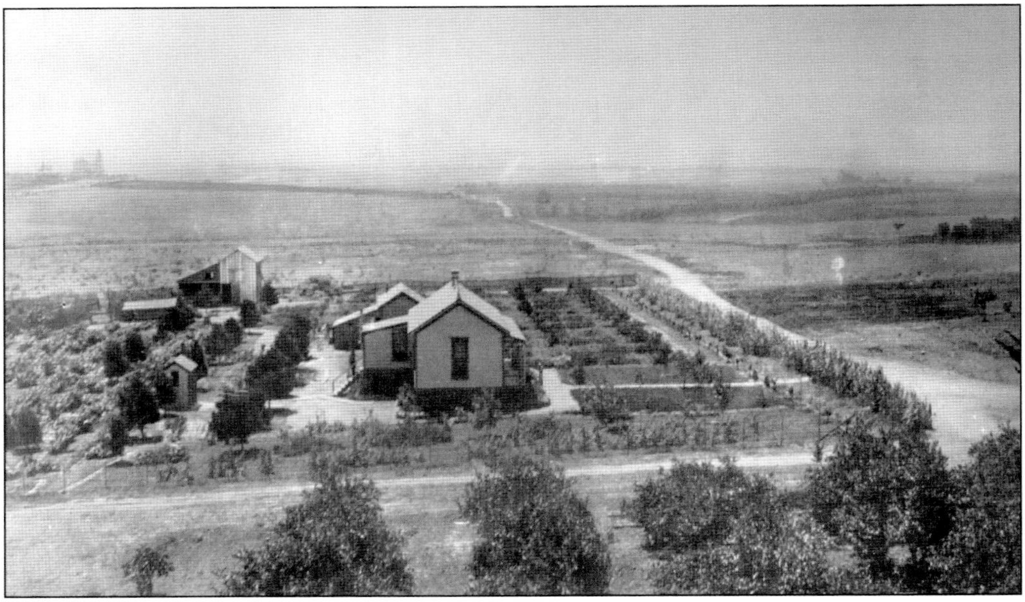

Looking South from George Kimball House, 1892. The George Kimball House at 1515 L Avenue has a hatch door that opens onto its flat roof. From this vantage, there is a wonderful view of the surrounding area, particularly so since the house stands on a hill. In this view across the fields, William Dickinson's imposing three-story home can be seen in the distance (left). The ranch house in the foreground is today at Sixteenth Street and L Avenue.

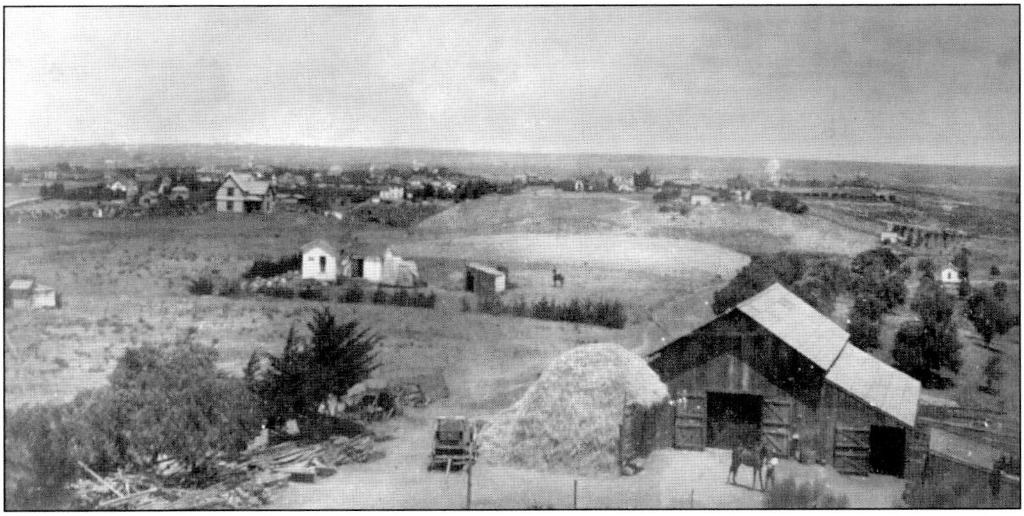

Looking North from George Kimball House, 1892. From this vantage, one could see the Kimball barn with farm wagon and haystack. One of the Kimball boys stands with a horse ready to hitch to the wagon. Plaza Boulevard would be built years later, down the hill behind the barn, running along the riverbed from left to right. Outbuildings and farmland surround the many houses in the distance.

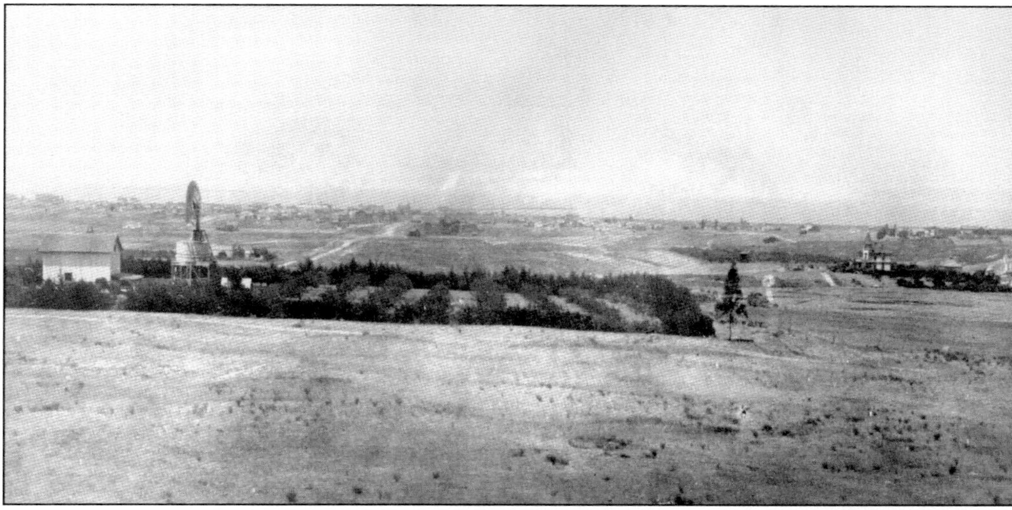

LOOKING WEST FROM GEORGE KIMBALL HOUSE, 1892. From the roof, the Kimballs had an expansive view of the entire San Diego Bay, the Silver Strand, and the ocean beyond. Point Loma could be clearly seen to the northwest, and the Coronado Islands to the southwest. This was a great place from which to watch the ships coming in to dock at the wharf at Seventeenth Street, which is in the center distance.

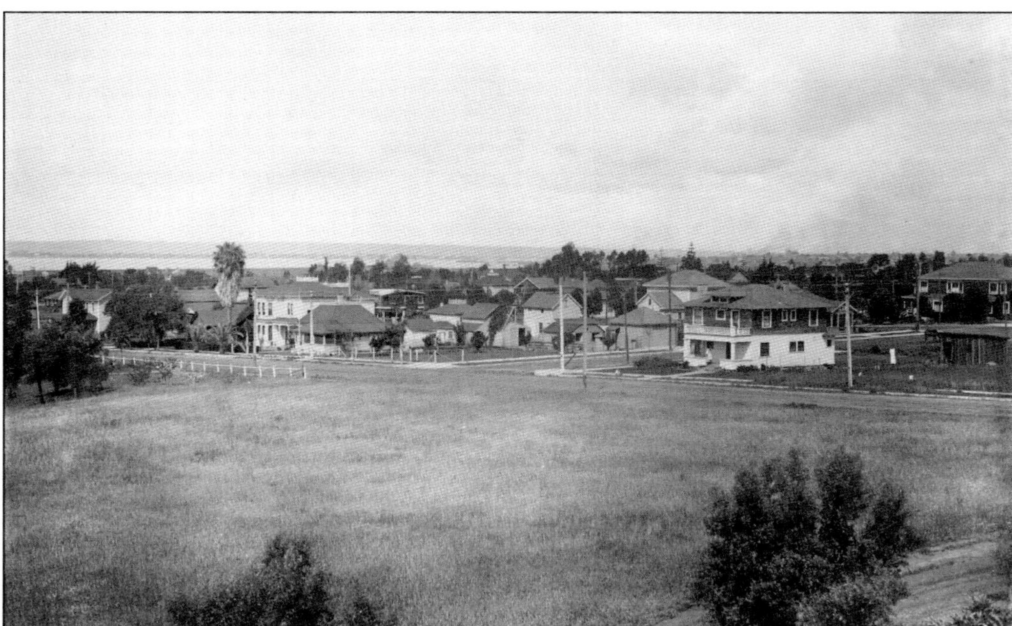

NATIONAL CITY VISTA, 1913. This westward view, taken 21 years after the image above, albeit from a different vantage point, shows the growth that occurred in National City over a relatively short period of time. By 1911, the population of National City had grown to 1,733, while that of San Diego city was 39,578.

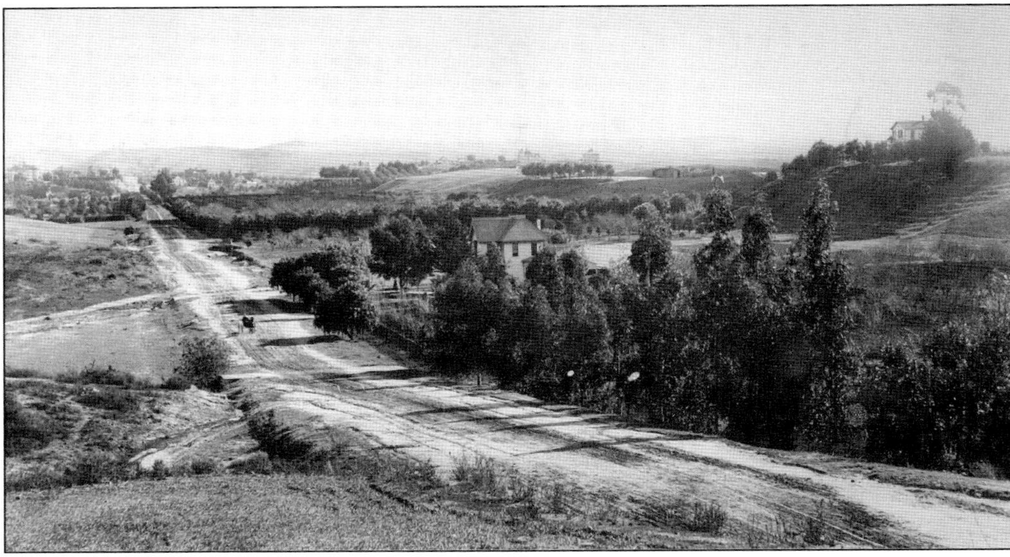

PARADISE VALLEY, 1899. This view, looking east along Eighth Street, was taken atop the hill at K Avenue. A horse with buggy can be seen plodding up the hill along the rutted road. In the distance, Dr. Potts' Sanitarium stands on the far left. The house left of center is La Corona, owned by Harry L. Titus. In the distance, right of center, is Roseway Ranch, the home of Moses C. Kimball, with a two-story carriage house to its right.

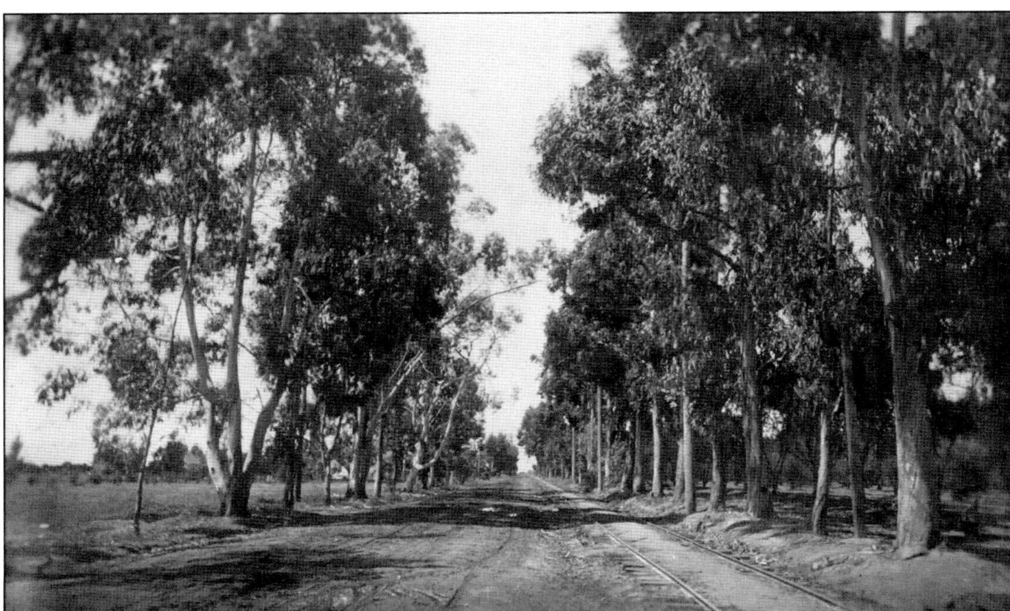

EUCALYPTUS-LINED TWENTY-FOURTH STREET, C. 1910. Looking west from F Avenue along this dirt road, one can see the railroad tracks that carried the National City and Otay Railroad up the hill to the summit on the Terrace (N Avenue). On April 10, 1875, Frank Kimball mentioned in his diary that he planted 10 acres of eucalyptus trees in Sweetwater Valley. Flora Kimball planted trees along the streets, and soon the eucalyptus became part of the National City scene.

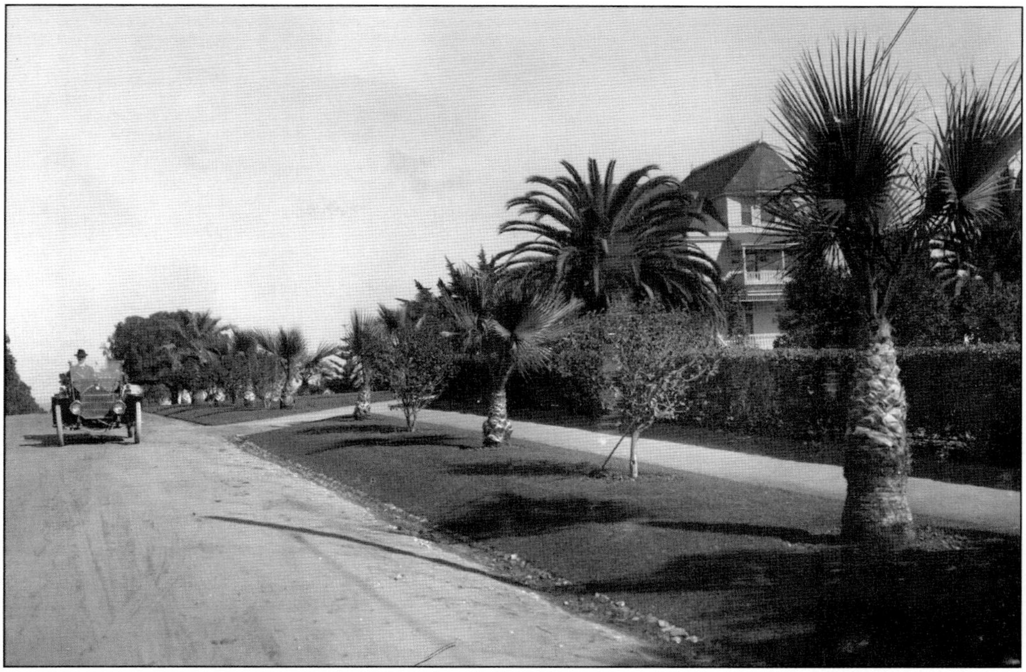

WALLACE D. DICKINSON HOUSE. The Terrace, N Avenue at Twenty-fourth Street, was the fashionable place to live. Wallace Dickinson came to National City with his wife, Marian, and young daughter Adelaide and built this house at 1430 East Twenty-fourth Street in 1887. It was directly across the street from the home of his parents, William and Sarah Dickinson. This large Queen Anne with dominant hipped gable has a wonderful view of the ocean.

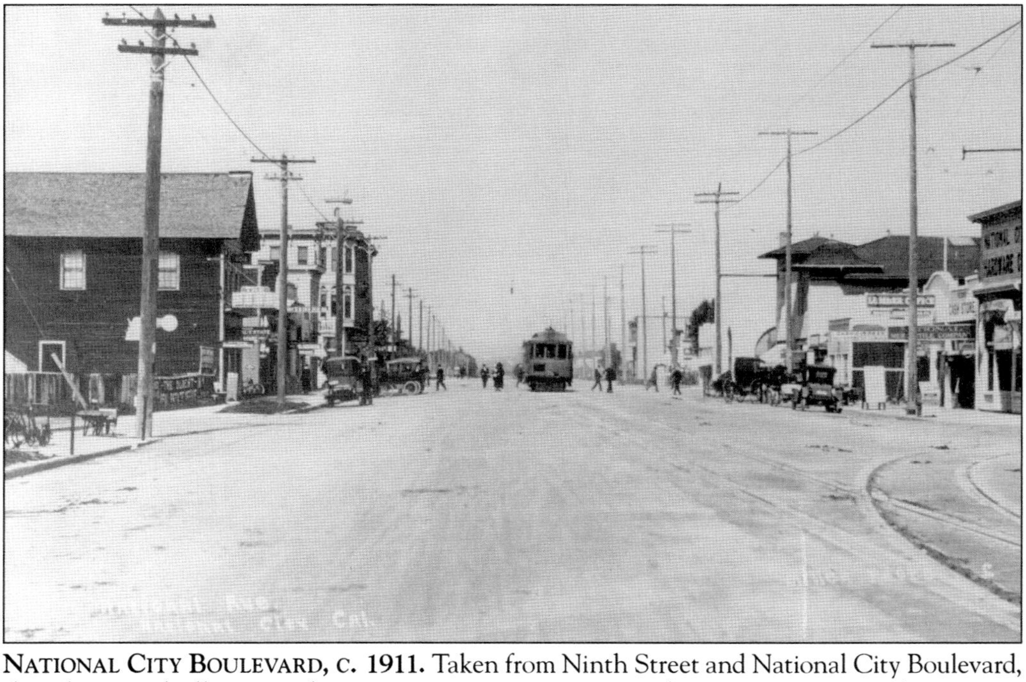

NATIONAL CITY BOULEVARD, C. 1911. Taken from Ninth Street and National City Boulevard, this photograph illustrates the transition occurring in regards to transportation. A streetcar, automobiles, and horse-drawn buggies are represented, as well as bicycles and wheelbarrows.

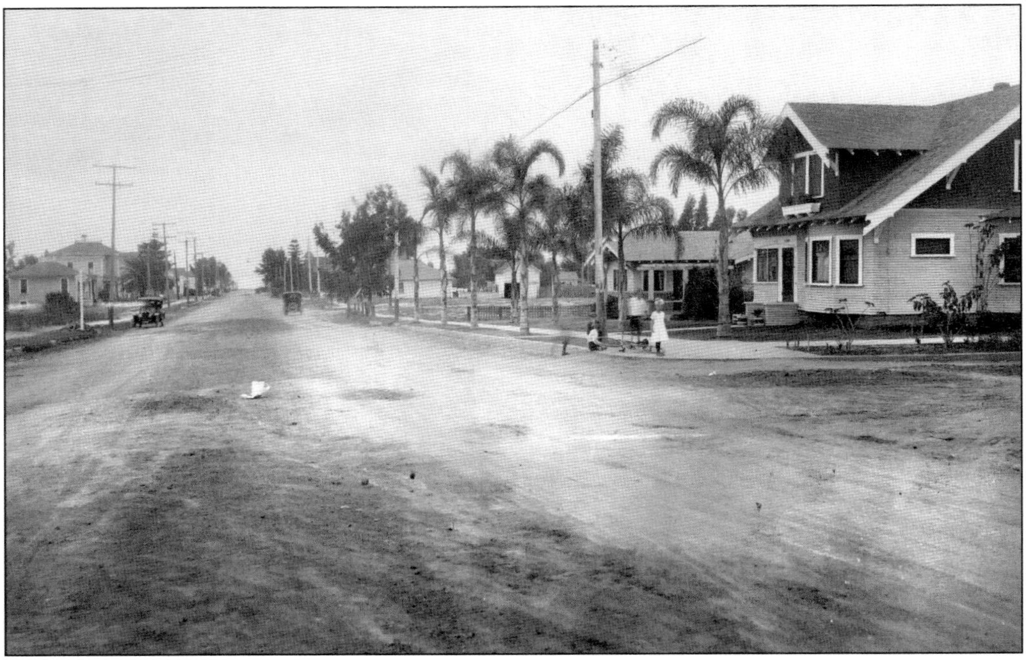

Eighth Street and E Avenue. During the second decade of the 20th century, craftsman bungalows became the popular style of architecture. Houses were filling in what once had been farmland. By this time, electricity was commonly available to the community, but the unpaved streets revealed ties to its recent agricultural past.

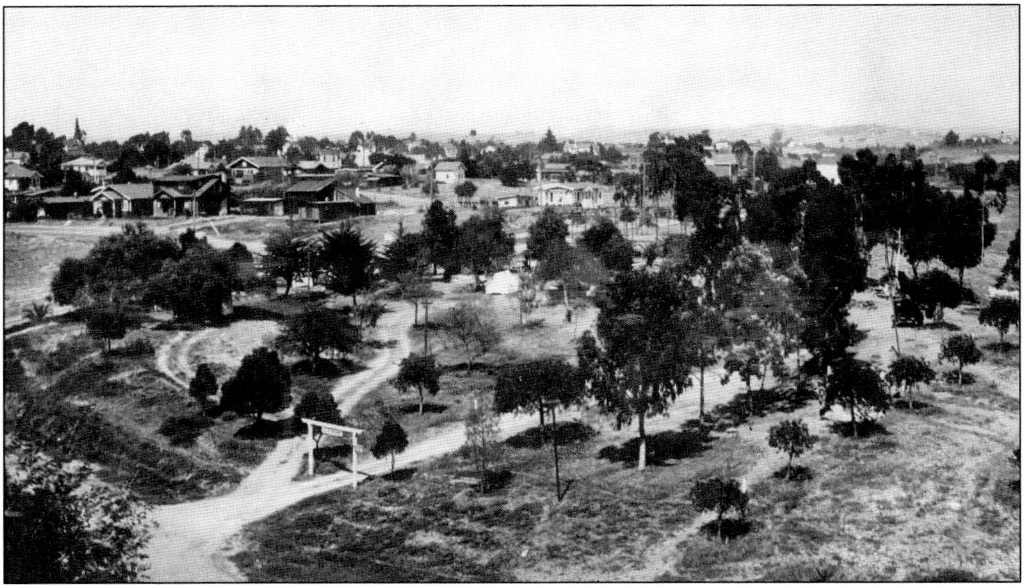

Kimball Park. Viewed atop the fire station roof on National City Boulevard, looking northeast, Kimball Park sprawls in the foreground. On May 4, 1909, the citizens of National City voted in favor of a park to be located on 15 acres of block 12, on the east side of National City Boulevard. The National City Rodeo was held here for years, while later a small zoo provided enjoyment for many children.

Two

FIRST FAMILIES
NATIONAL CITY PIONEERS

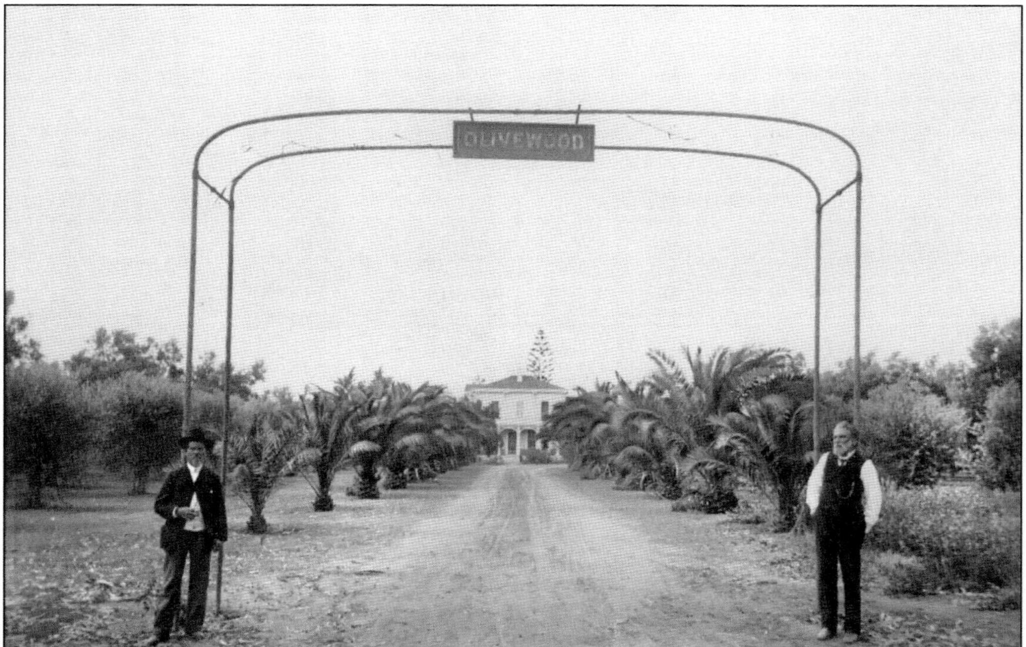

KIMBALL BROTHERS AT OLIVEWOOD GATE. Francis Kimball (left) and Warren Kimball stand at the entrance to Warren's estate, Olivewood. This is the only known photograph of the two brothers together and is significant in the fact that Frank and Warren were the two forces behind the development of National City. In business, they were known as the Kimball Brothers, who purchased the Rancho de la Nacion and orchestrated its development. Levi Kimball was initially the third member of this partnership, but by 1873, he sold his share and moved back to Oakland. Frank took the lead in promoting the city, while Warren, although active in business development, always seemed to play a supporting role to his younger brother.

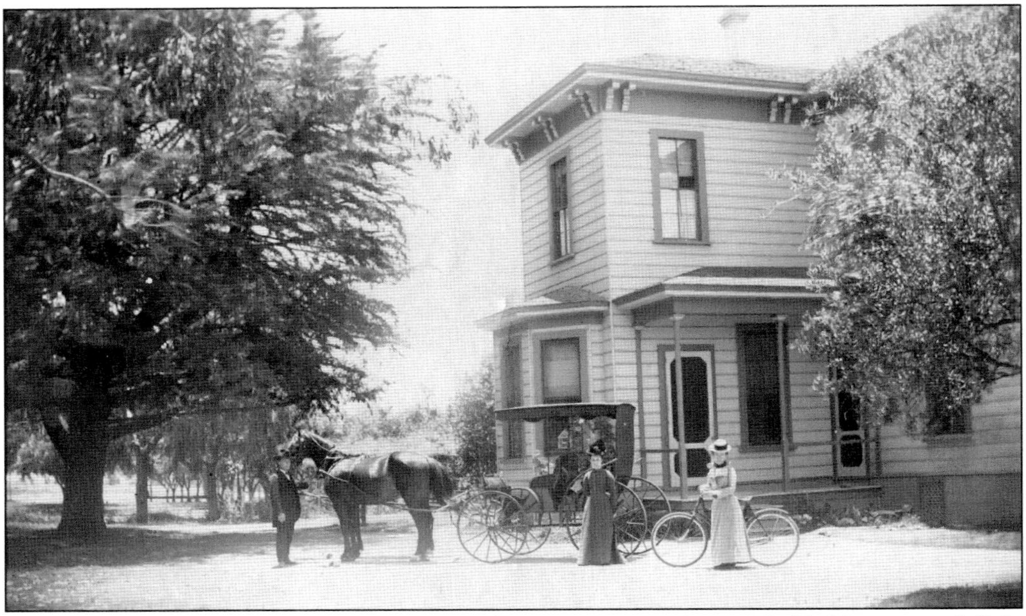

FRANK KIMBALL HOUSE, C. 1906. The October 10, 1868, *San Diego Weekly Union* stated, "Mr. Frank Kimball is putting the roof on his large two-storied house. He will have hot and cold water in every room. The house overlooks the Bay and has a wonderful view." On the grounds surrounding the house, which extended from Ninth to Eleventh Streets and from National City Boulevard to Hoover Avenue, Frank carried out his horticultural experimentation.

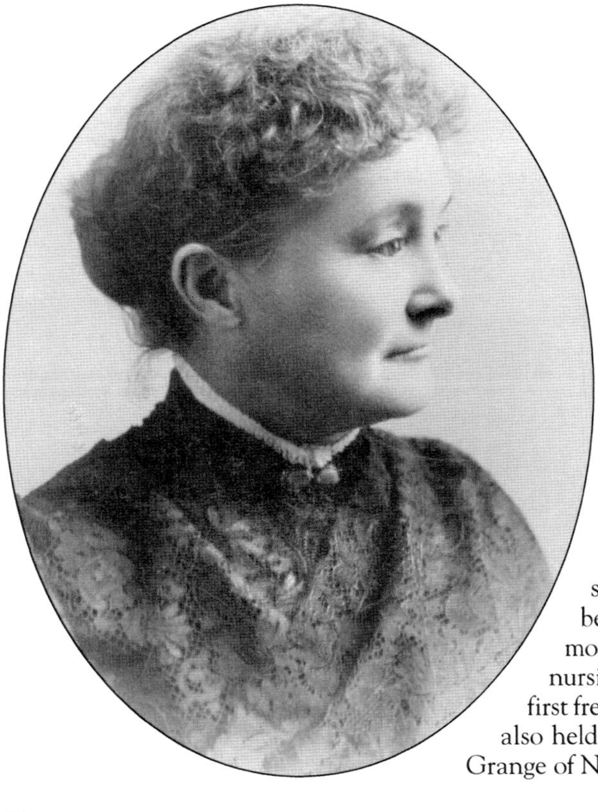

SARAH CURRIER KIMBALL. No woman could have been a better helpmate to her husband; while Frank was promoting business development, Sarah was quietly spending her time helping others. No beggar left her door without a gift of food or money. Frank's diaries often mention Sarah nursing a sick neighbor. She sponsored the first free kindergarten in San Diego County and also held the office of recorder for the National Grange of National City.

FRANK A. KIMBALL. Overcoming obstacles of health, and later finances, this man was the force behind the Kimball Brothers in promoting the growth of National City. His interests were many; he was active in horticulture, the olive oil industry, real estate, banking, general entrepreneurship (helping promote many new local businesses), and philanthropy (donating land for the cemetery, schools, and churches).

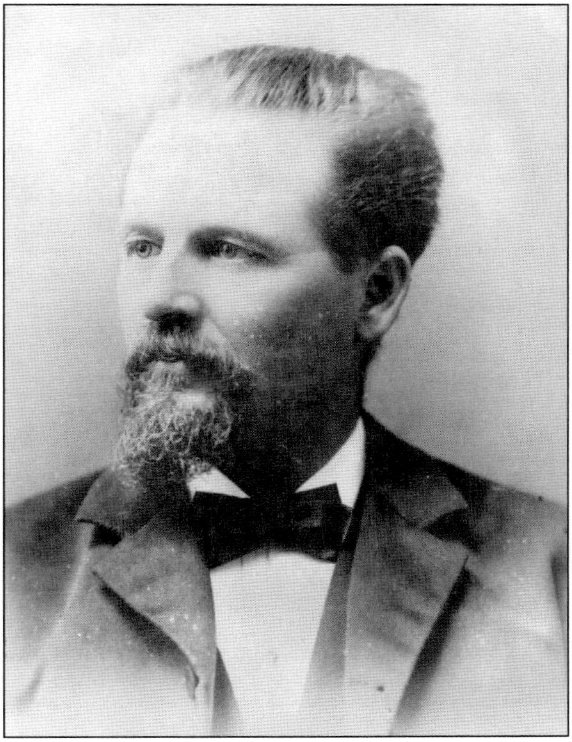

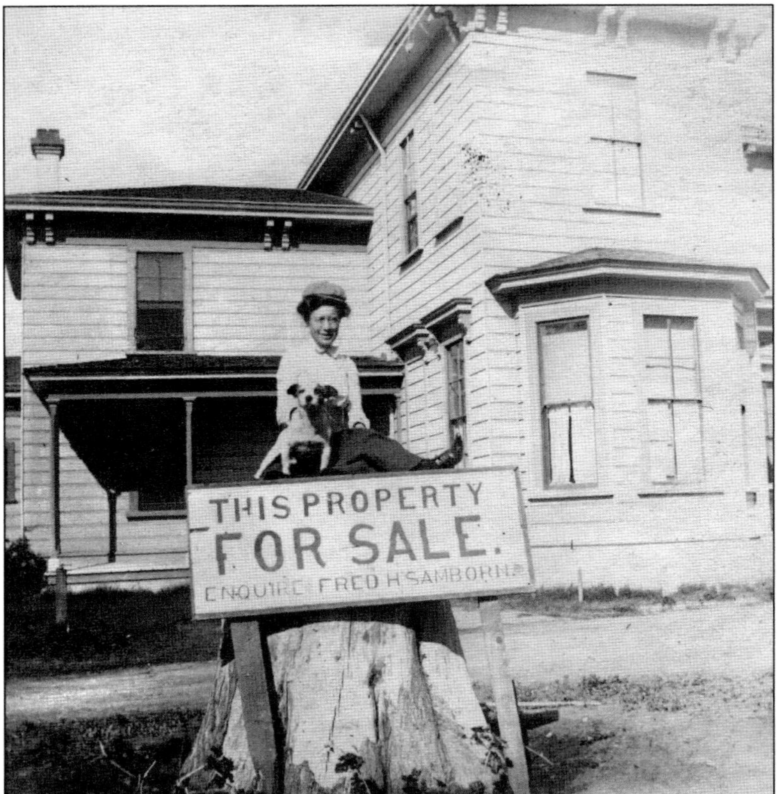

KIMBALL HOUSE FOR SALE. When Frank could not pay the mortgage he had taken out on this residence, thanks to unscrupulous associates who had swindled him, he and Sarah were forced out of their beloved home of 30 years and sought shelter in a drafty apartment above their nephew's restaurant on McKinley Avenue. Before they left, Frank cut down a huge cypress tree that had stood at the front of the house and had meant much to him.

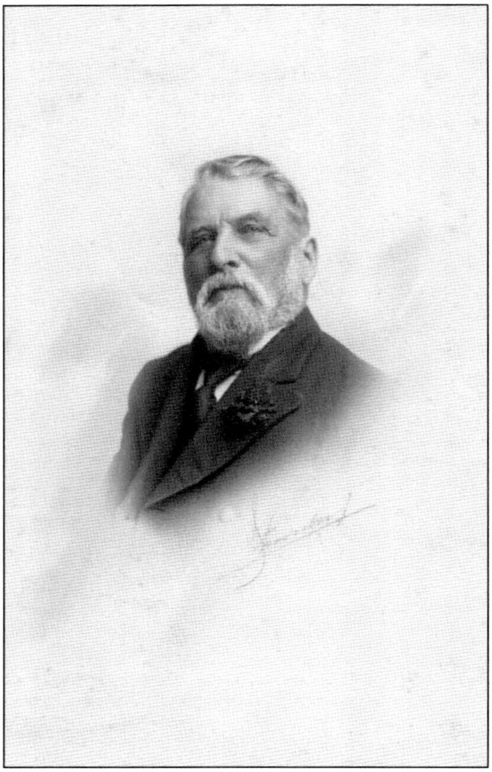

Warren Carlton Kimball. As partner with his brother Frank in the Kimball Brothers, Warren shared in the purchase of Rancho de la Nacion and its development. While active in farming, he was president of the West Coast Match Company, owner of the National Planing Mill (located at the foot of Seventeenth Street), and vice president of the Bank of National City. He also was a great supporter of his wife, Flora, and her many endeavors.

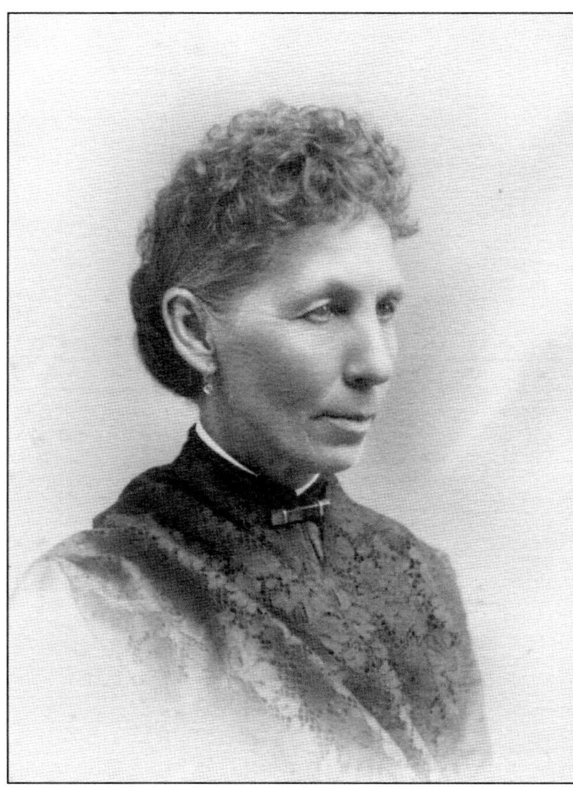

Flora Morrill Kimball. Her obituary boasted that she was the best-known woman in the state. Born in 1829, Kimball was a writer of note, lecturer, horticulturist, advocate for women's suffrage, and a promoter of education. In 1889, she was elected to the school board, distinguishing her as the first woman in the state of California to serve in such a capacity. In 1872, she wrote the first novel published in San Diego County and titled *The Fairfields.*

OLIVEWOOD. This stately Italianate home belonged to Warren and Flora Kimball. The beauty of Olivewood was often described in local and national publications after a visit from journalists or writers. Two such guests of the Kimballs were writer Kate Sanborn and suffragist leader Elizabeth Cady Stanton—the rare and exotic plants attracting the former and the hostess, Flora Kimball, the latter. This view is of the south side of the house, which stood on Twenty-fourth Street between D and F Avenues.

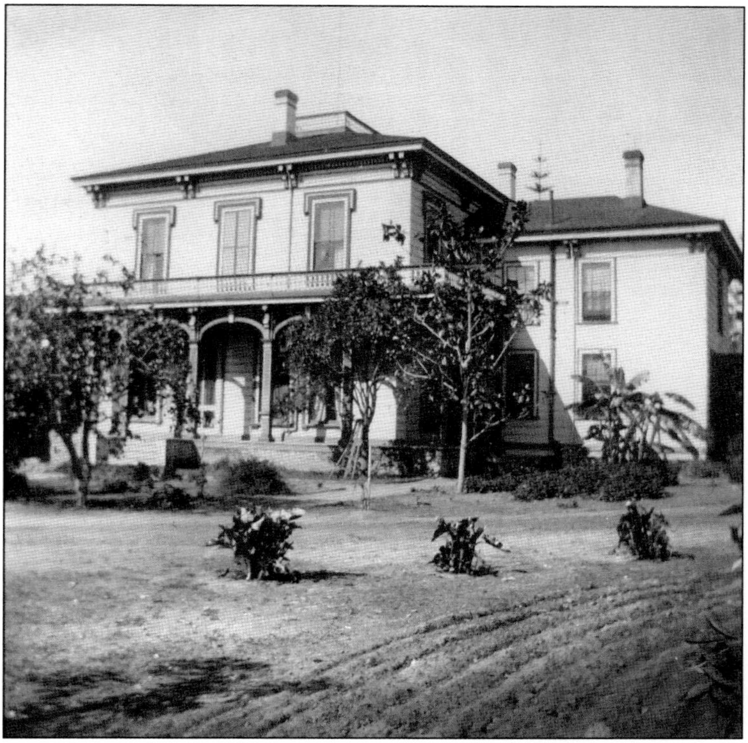

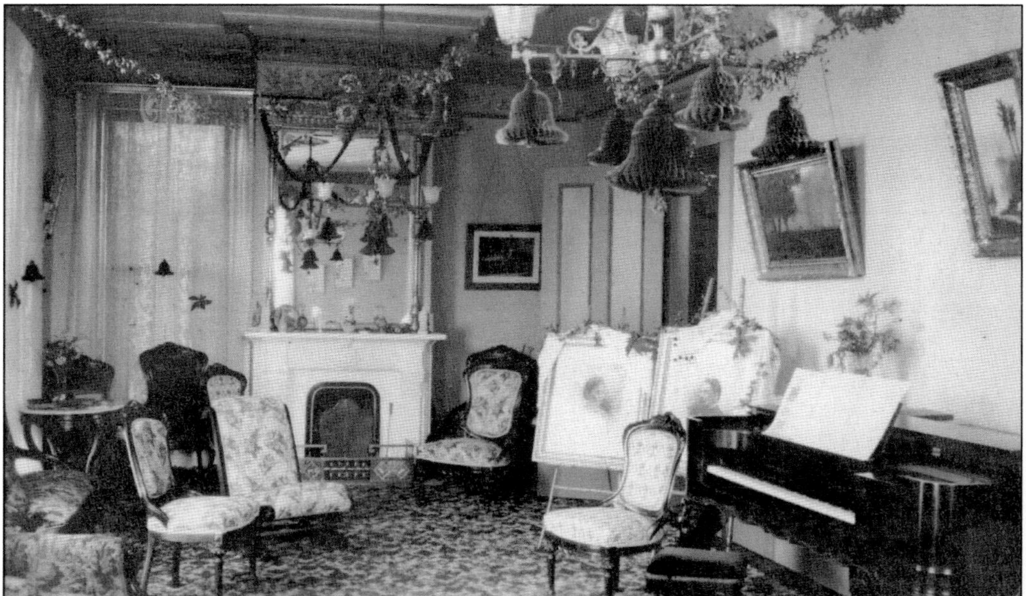

OLIVEWOOD INTERIOR, C. 1890. Decorated for a party, with paper bells hanging from the kerosene chandelier, this room depicts a family of wealth and culture. The mantle was made of white Carrara marble, while the large over-mantle mirror was gilded with gold leaf. In Victorian fashion, Flora and Warren's portraits are displayed on easels, garlanded with ivy.

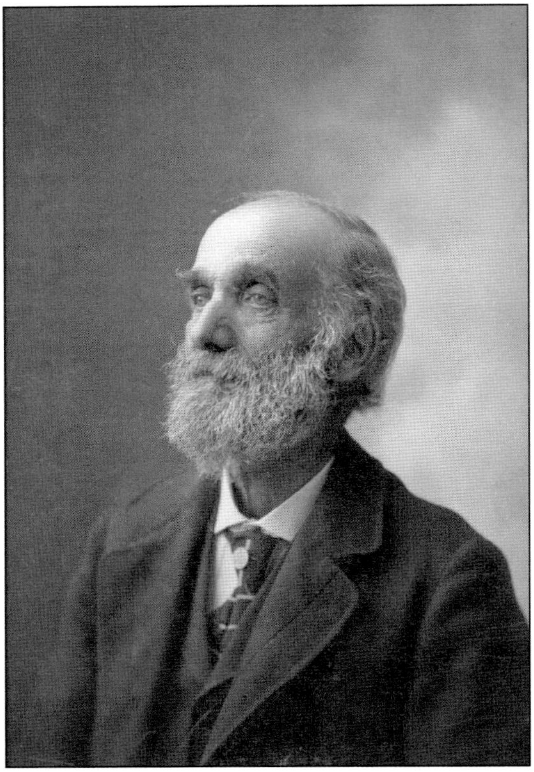

GEORGE LITTLE KIMBALL. George, the oldest of the Kimball brothers, born in 1824, responded to his brother Frank's entreaties and brought his family to National City in 1869, crossing the country on the new Union Pacific Railroad line. They arrived on November 16, 1869, by steamer from San Francisco. Their first home, at Tenth Street and National City Boulevard, became National City's first post office when George assumed the position as the city's first postmaster.

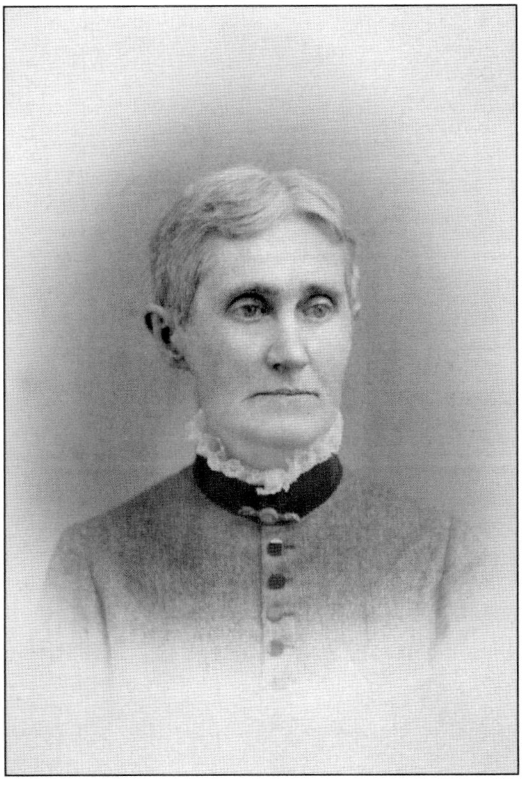

LUCY GORDON KIMBALL. George Kimball married Lucy Gordon Kimball in New Hampshire after his first wife, Harriet Floyd Kimball, died. Lucy gave birth to four children: Augustus, Gilbert, Clinton, and Laura.

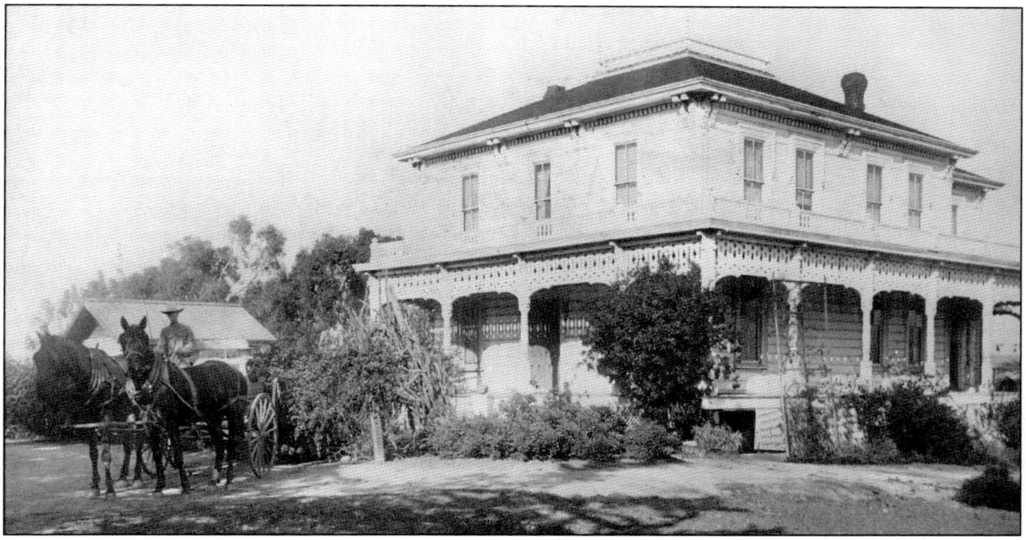

GEORGE KIMBALL HOUSE. In 1887, the local newspaper reported, "George Kimball is building an elegant residence on Nob Hill." This was built on the 20 acres Frank had given his brother in 1870 and which George had been farming for 17 years. This Italianate home cost the sum of $6,000, the millwork coming from Warren Kimball's planing mill and the bricks from the Kimball Brothers brick kilns in the Sweetwater Valley.

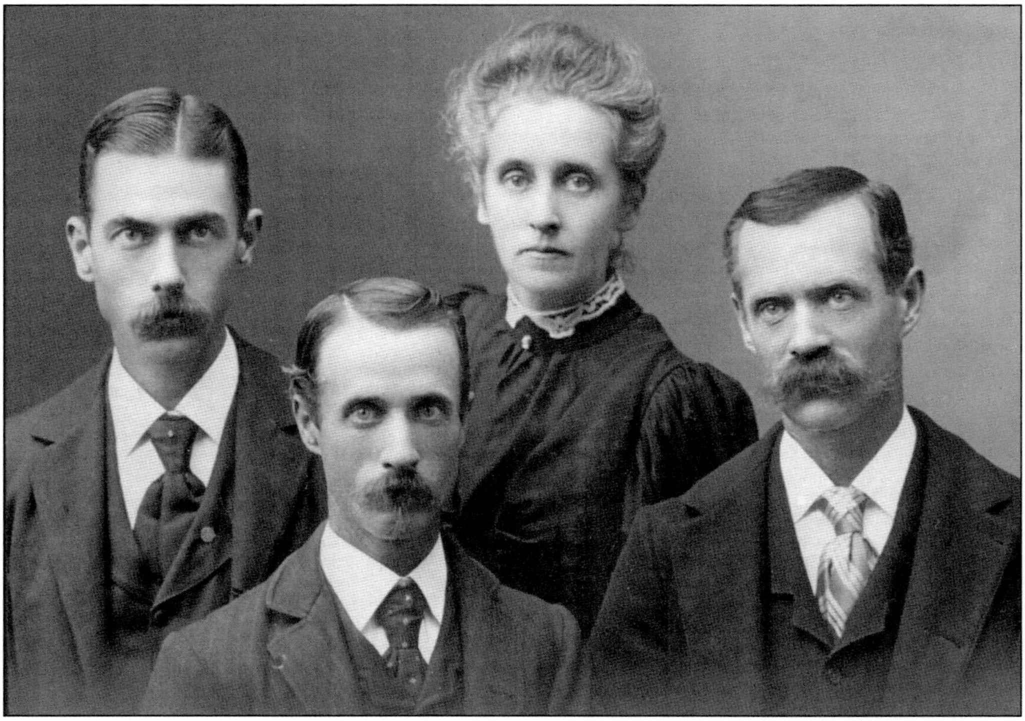

GEORGE KIMBALL CHILDREN. Pictured in no particular order are Augustus, Clinton, Gilbert, and Laura Kimball. Only one of the Kimball children married; the other three lived out their adult lives in the Kimball family home on L Avenue. Clinton and Gilbert continued to run the farm while Laura kept house. Augustus married Harriett Johnson and became editor of the local newspaper for several years.

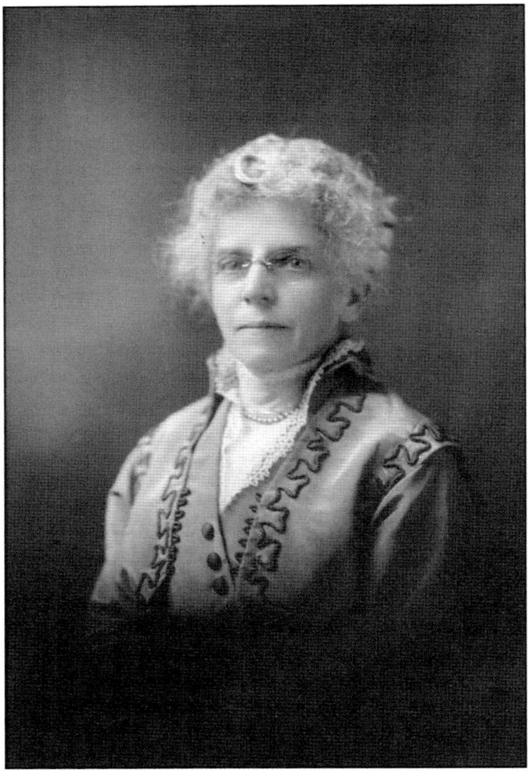

HANNAH JANE KIMBALL BARNES REED. Daughter of George Kimball and widow of George Barnes, Hannah came to National City from New Hampshire in July 1881. At this time, it took her 16 days by rail to Los Angeles, followed by a boat ride to San Diego, and finally a horseback ride to reach National City.

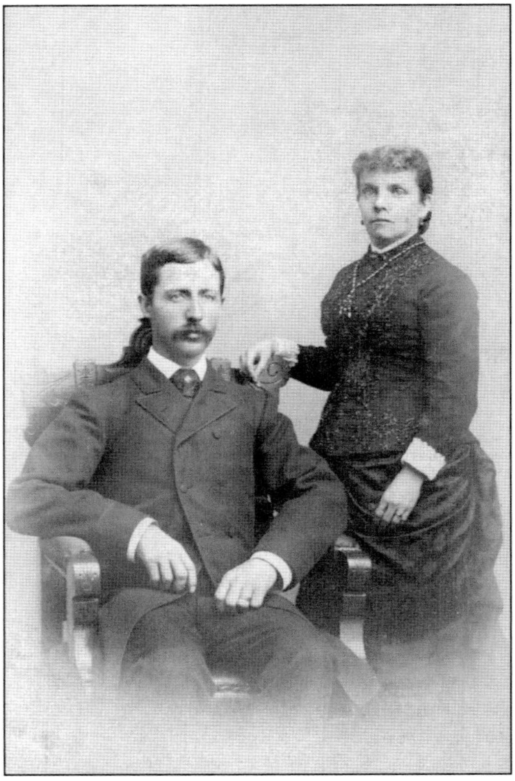

FRANKLIN PIERCE AND HANNAH REED. Franklin Reed, born in Pennsylvania in 1853, migrated to National City and married Hannah Barnes on June 21, 1884. Together they had two daughters, Chassie Frances and Hazel Kimball. Franklin owned a hardware store, while Hannah Reed participated in community life by joining the New England Society and the National Grange.

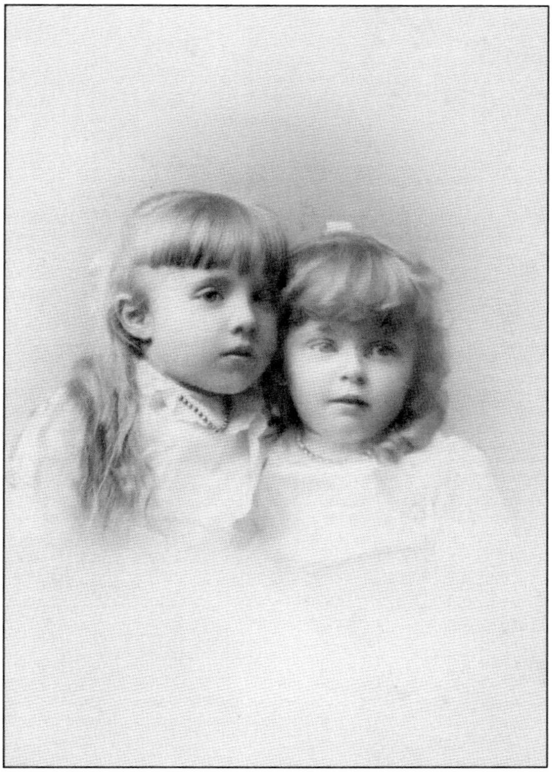

Reed Sisters, c. 1892. The Reed sisters, Chassie Frances and Hazel Kimball, were granddaughters of George Kimball; they were raised surrounded by the many aunts, uncles, and cousins of the Kimball family. As young girls, they benefited from the free kindergarten sponsored in National City by their great-aunt, Sarah Kimball.

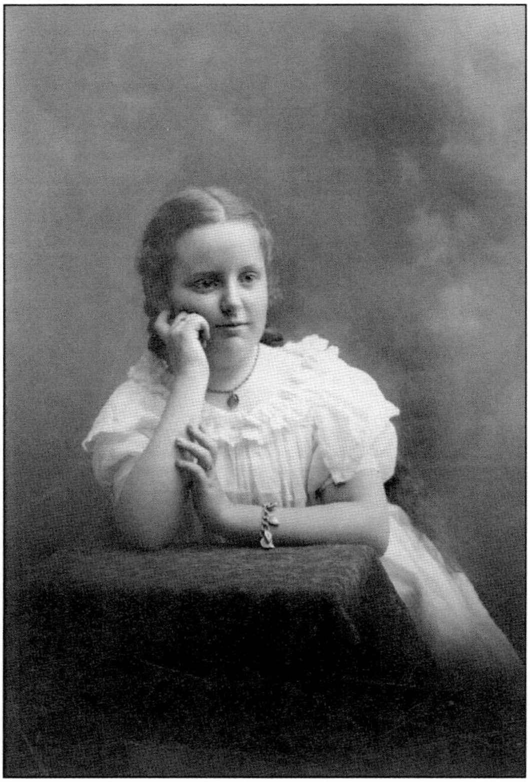

Hazel Kimball Reed, c. 1900. Hazel was born in National City in December 1888, and like many youths, her life involved social clubs, parties, church functions, and picnics. After graduating from high school in National City, Hazel went to Leland Stanford Junior University, where in 1911 she was awarded a degree in English. As an adult, she moved to San Diego, where she taught school for 25 years.

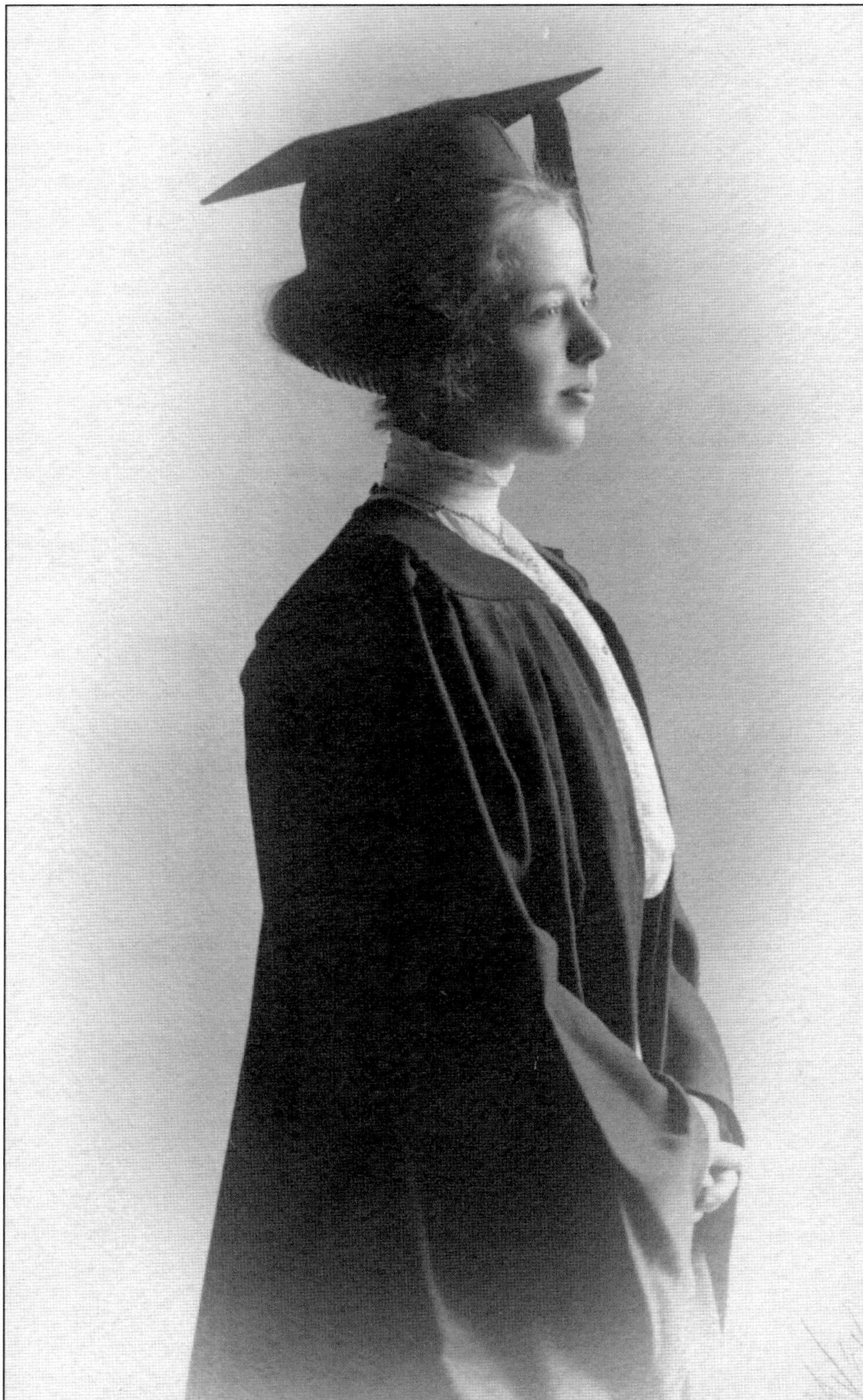

CHASSIE FRANCES REED, 1911. Chassie was born in National City in February 1887, the same year the city became incorporated. She is pictured here as a Stanford graduate, class of 1911, with a degree in graphic arts. She returned to Southern California to teach school in San Diego. In 1926, she married Lloyd Chapman, who worked for Acme Sheet Metal in San Diego.

LEVI WOODBURY KIMBALL, 1886. The second eldest Kimball brother, Levi joined his brothers Warren and Frank in Oakland in 1860, where they worked in the construction trade. Levi became a partner in the Kimball Brothers with the purchase of the National Ranch in 1868. After five years, he decided to withdraw from this partnership, sold most of his holdings to his brothers, and returned to Oakland with his wife, Grace.

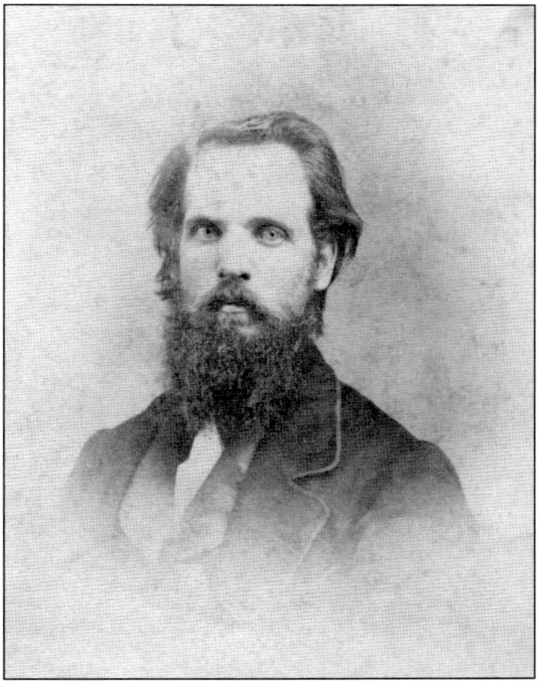

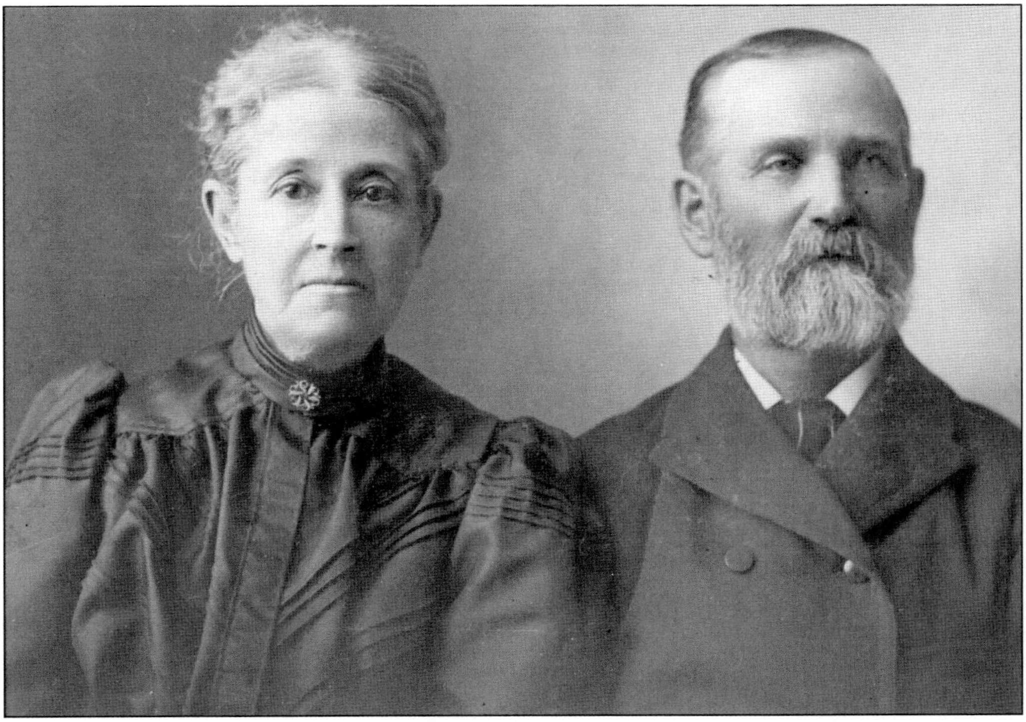

CHARLES HENRY AND ELLEN CLARK KIMBALL. Charles, born in 1836, chose to remain in New Hampshire while his parents were alive. After their death, he, his wife, Ellen, and their daughter Frances moved to National City. They lived at 539 East Twentieth Street, across the road from Warren and Flora Kimball's Olivewood estate. Charles did some farming, was a carpenter, and also worked for the San Diego Land and Town Company.

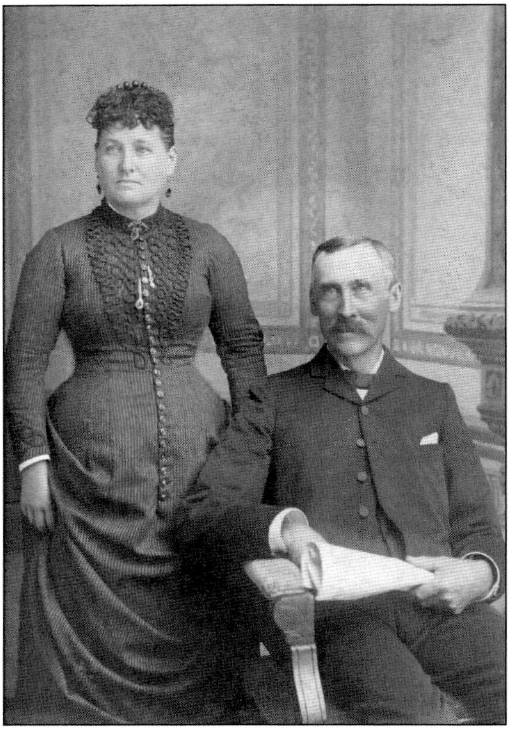

Fred and Mary Kimball Copeland. Mary, born in 1838, was the younger sister to the five Kimball brothers. In 1869, the Copelands arrived in National City with their four children: Albert, Fred, Charles, and Edna. Fred capably served as National City's first civil engineer, laying out the streets in the new city and building the wharves. He was also in demand for drilling wells and building windmills.

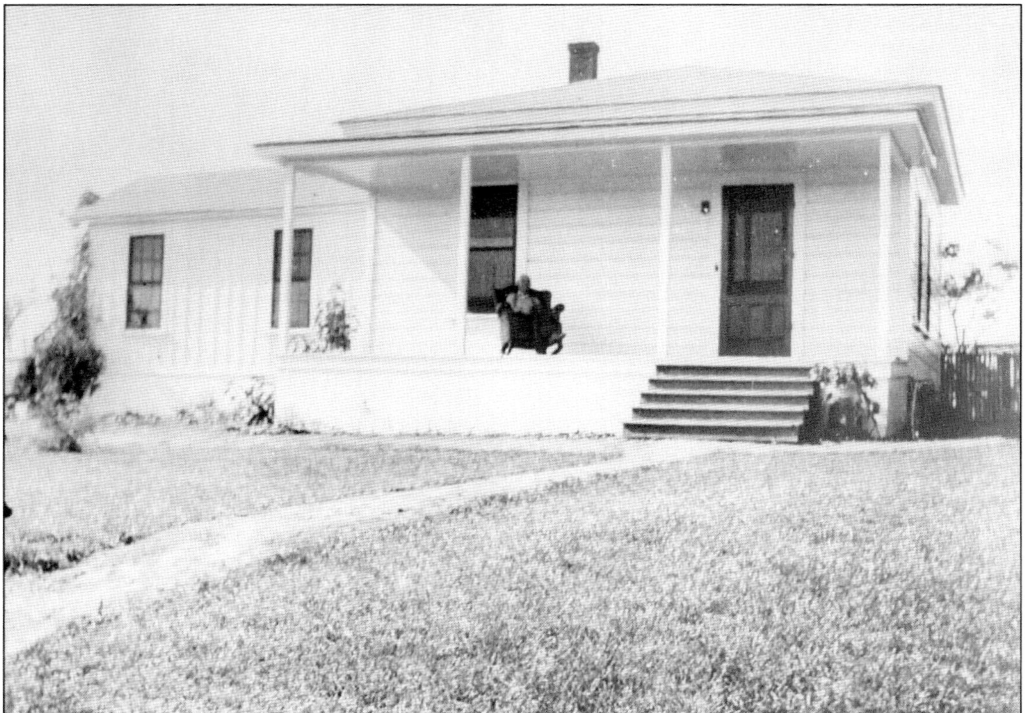

Fred Copeland House. This simple one-story Victorian house stands at 1108 D Avenue. The Copelands' home, with its unpretentious clean lines, stands in contrast to the more elaborate two-story homes of brothers-in-law Warren, Frank, and George Kimball.

MYRNA PATTERSON EGGLESTON SNOW. Myrna was the daughter of John and Edna Copeland Patterson and granddaughter of Fred and Mary Kimball Copeland. Myrna married William Eggleston, the city marshal, in 1896 and had daughters Helen and Mabel. After Eggleston's death, Myrna married Henry Packard Snow and had one more daughter, Alice. Henry Snow was an agent for the National City and Otay Railroad.

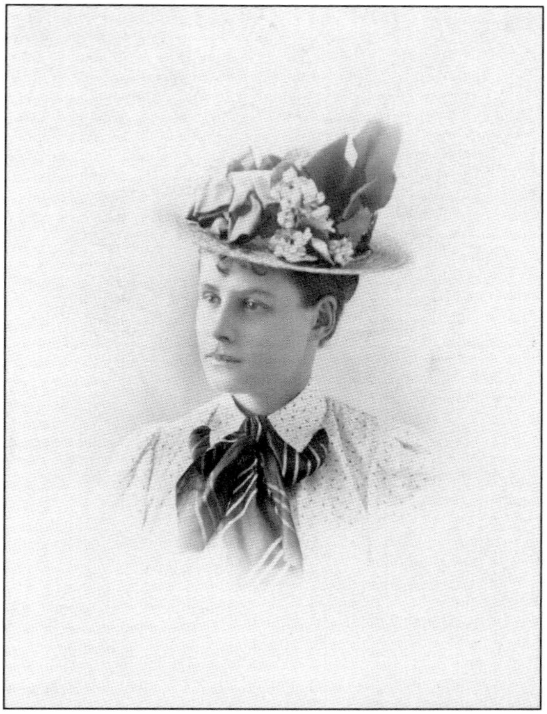

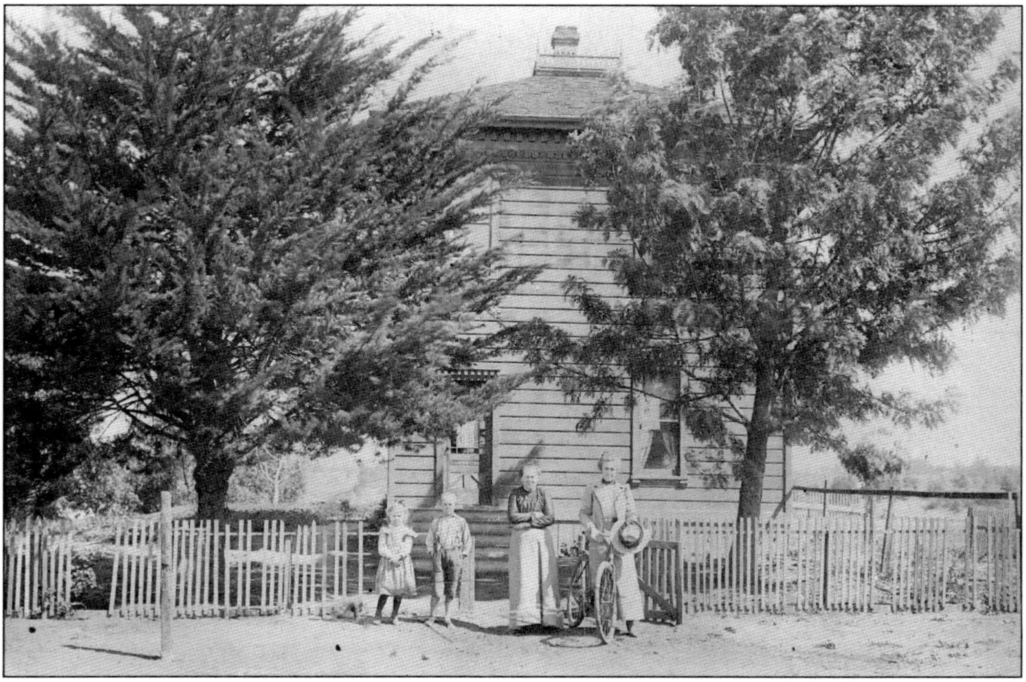

PATTERSON FAMILY HOME, C. 1900. John and Edna Patterson's home was located on Coolidge Avenue at the corner of Eighteenth Street. John served as a member of the National City Volunteer Fire Department. In 1896, while working for the San Diego Land and Town Company, he confronted thieves in a company citrus orchard and was mortally wounded. After this tragic event, his wife, Edna, daughter of Mary Kimball Copeland, was left to raise their eight children.

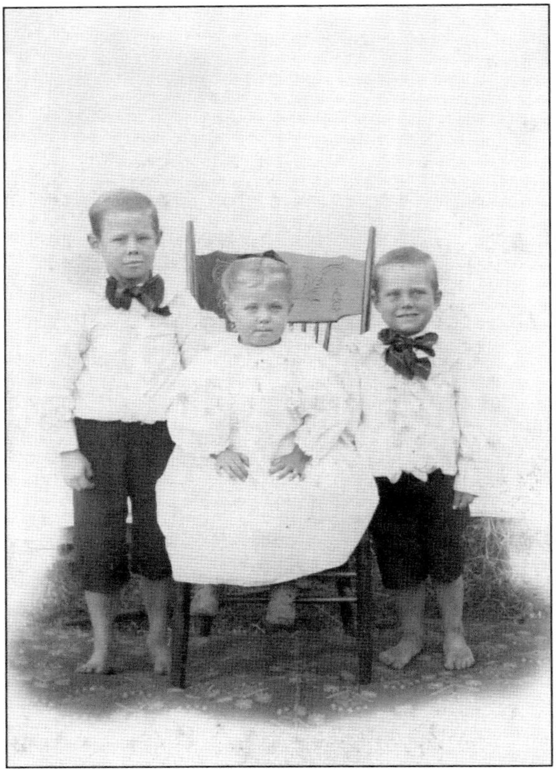

JOHN, ARTHUR, AND MYRTLE PATTERSON, C. 1897. The three youngest children of John and Edna Patterson pose for a formal portrait. The barefoot boys, standing on a carpet apparently laid out on the grass, suggest a traveling photographer going door to door took the photograph.

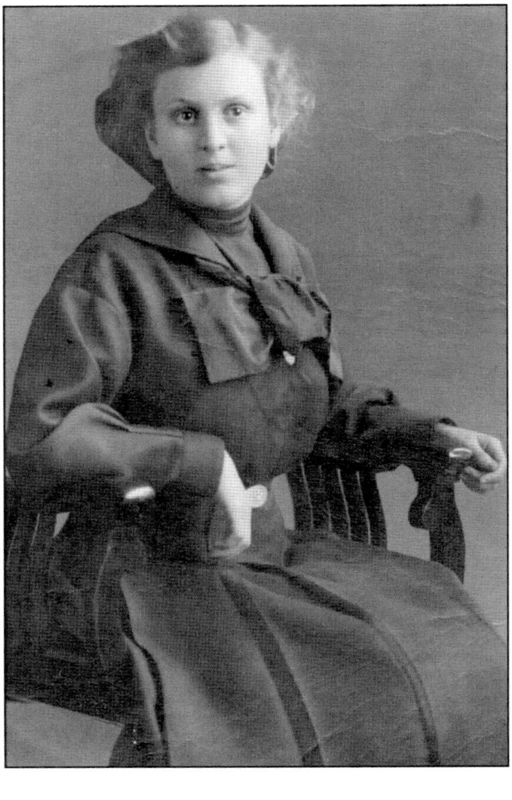

MARY "TOT" COPELAND, C. 1910. Named after her paternal grandmother, Mary Kimball Copeland, Tot was the daughter of Fred W. and Nellie Copeland. Fred was a carpenter by trade. By 1916, Tot had married William Alexander McLean and, like many of the Kimball-Copeland offspring, moved away from National City.

CICERO P. AND ALICE FINCHER EVANS. Born in Alabama, Cicero Evans came to California and taught school in various cities before becoming principal of National City High School in 1902. After 33 years of working in the educational field, Evans retired and purchased a lemon grove in National City, becoming a fruit rancher. In social activities, he held the position of secretary in the Woodmen of the World organization.

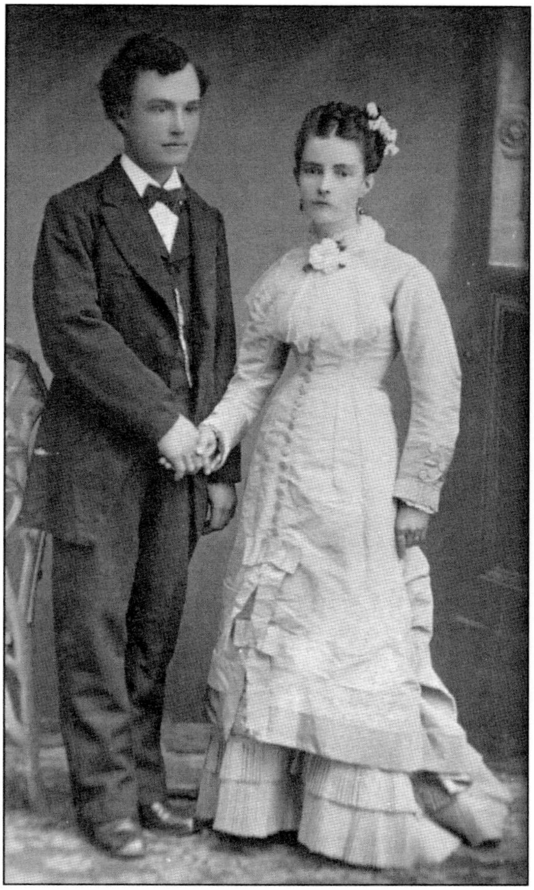

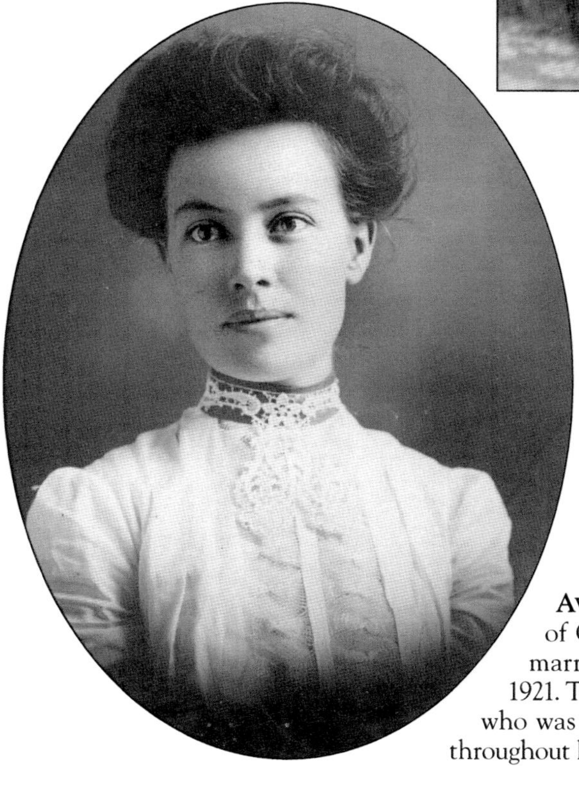

AVA EVANS SMITH. Ava was the only child of Cicero and Alice (Fincher) Evans. She married Dale Smith, the deputy assessor, in 1921. Together they had one child, Donald Smith, who was raised in National City and lived there throughout his adult life (see page 50).

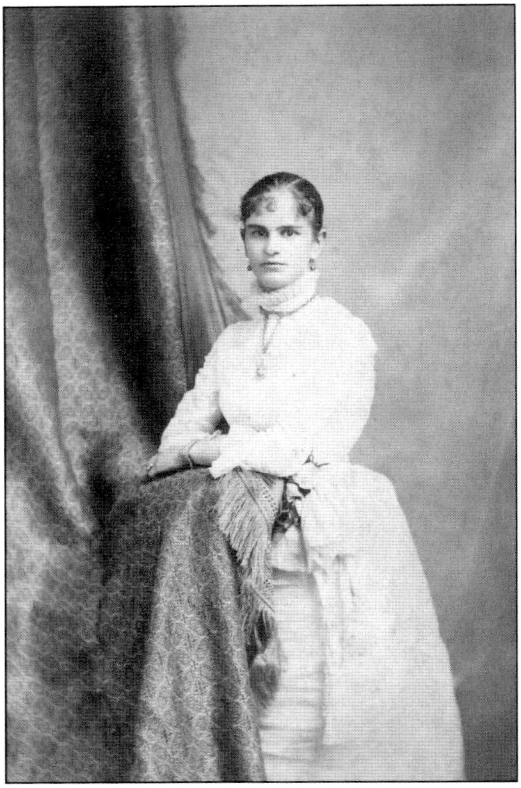

MARY DICKINSON. Mary was the daughter of William and Sarah Dickinson. The family came from Topeka, Kansas, in 1886, when the elder Dickinson was appointed general manager of the San Diego Land and Town Company.

HOME OF WILLIAM G. DICKINSON. Built in 1887 for William Dickinson, this elegant Queen Anne stands at 1433 East Twenty-fourth Street. After his wife chose the site for the house, Dickinson purchased 40 acres on which to build. The San Diego Land and Town Company was the real estate arm of the California Southern Railroad. As general manager, Dickinson is credited with developing Chula Vista, the Sweetwater Dam, and the National City and Otay Railroad.

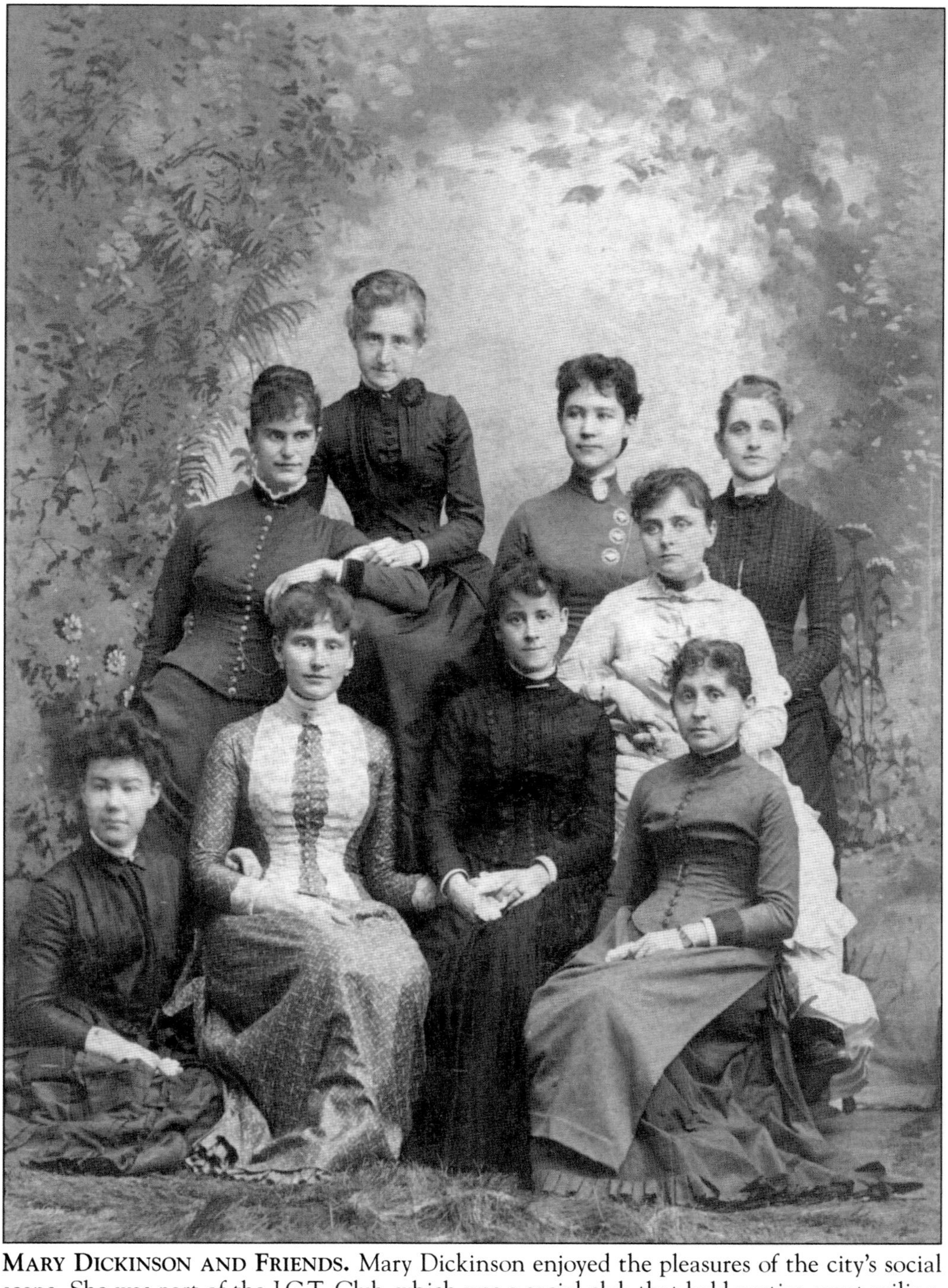

MARY DICKINSON AND FRIENDS. Mary Dickinson enjoyed the pleasures of the city's social scene. She was part of the J.G.T. Club, which was a social club that held parties, went sailing, and attended dinner dances at the Hotel Del Coronado. She married John Boal in 1888. They became the parents of three children: Helen, Marion, and Edgar. Boal worked with his father-in-law at the San Diego Land and Town Company, assuming his role of general manager after Dickinson died in 1891. In this photograph, Mary appears in the back row on the left; the other young ladies are unidentified.

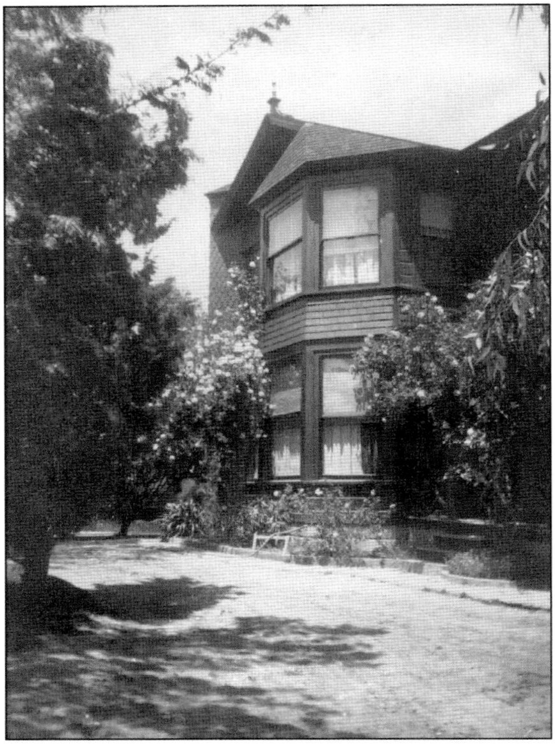

JULIUS A. RICE HOUSE. Julius Rice, born in Vermont in 1854, came west to teach school. In 1880, he married Laura Steele. He served as a teacher then principal in National City schools, as well as a member of the school board. In 1900, he held the position of deputy county superintendent of schools. He was also involved in several other enterprises to supplement his income; he sold real estate and insurance and grew fruit.

RICE HOUSE INTERIOR. Julius Rice had this house built in 1887 at 740 East Second Street. This interior view shows a typical Victorian parlor, the mantel decorated with various art objects and the piano draped with a heavy shawl. Rice's wife, Laura, the daughter of National City developer John Steele, enjoyed painting and fostered artistic interests in her daughter Lilian Jenette, who later gained fame as a noted architect.

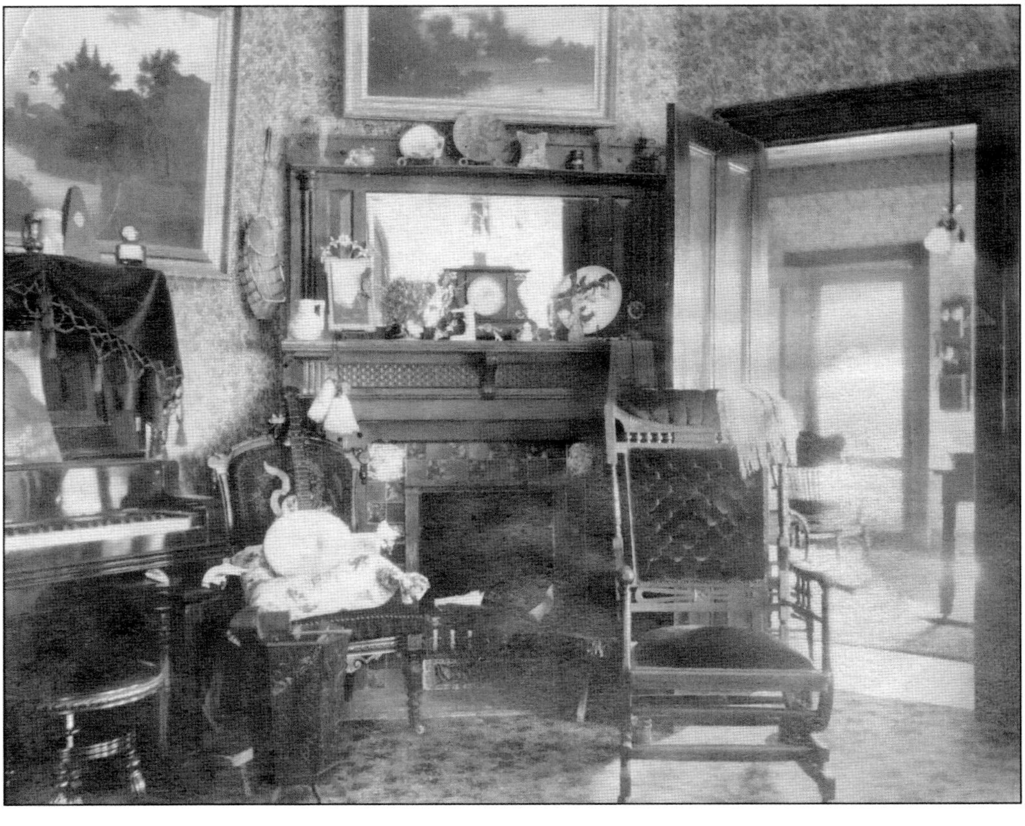

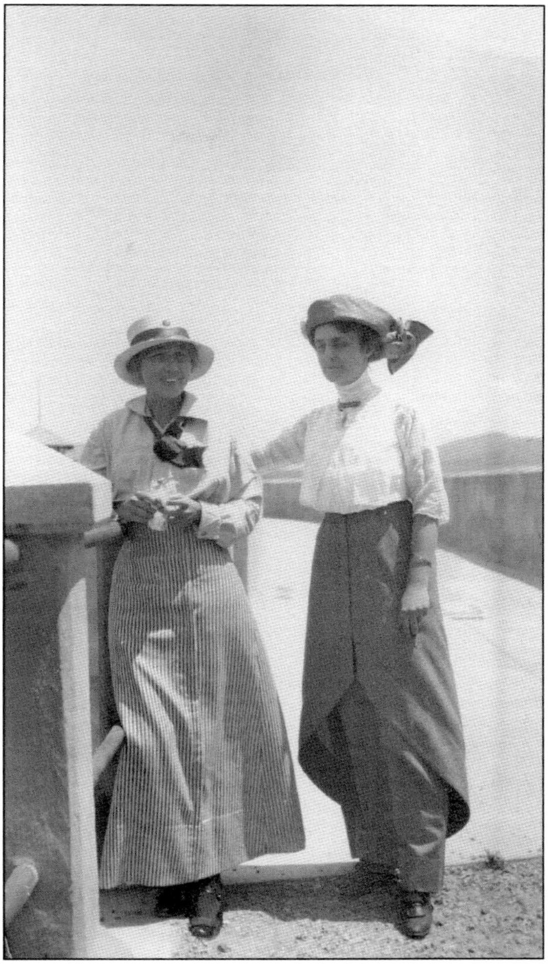

LILIAN JENETTE RICE. Born in National City in 1889, Lilian graduated from the University of California, Berkeley School of Architecture, one of the first women to do so. After returning home from school, Lilian became associated with the architectural firm of Richard Requa and Herbert L. Jackson. Through this firm, in 1921, Lilian planned and supervised the development of Rancho Santa Fe. Lilian is pictured here on the left with an unidentified friend.

LILIAN RICE'S CAR, C. 1910. Lilian defined the new woman of her generation coming out of National City—single, educated, and professional. She enjoyed her job, a social life with friends, picnics, sports (she belonged to the ZLAC Rowing Club), and she tooled around in a very fashionable Cole, a rare automobile even in its day. Lilian is pictured here at the wheel with an unidentified friend.

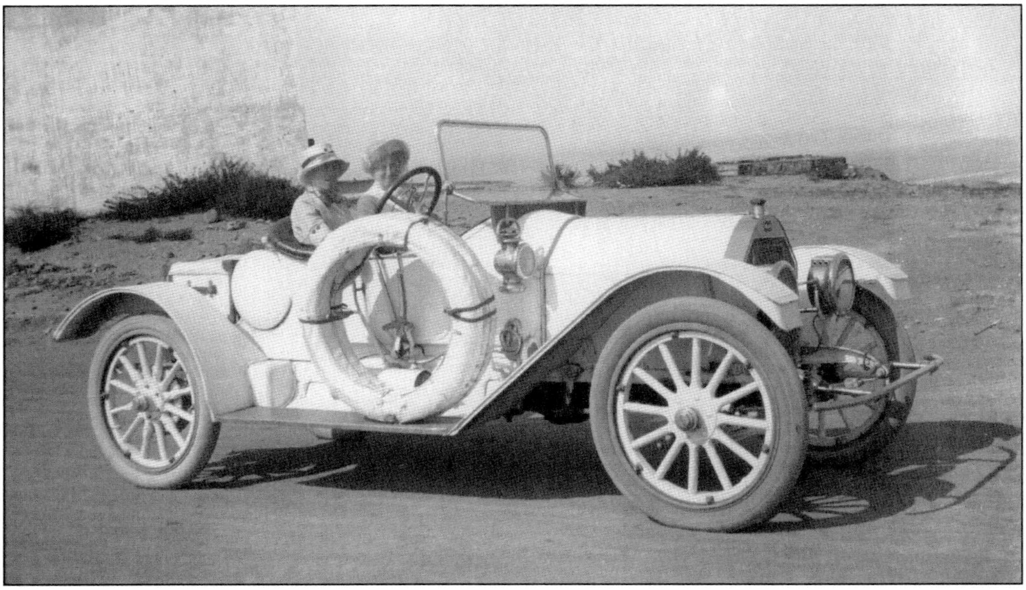

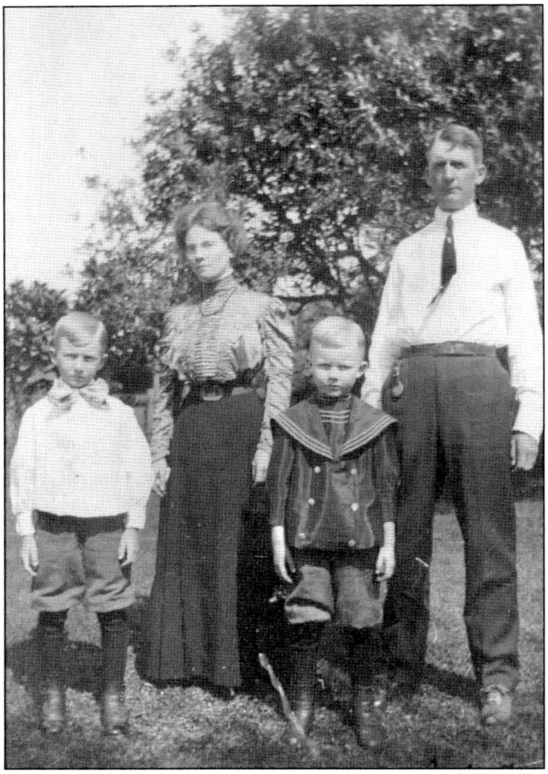

THE BULLEN FAMILY, 1912. Dressed in fine Sunday attire, the Bullens posed for a family portrait in their backyard. Standing from left to right are Clayton, Mattie, Howard, and Claude Bullen. Claude worked for Tyler Canter Company and clerked for D. E. Lozier and Company. He ran for city clerk in 1910. His brother, Ernest Bullen, was secretary treasurer for the Homeland Building Company and city attorney from 1909 to 1911.

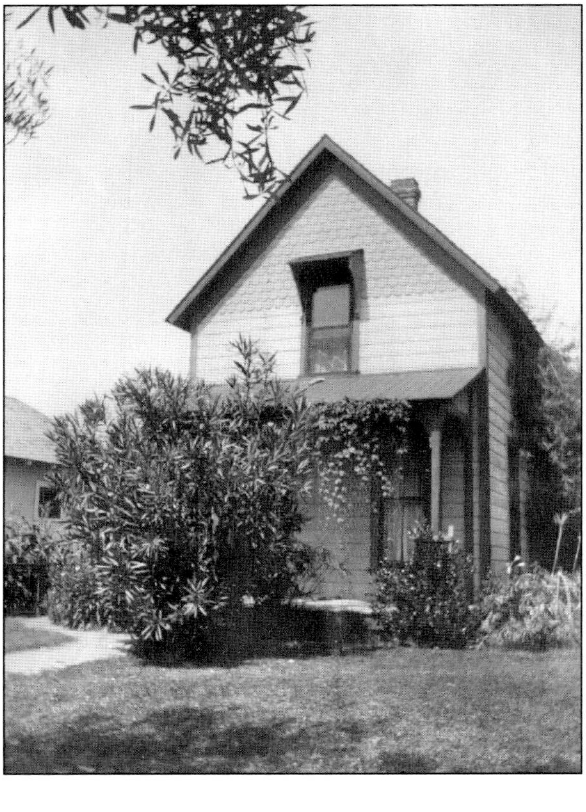

THE BULLEN HOUSE, 1912. Located at 721 B Avenue, the Bullen home represents the simple Victorian vernacular home common for the middle class in National City at the turn of the 20th century.

Three

PIONEER HOMES

THE FAMILY HEARTH

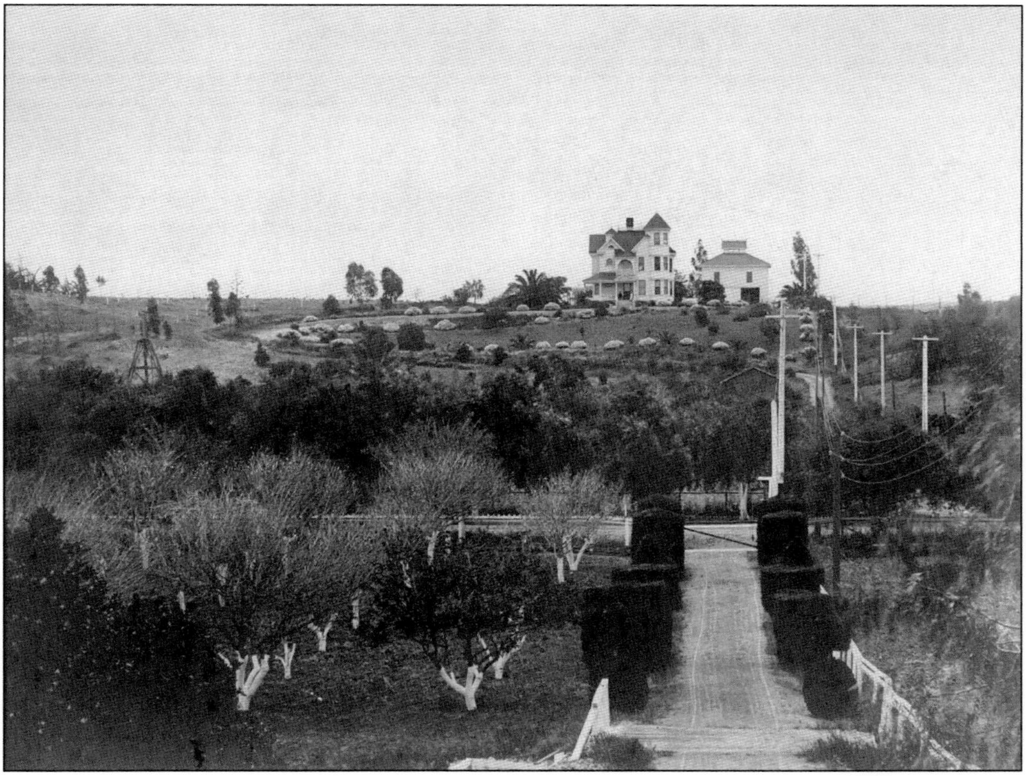

MOSES C. KIMBALL HOUSE. Built in 1893, this home at 2202 East Tenth Street stands overlooking Paradise Valley with a view eastward to Mount Cuyamaca and westward to the Pacific Ocean. Kimball, a retired farmer from Ohio, purchased the property from Elizabeth Brewster and commissioned National City architect Lewis Curtis to build a Queen Anne home for his wife, Sarah, and adult son, Edward. In the front entry hall, the oak staircase, with carved newel post, rises up to the third story. The four sets of pocket doors, which separate the entryway, the dining room, and the front and back parlors, are distinctive features of this house. When Moses Kimball purchased the property from Elizabeth Brewster, he gutted the home she had formerly occupied (see page 48) and converted it to be his carriage house (shown to the right in this photograph). This home turned carriage house predated Brewster. Josephus Asher, who owned a nursery in Paradise Valley in 1870, had originally built the house; it was one of the earliest residences on the National Ranch. The materials that were removed from this home, such as doors, trim, hardware, and mantel, were incorporated into Kimball's 1893 home.

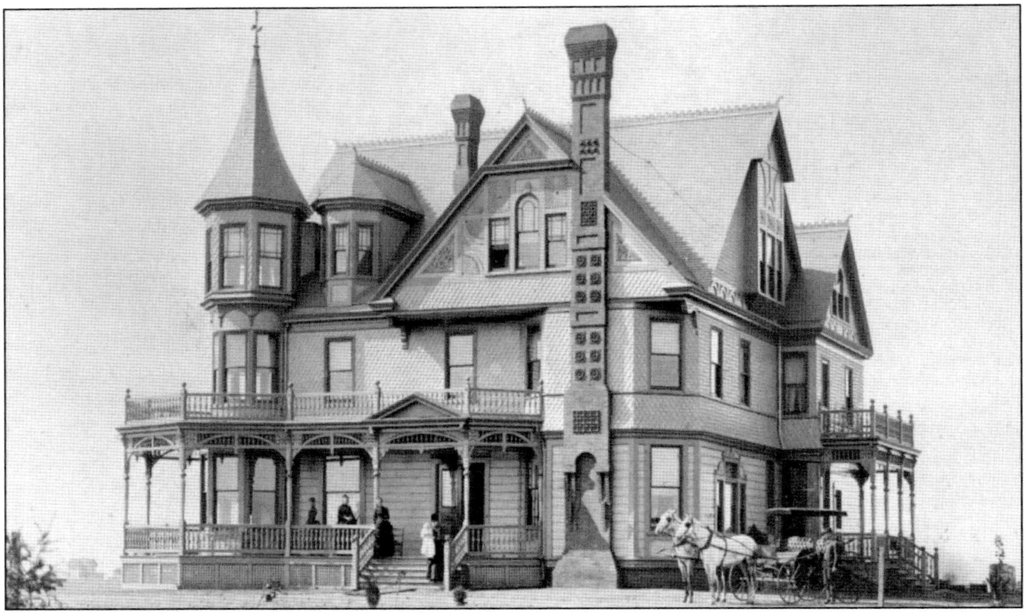

Dickinson-Boal House. In this photograph, Sarah Dickinson stands on the porch with arms folded, while Mary Dickinson Boal is holding her daughter Helen. Also included is ? Cumey (nurse), May Laurie (friend), Michael ? (the coachman), and the gray horses Jim and Lucy. This spectacular Queen Anne home, built in 1887, with its third-story ballroom was the scene of many happy parties.

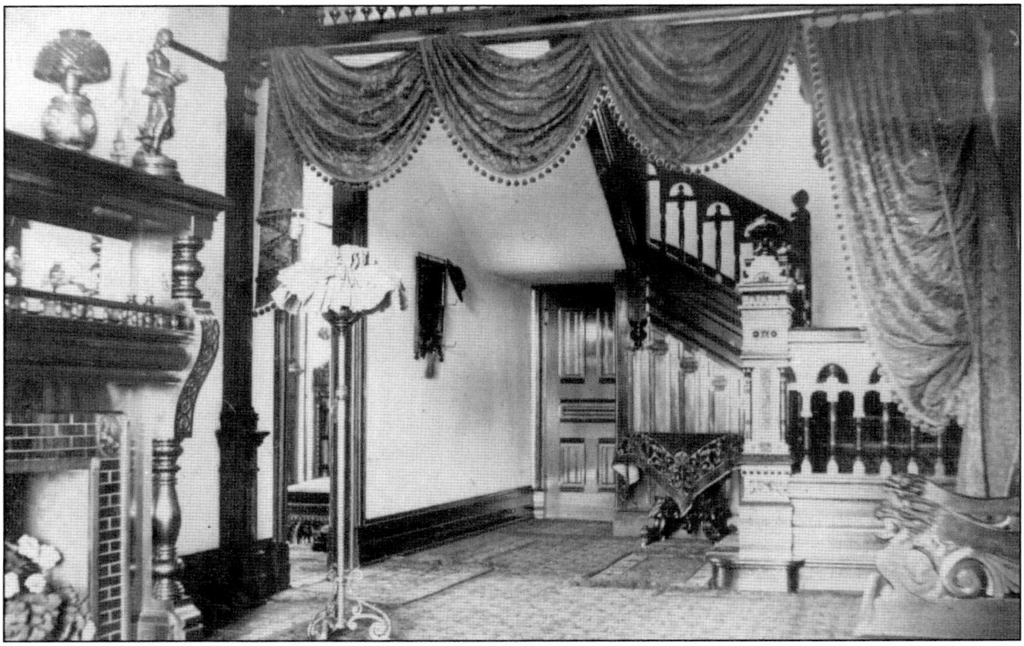

Dickinson-Boal House Interior, c. 1888. Queen Anne houses typically had a large front entry hall with an ornate fireplace and impressive stairs ascending to the second floor—and this house was no exception. Portieres separated the front entry, leading the eye back to the magnificent stairway and newel posts made of black walnut. Beautiful stained-glass windows adorned the parlor to the left and the dining room to the right. In 1887, the house cost $20,000 to build.

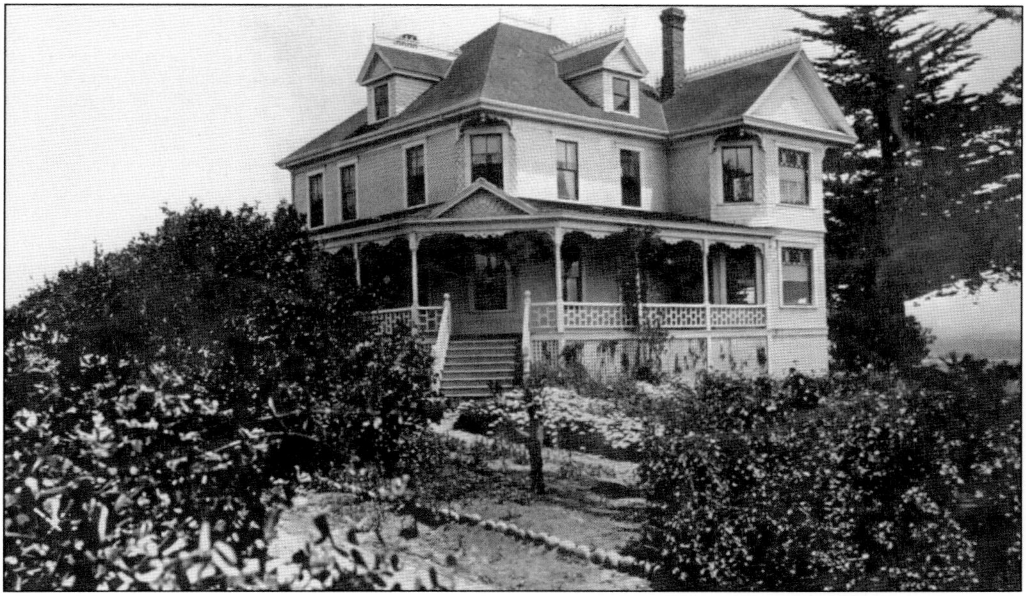

OLIVER NOYES HOUSE. Noyes, a friend of the Kimball family in New Hampshire, served as National City postmaster from 1893 to 1898. His home, built in 1896 at 2525 N Avenue, shows the characteristics of a simplified Queen Anne, with wraparound front porch, fish-scale shingles, and ridge cresting along the roof. The square panes of stained glass, which surround many of the windows, were meant to evoke the era of Shakespearean England.

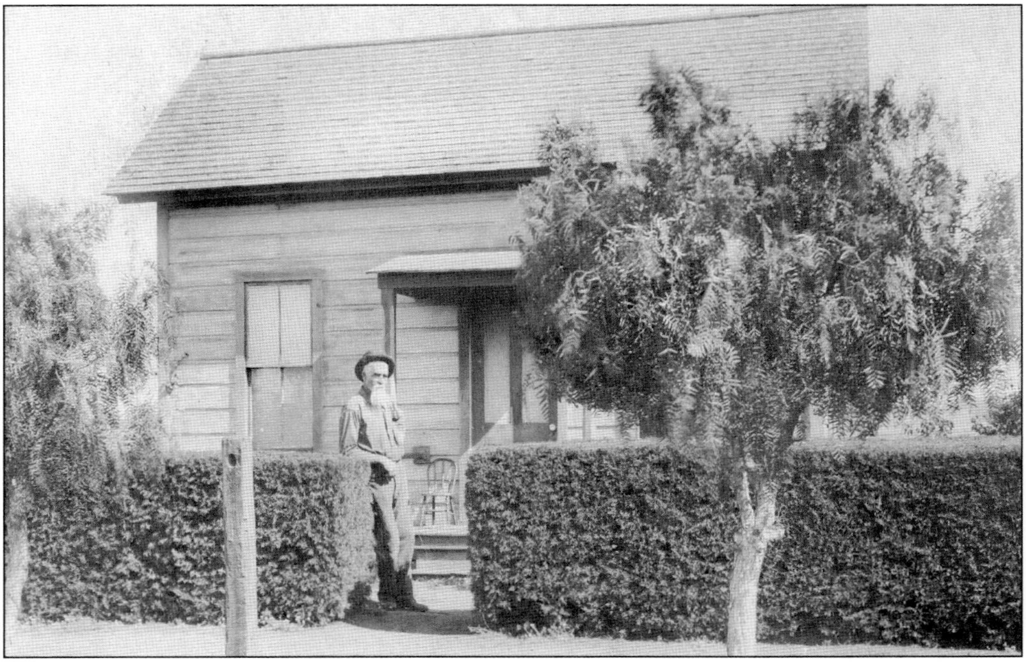

WILLIAM EGGLESTON, C. 1907. Frank Kimball noted in his diary, "Gus and I called on William Eggleston and saw his immense Kelsey plums, also peaches, pears, grapes and various other fruits. Also squashes." The Eggleston place, located on the east side of Roosevelt Avenue between Fifteenth and Sixteenth Streets, boasted an arbor on the south side of the house, which when covered with ripe grapes was said to have been a very beautiful sight.

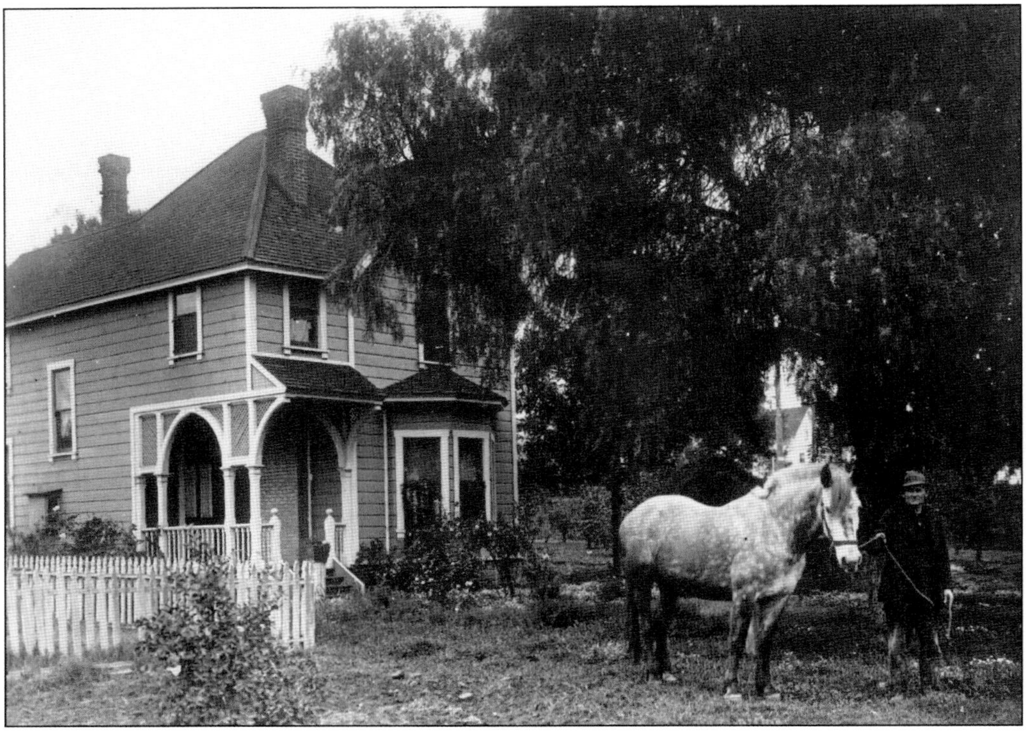

Elbridge F. Osborne House. Osborne, a native Californian, settled with his wife, Elizabeth, in this house on Twenty-third Street and C Avenue in the late 1890s. Like so many others in National City, Osborne was a fruit rancher. By 1910, the Osbornes had four children living with them: Florence, Marie, Myrtle, and Lloyd.

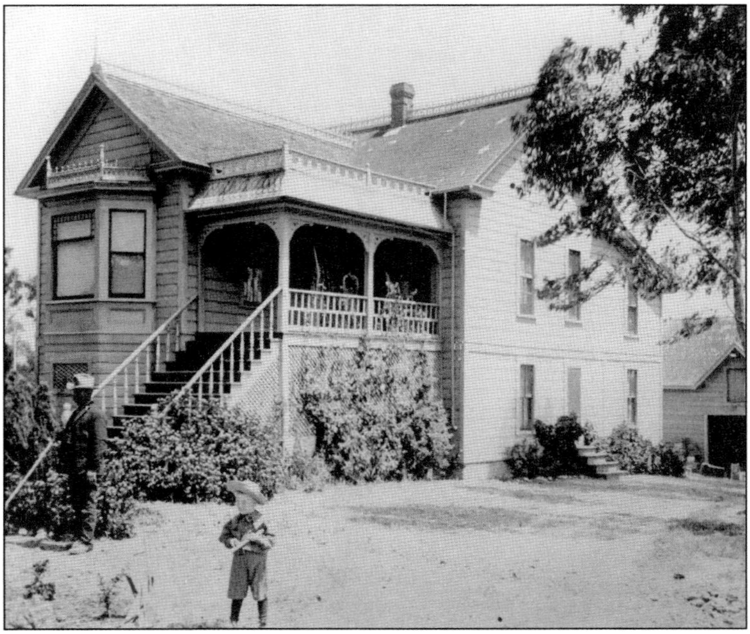

David Harbison House. The first home of David and Carrie Floyd Harbison was located on the south side of Eighth Street, east of Euclid Avenue. Carrie had come to National City as a child in 1876 and was an artist of note. The Harbisons had three children: Mary, Ira H., and Charles. Ira later served as a municipal judge in National City, while Charles became head of the entomology department at San Diego State University.

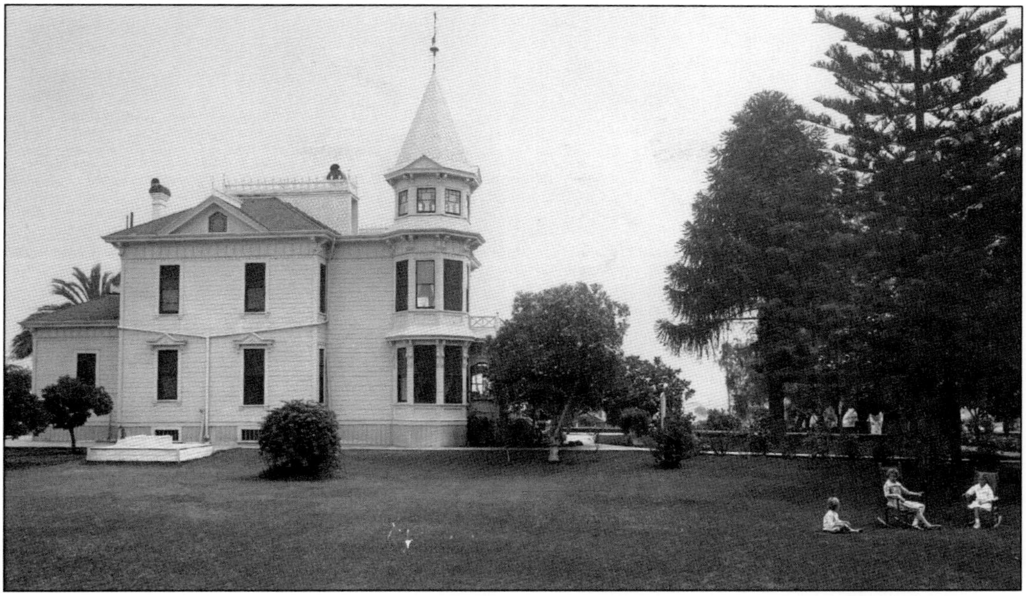

SHADOW CREST. Built around 1886, this house stood on the northwest corner of Second Street and Highland Avenue. Later it was moved north on Highland to Division Street. This was not the only National City home with a name—others included Olivewood, La Valencia, La Corona, Roseway Ranch, and the Willows. Note the gutters that channeled rainwater from the roof to an underground cistern—necessary in a dry climate.

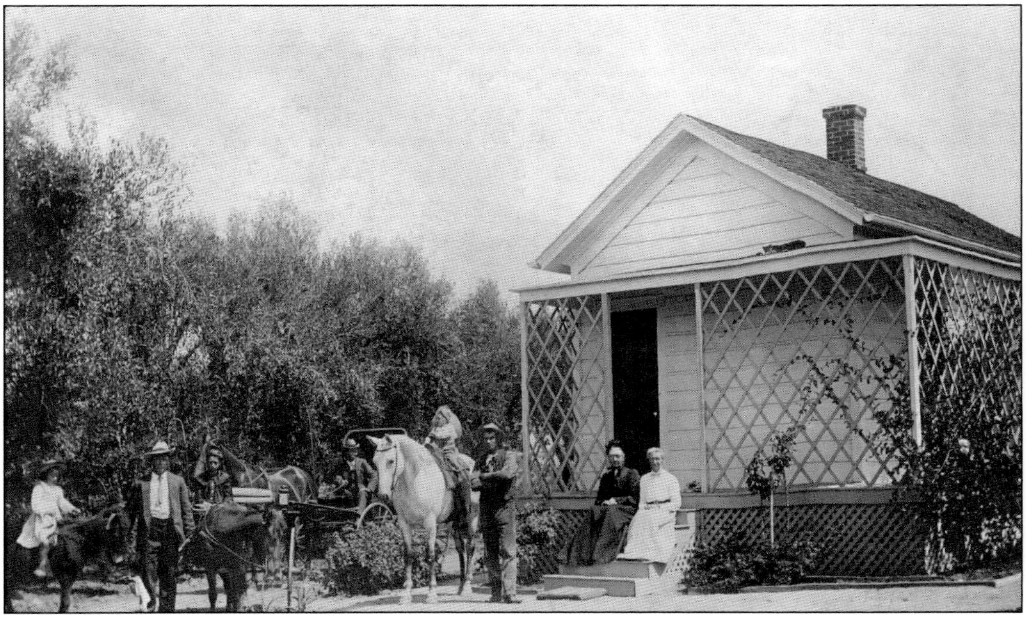

JOHN FLEMING HOUSE. Fleming built this ranch house in Paradise Valley in the 1870s, at Eighth Street east of Palm Avenue. Pictured from left to right are Marie Titus (on the Shetland pony), James Fleming, Jean Titus, Alex Burnside (in buggy), Lucile Fleming (on the white horse), and Jack Fleming. Seated on the front step is Elizabeth Fleming, John's wife, on the right. The Titus girls were neighbors.

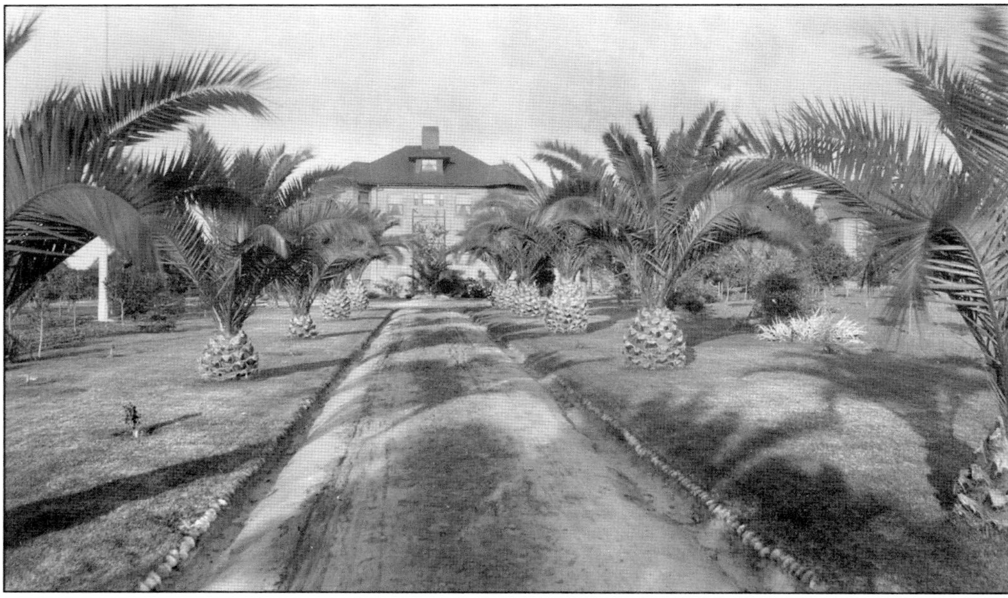

PALM DRIVE TO THE HORTON HOUSE. Frank Kimball encouraged his friend David K. Horton, an influential stockholder in the San Diego Land and Town Company, to move west for his health; unfortunately he only lived three years after arriving in National City. Horton lined the drive to his house with palm trees, the quintessential tree for Victorian Southern California. This house still occupies the property at 1504 East Twenty-second Street.

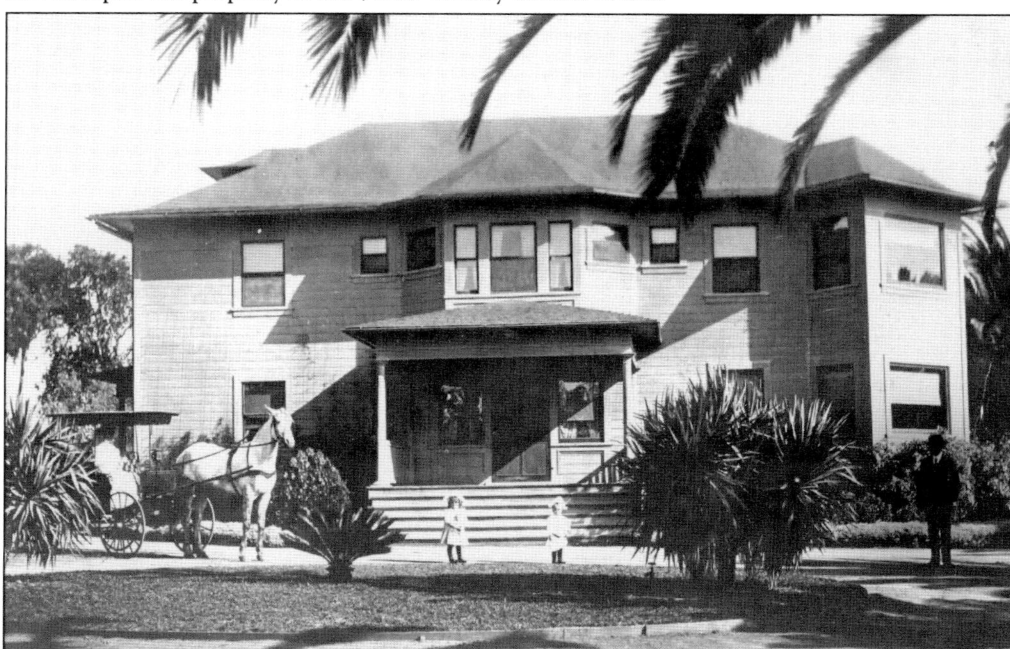

DAVID K. HORTON HOUSE. This home, designed by architect Irving Gill in 1895, is a wonderful example of his transition between the Victorian and his later style of architecture. Besides entry hall, living room, study, and sunroom, the first floor contains a formal dining room and breakfast room. Modern conveniences at the time of construction included electric wiring, indoor plumbing, central heating, and a skylight in the kitchen (a Gill feature).

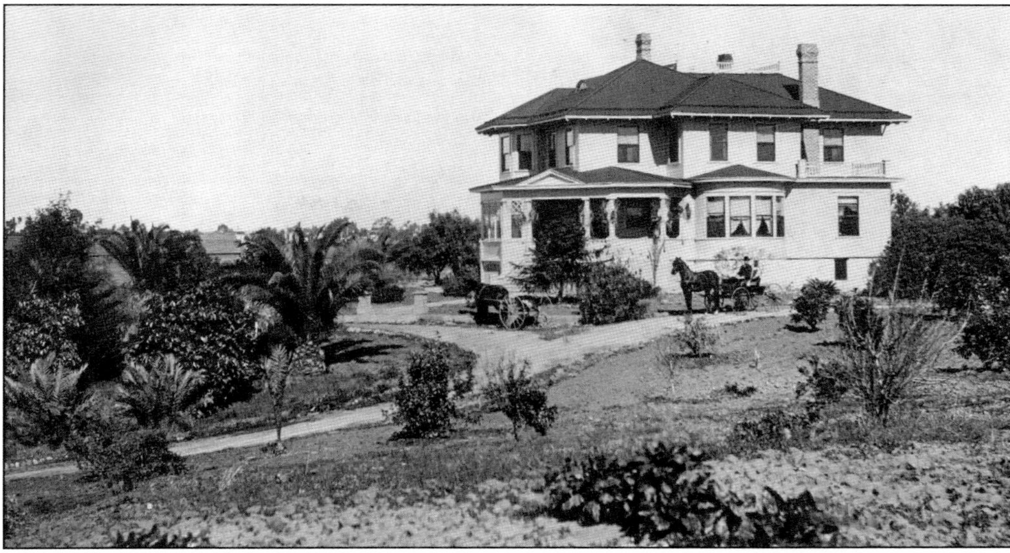

George W. Deford House. Deford came to National City in the late 1880s to operate the National Barley Mill as well as a feed store on Sixth Avenue. He built his Colonial Revival home—named Ronellaheim after his two children, Ronald and Estella—in 1909 at 1889 National City Boulevard. He served as a city trustee for several years in the 1890s. By 1910, he was out of the grain business and running a tobacco shop.

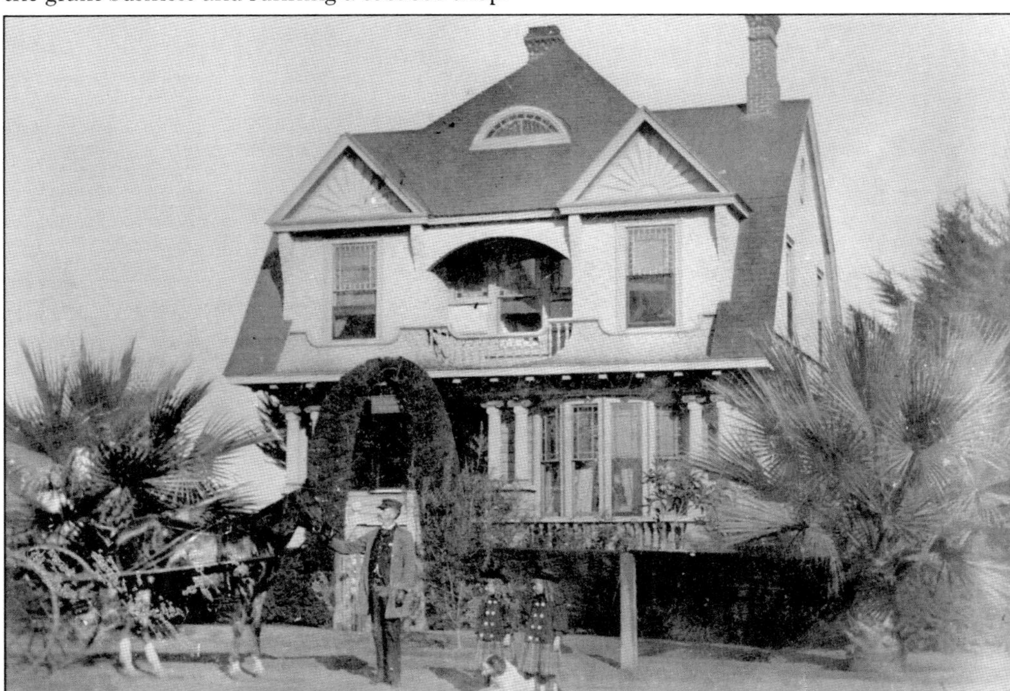

A. A. Robinson Home. Robinson worked for Warren Kimball as the manager of the National City Planing Mill. His Queen Anne–style house, with Colonial Revival elements, stood at Twenty-fourth Street and Highland Avenue surrounded by five acres with its own well. George Burnham, president and general manager of Scott Burnham Investment Company, lived here in 1904 with his wife, Neva, and their six children.

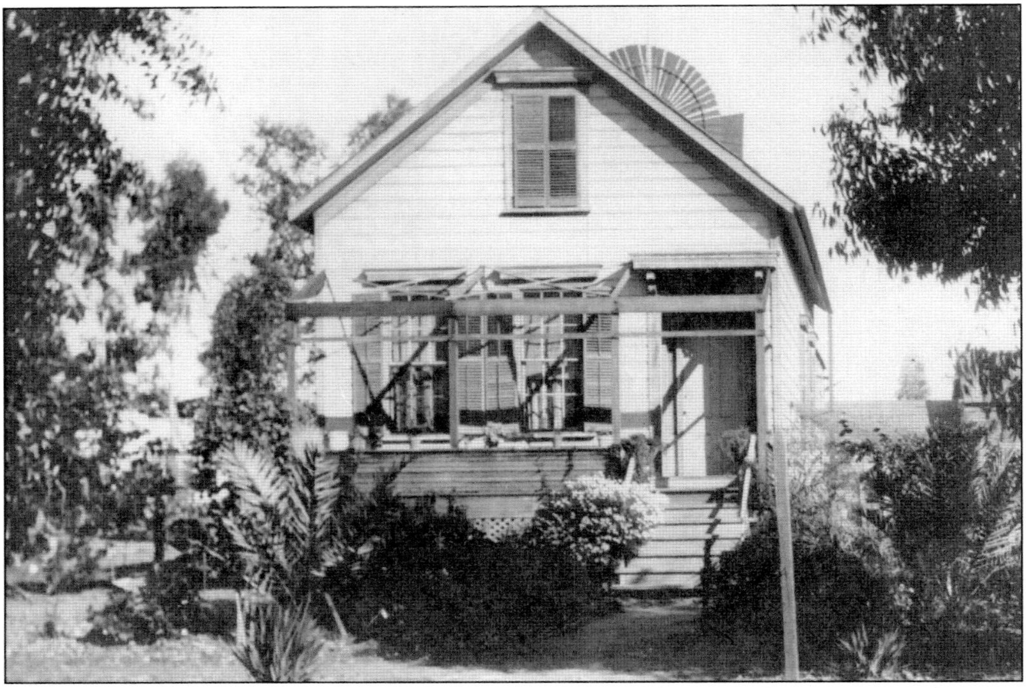

CAPT. F. T. MOORE HOUSE, C. 1904. This home stood on the east side of F Avenue, between Fifth and Sixth Streets. Moore had a reliable well in his backyard from which he obtained water to sell to his neighbors during dry spells. The windmill can just be seen peeking beyond the house roof. When not selling water, Moore was a woodworker and served as city recorder.

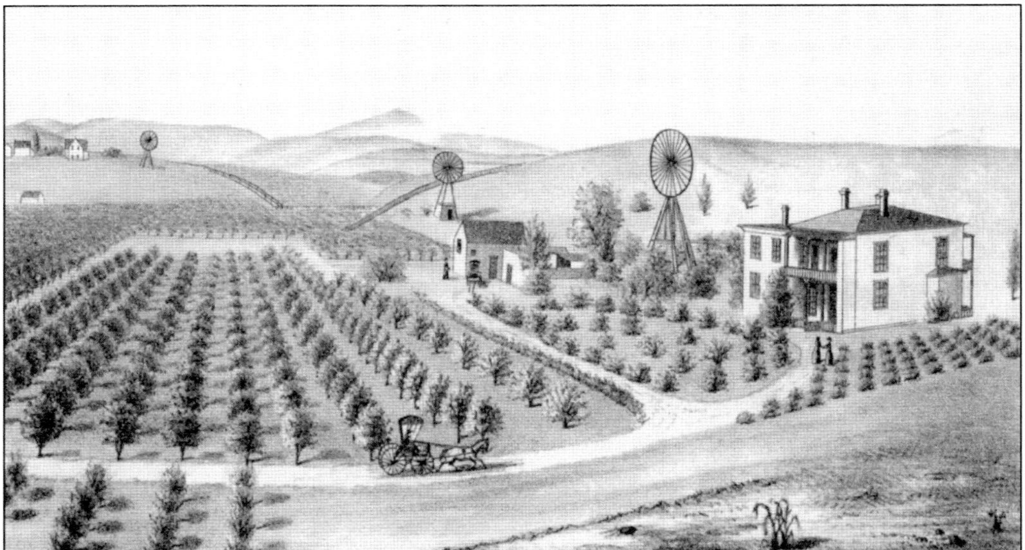

BREWSTER MEMORIAL HOME, PARADISE VALLEY. Elizabeth Brewster purchased the 1870 Josephus Asher house in Paradise Valley and converted it into a sanitarium for consumptives in honor of her son, who suffered from the disease. The home stood on the south side of Eighth Street at V Avenue. Besides caring for patients, she managed the gardens and orchards surrounding the home, winning several awards at local agricultural fairs for her produce. This lithograph is from the 1883 publication *History of San Diego County*, by Wallace W. Elliott and Company, Publishers.

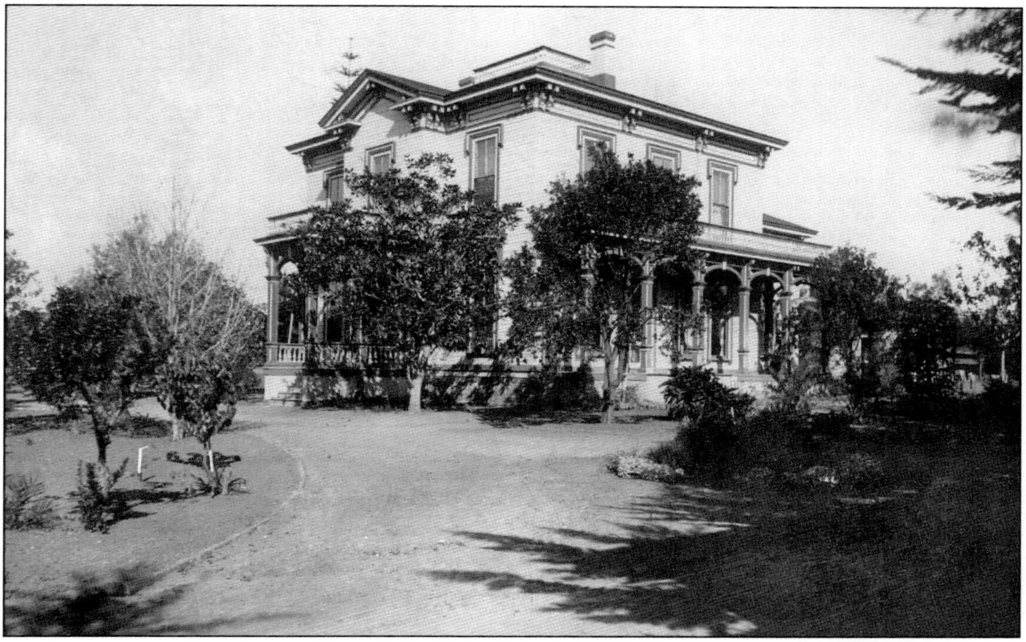

OLIVEWOOD. Built in 1887 for Warren and Flora Kimball, this Italianate house faced west toward the ocean. Flora, a noted horticulturist, surrounded her home with olive, orange, and lemon groves, rare plants, and ever-blooming flowers. Her gardening pursuits did not stop at her gate; she is credited with planting trees along the streets of National City, which she would water by hand with buckets she hauled in a wagon.

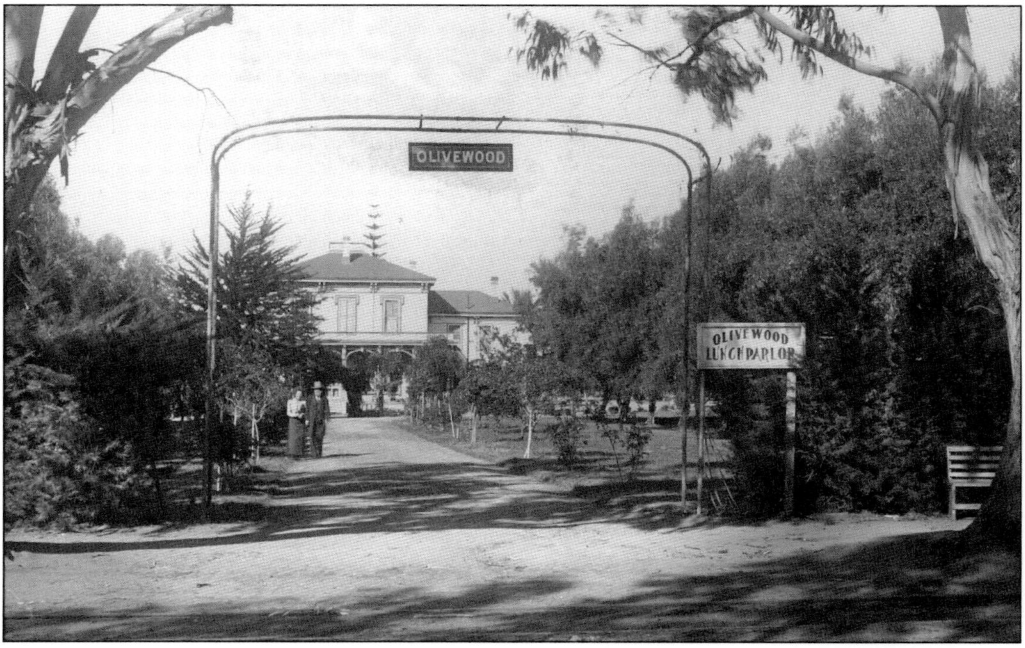

THE ENTRANCE TO OLIVEWOOD. Olivewood was a regular stop on the National City and Otay Railroad, whose tracks ran up Twenty-fourth Street. The sign to the right of the gate advertised the Olivewood Lunch Parlor, located east of the house, which offered guests a tasty meal and respite before touring the verdant grounds, which contained over 1,300 olive trees and 2,000 roses.

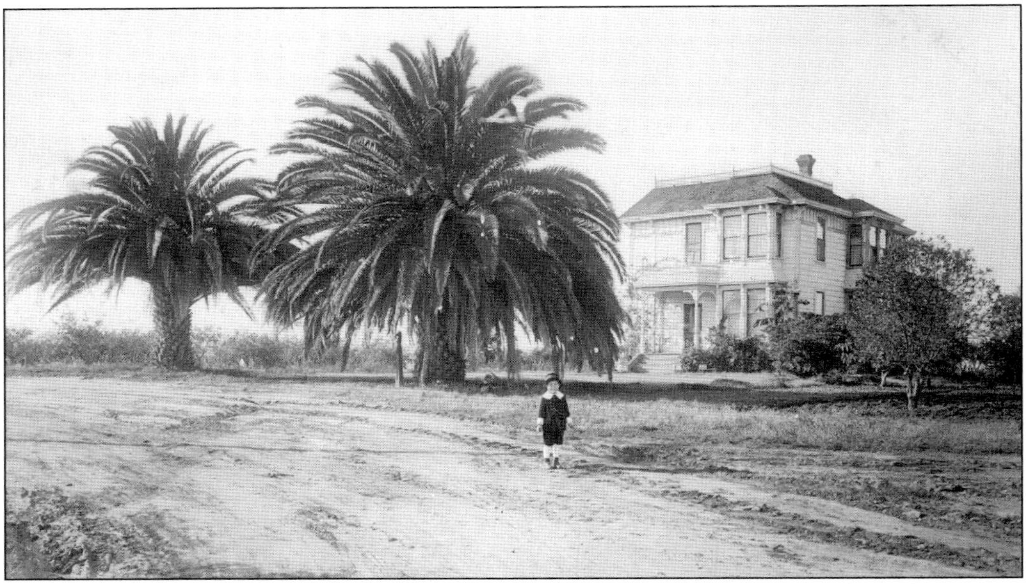

ORSMOND BARRETT HOUSE, C. 1880S. This Victorian Stick–style house stands on the summit of the hill at 1129 East Sixteenth Street. Dale Smith, a deputy assessor, and his wife, Ava, purchased the house in 1918. Their son Donald, the little boy in the foreground, is wearing a blue velvet suit now in the collection of the Kile Morgan Local History Room at the National City Public Library.

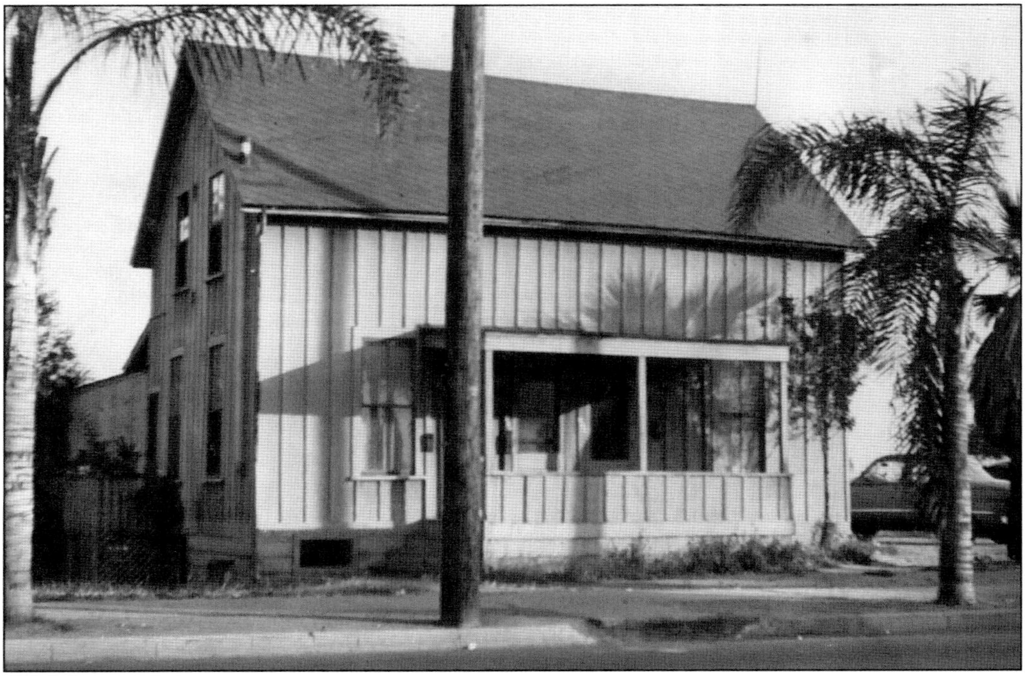

A CALIFORNIA HOUSE, 1885. Theron Parsons built this house at 606 East Eighth Street in anticipation of the boom expected with the coming of the railroad. Board-and-batten houses could be constructed quickly and cheaply in the temperate Southern California climate. The exterior was made with 1-by-12-inch boards, each placed on end, with batten boards holding them together. Cheesecloth, covered by wallpaper on the interior, kept out the drafts.

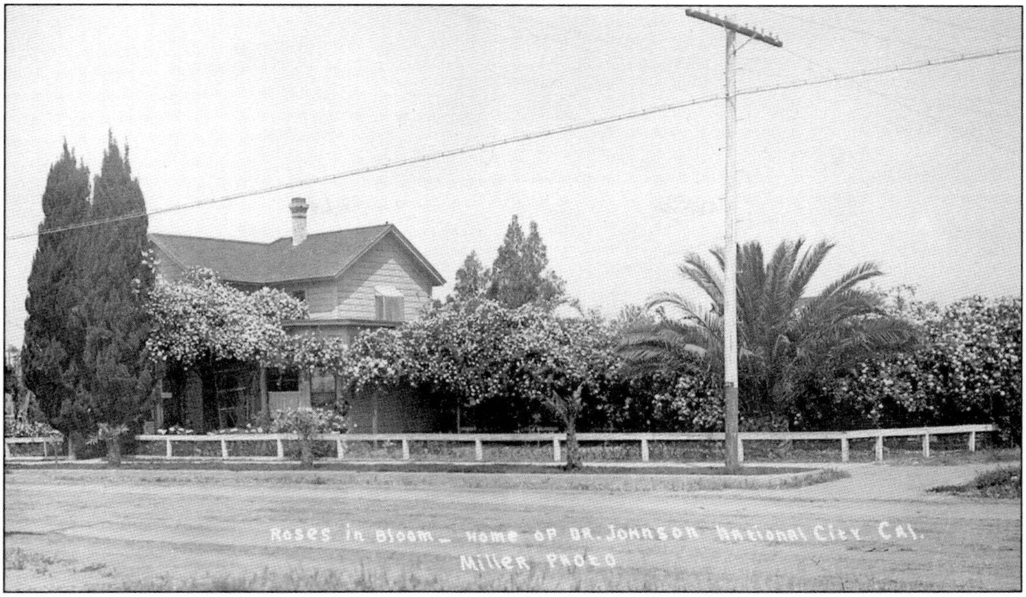

DR. THEODORE F. JOHNSON HOME. In 1889, Dr. Johnson left Vermont for California. He purchased a home at Eighth Street and B Avenue in National City, where he lived the next 45 years. As a physician, he served as the city health officer and as a civic-minded citizen, a school trustee, a member of the library board (for 30 years), and a deacon in the First Baptist Church. His daughter, Dr. Myrtle Johnson, graduated from University of California, Berkeley, and chaired the biology department at San Diego State College.

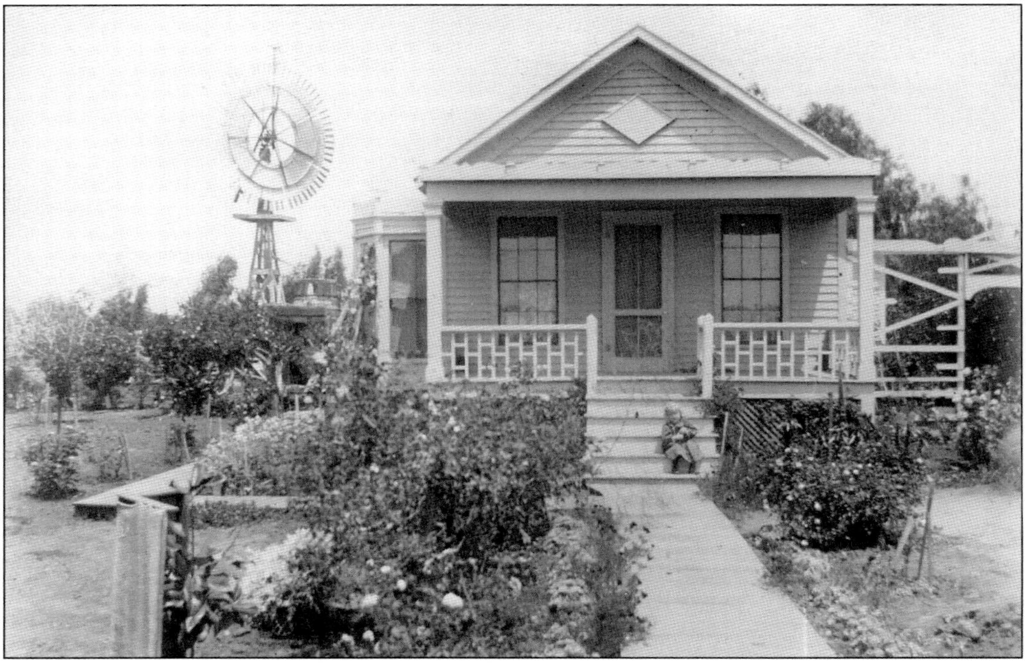

CHARLES H. SWEET HOUSE. The Sweet house stood at 641 East Eighth Street. This simple house typifies that of the common workingman. Sweet and his son were employed by the California Southern Railroad to clean cars in the railroad shops. In 1904, Sweet was promoted to engineer for the railroad. He later worked as a house painter.

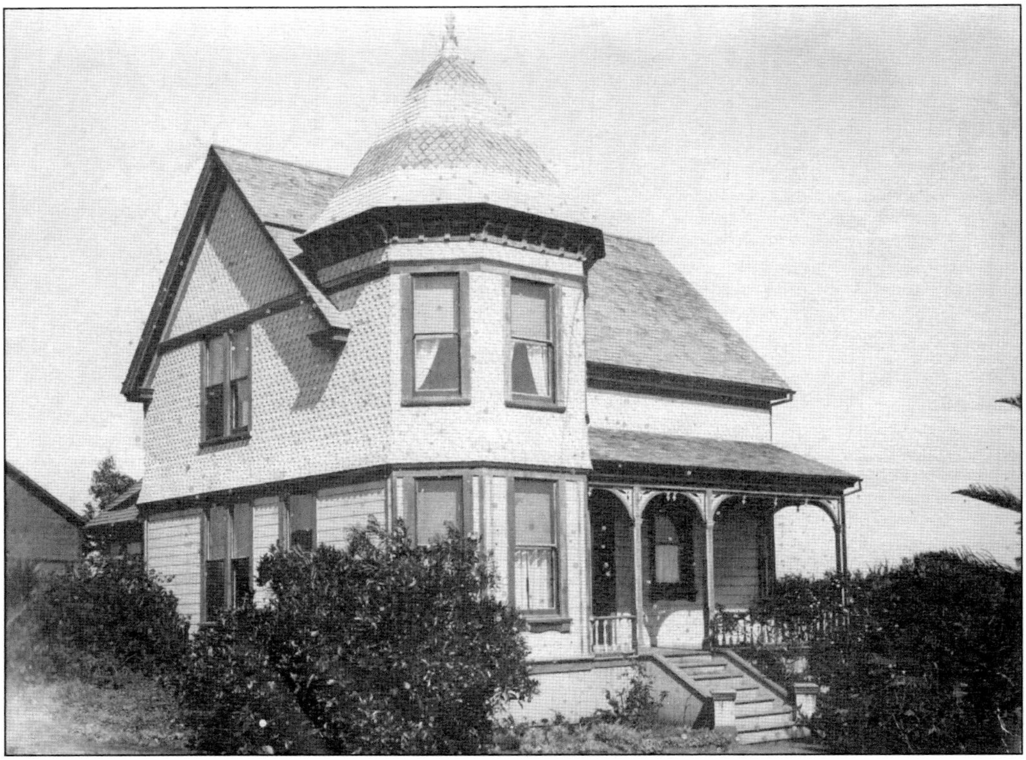

R. E. GATISS HOUSE. This house, located on Summit Heights at Twelfth Street and J Avenue, was built in 1892. The tower shows the popular Victorian custom of painting roof shingles in stripes, a common decoration not only for cupola roofs but for flat porch roofs as well. The colors used would commonly be gold ochre, olive green, and rust red. Since the shingles were made of wood, this decorative addition also helped preserve the roof. Gatiss was a rancher who purchased 10 acres between J and K Avenues and Eleventh and Fourteenth Streets. Cicero P. Evans, the local school principal, later owned the home.

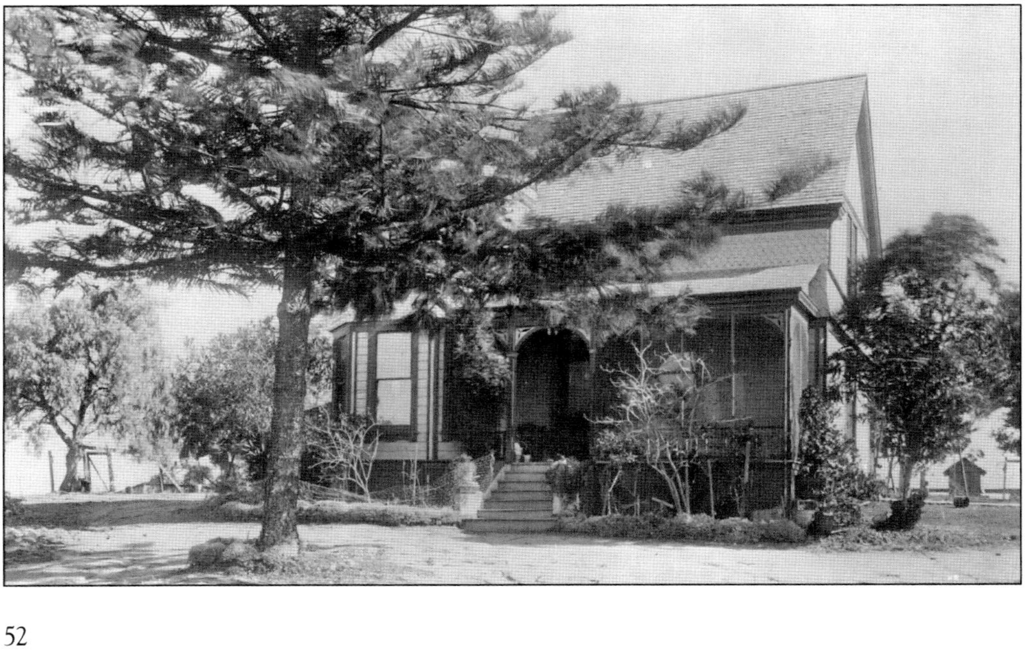

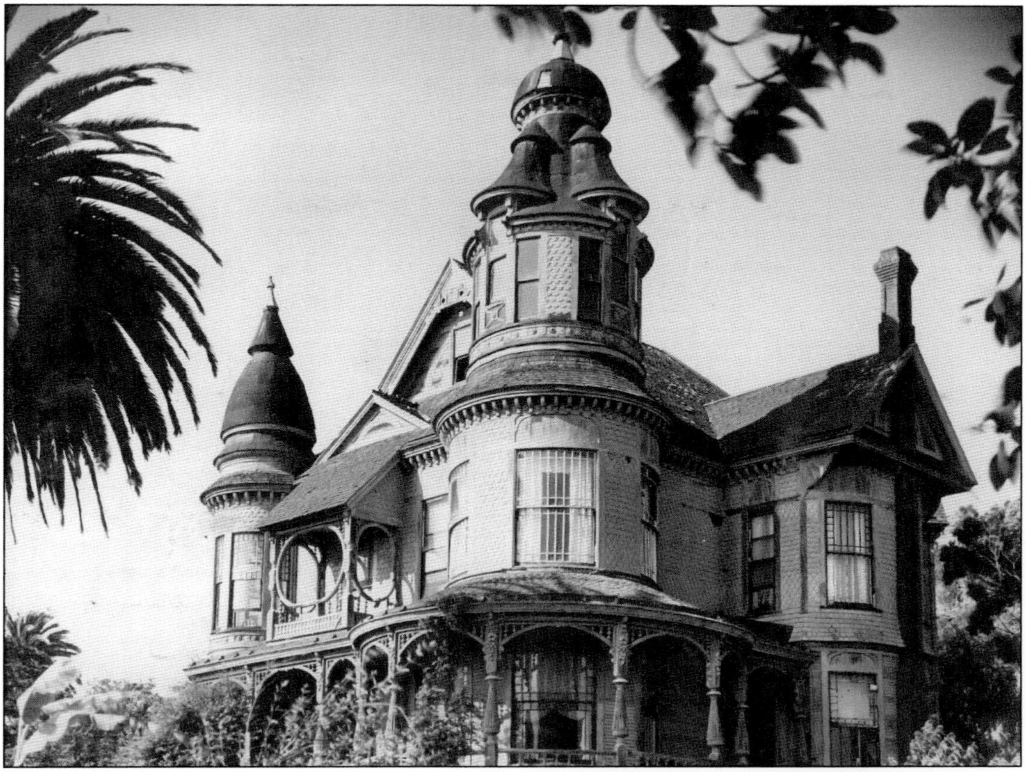

JAMES S. GORDON HOUSE. Frank Kimball sold Gordon the five acres of land on which he built this magnificent Queen Anne house in 1887. Located on the Terrace (N Avenue), this house was designed by National City architect Lewis Curtis. It sported two towers, one with an unusual Russian-inspired cupola, which can be seen in the center of the photograph. Gordon started out as a cashier at the Bank of National City when Frank Kimball was president.

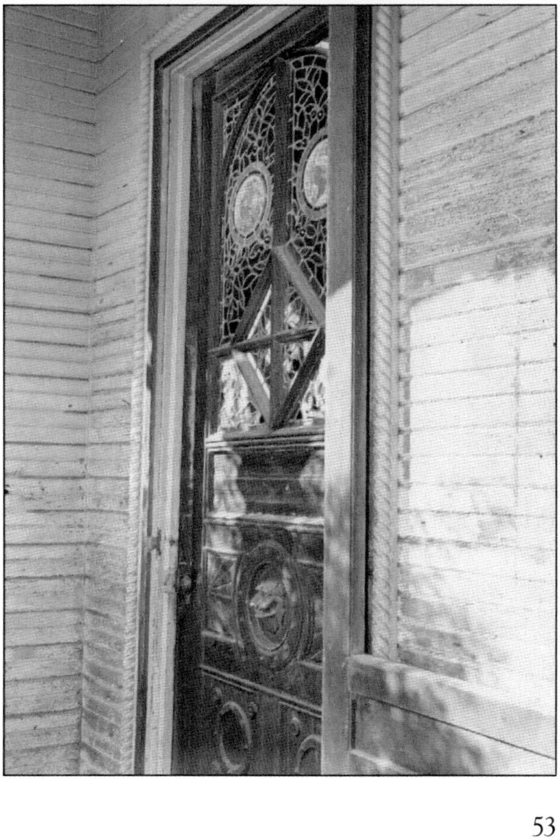

FRONT DOOR OF GORDON HOUSE. This carved door with stained glass served as a fashionable entrance to Gordon's impressive home. Gordon went into partnership with Alfred H. Isham in a wholesale and retail agricultural implements company that sold such items as wagons, carriages, lime, and cement. Unfortunately Gordon and Isham forged Frank Kimball's name on checks, which greatly added to Kimball's financial ruin.

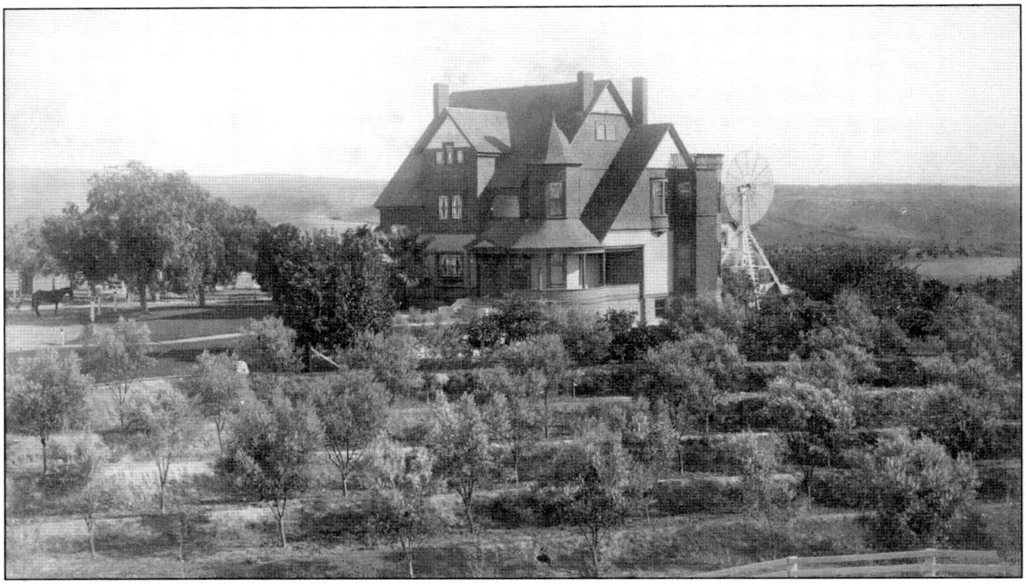

RALPH GRANGER HOUSE. Ralph Granger purchased this picturesque home, built by E. P. Fowler in 1889 at the east end of Paradise Valley, in 1893. At the time Granger arrived in National City, his Colorado silver mine was producing $5,000 a day. He owned business property both in National City and San Diego, raced horses on his private racetrack, and purchased the first automobile in National City.

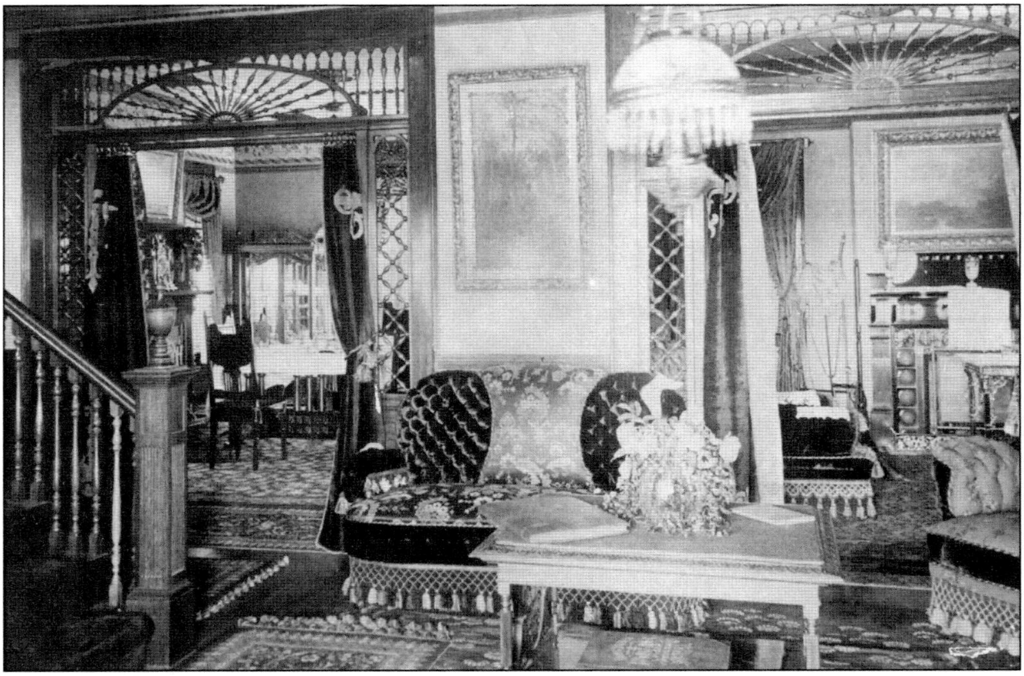

GRANGER HOUSE ENTRY HALL, 1899. From this elegant reception area, one can see the dining room on the left, the drawing room on the right, and the stairway to the second floor at the far left. There was also a second stairway located in the kitchen for the servants. Elaborate spindle work decorates the doorways. The tufted Turkish settee and chairs, trimmed with tassels, were very fashionable at the time, as were the Oriental carpets that covered the floors.

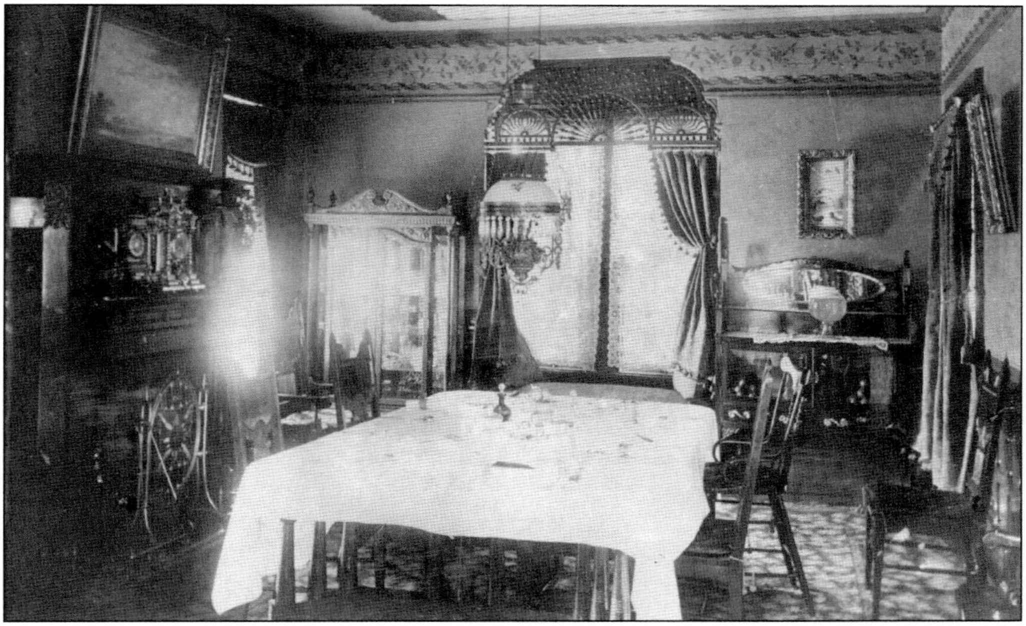

GRANGER DINING ROOM, 1899. In the Victorian fashion, a wallpaper frieze topped the walls and patterned wallpaper decorated the ceiling of Granger's dining room. Kerosene lamps provided light for country homes such as this, since electric or gas lines did not arrive until after 1910. The mirror over the fireplace and the prisms on the lamp helped to reflect light throughout the room. Heavy fringed curtains covered panels of lace at the windows.

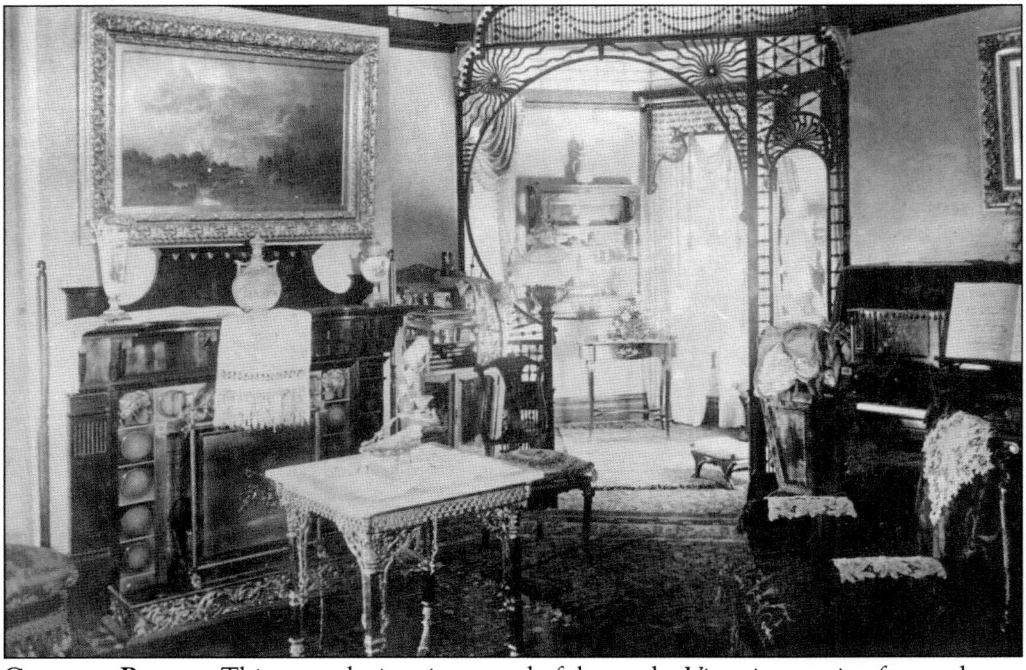

GRANGER PARLOR. This room depicts, in a wonderful way, the Victorian passion for good taste and overabundance. A large oil painting hangs over the well-appointed fireplace mantel. Embossed tiles cover the fireplace surround. The table in the center of the room shows the excellent taste of its owners. The piano on the right denotes Ralph Granger's love of music.

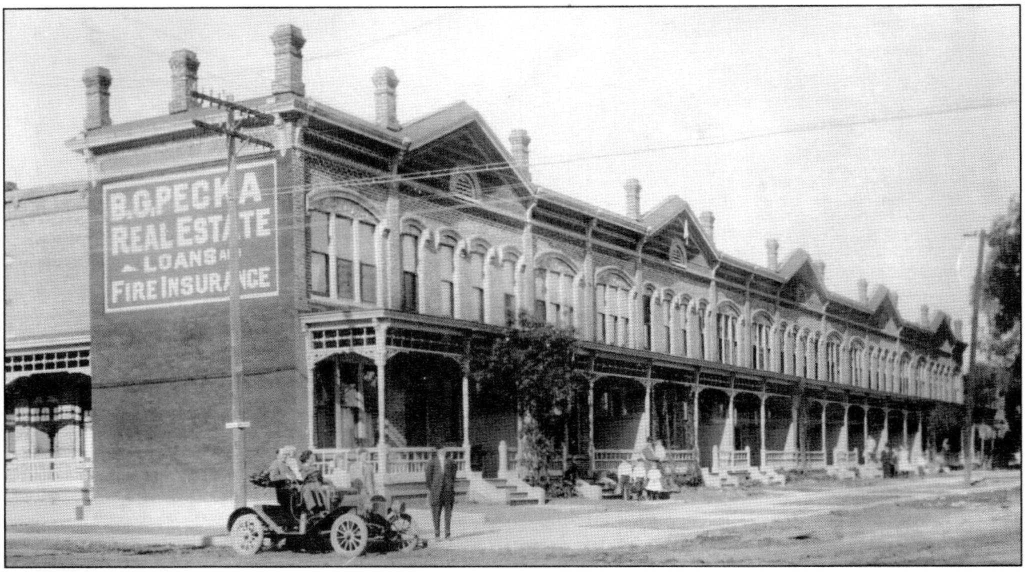

BRICK ROW, 1911. On September 23, 1887, Frank Kimball contracted with J. J. Hunt to build 10 row houses covering a footprint of 250 feet by 45 feet. This was during the economic boom, when visitors were sleeping in the hallways and on the veranda of the International Hotel for lack of rooms. The bricks were supplied from the Kimball brick kilns; the staircase balusters and newel posts were solid oak. It cost $22,000 to build all 10 units.

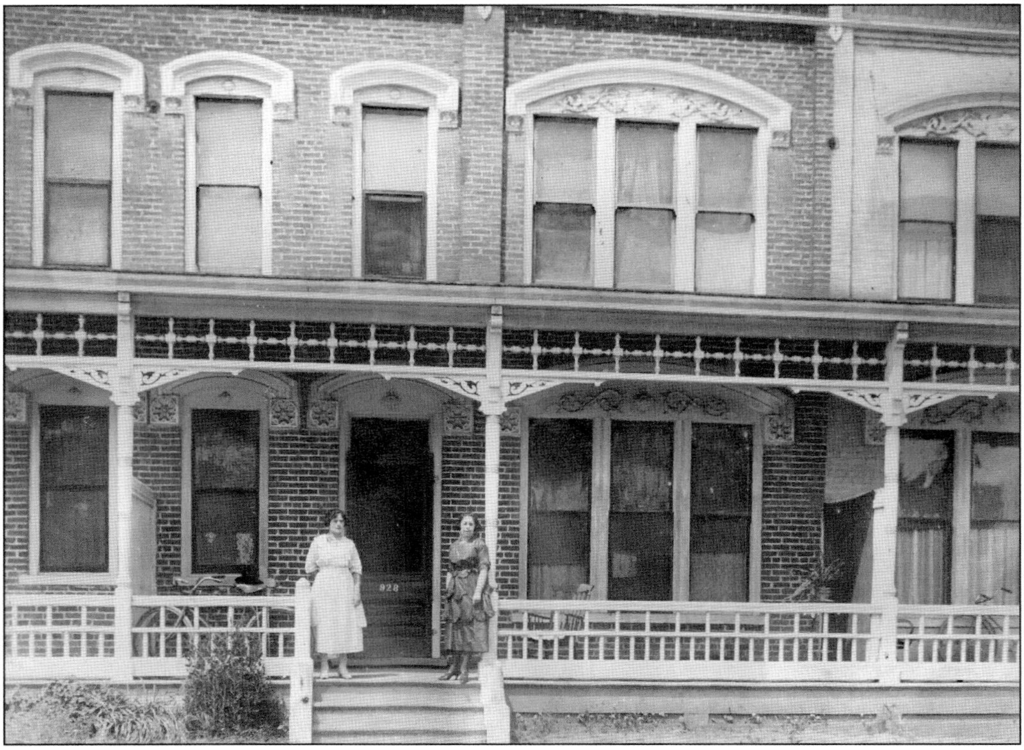

BRICK ROW UNITS. Each row house had its own front porch. Here the Cesena sisters, Augie (left) and Amparo, stand on their front stairs. The Brick Row, listed on the National Register of Historic Places, covers the west side of A Avenue, from Plaza Boulevard to Ninth Street.

Four

BUSINESS AND INDUSTRY

THE EMERGING CITY

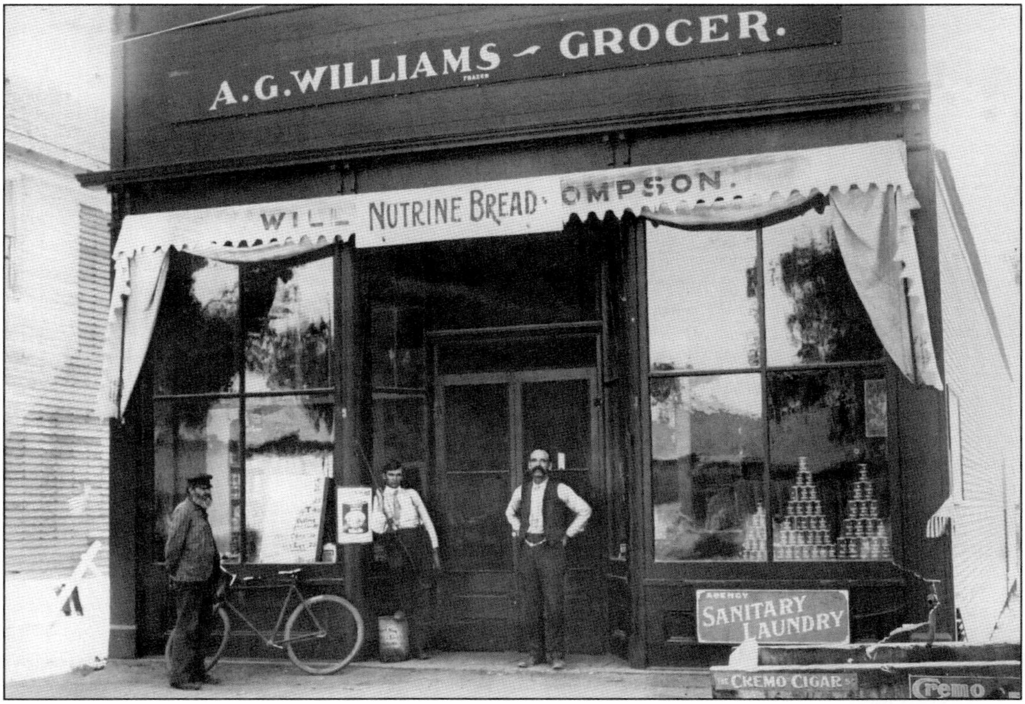

A. G. WILLIAMS GROCERY, C. 1880. Arthur Williams's grocery, located on National City Boulevard between Eighth and Ninth Streets, provided bread, canned goods, and other groceries along with hay, wood, and coal. Williams (wearing a vest) stands in front of the double doors. Originally known as the Horticultural Hall, it housed the first county Citrus Fair on September 22, 1880. This event continued to be held, first in National City, then in other parts of the county, and expanded to what is known today as the San Diego County Fair.

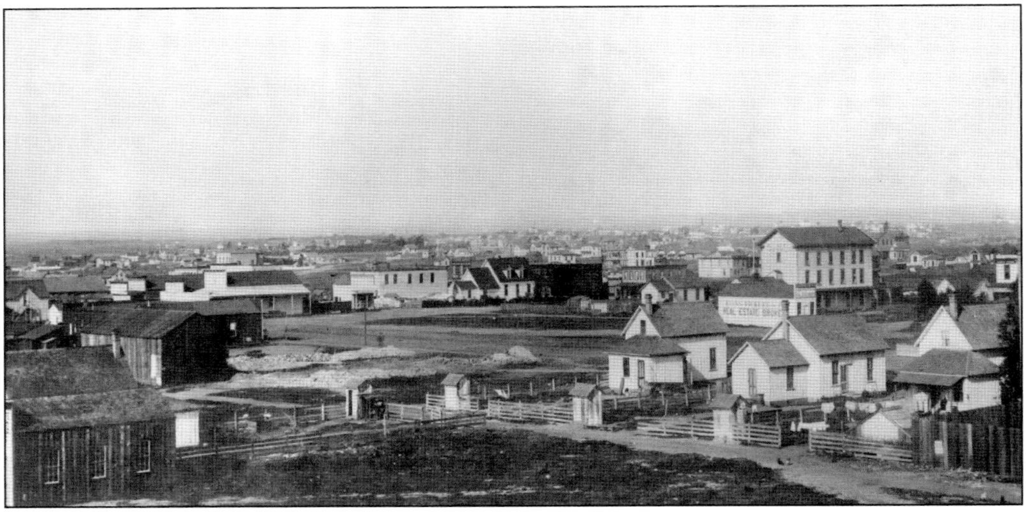

VISTA OF BUSINESS DISTRICT, 1887. During National City's early years, the business district stretched west of National City Boulevard along McKinley Avenue. The photographer most likely took this picture from the top of the Bank of National City, located at the corner of McKinley Avenue and Twenty-first Street.

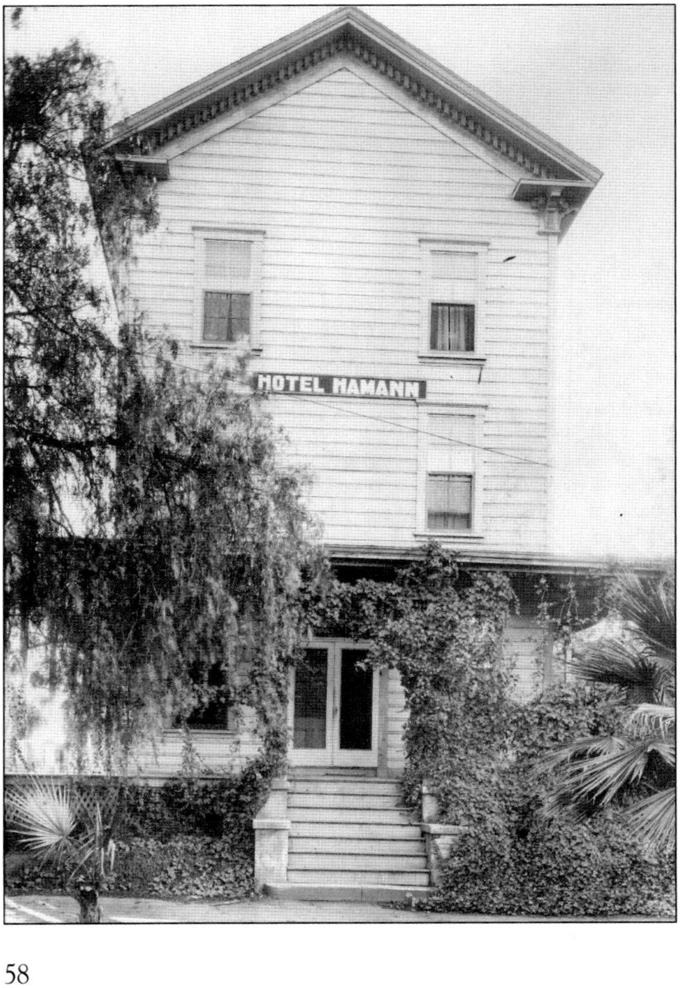

HOTEL HAMANN, C. 1913. In the fall of 1886, Frank Kimball built the Sixth Avenue Hotel on Twelfth Street and what is now Interstate 5 to accommodate increased visitors during the land boom. The hotel had a wide veranda that wrapped around the building and room for 100 guests, who were charged $6 a week for meals and lodging. In 1912, a new owner, William Hamann, renamed it Hotel Hamann.

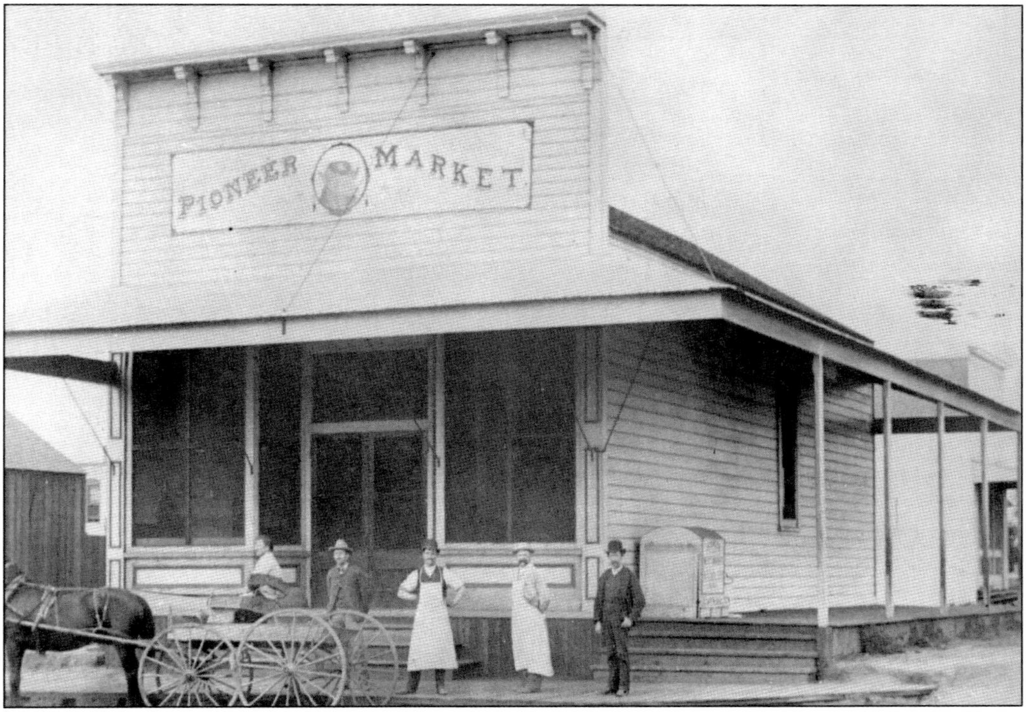

PIONEER MARKET. John T. Bohnert, a butcher by trade, owned the Pioneer Market located at McKinley Avenue and Nineteenth Street. In this photograph, Bohnert stands third from the left. He immigrated to this country from Germany in 1886, and his wife, Mina, arrived eight years later. They were married in 1898 and lived a block away from their market on Sixth Avenue with their two children, Karl and Bessie.

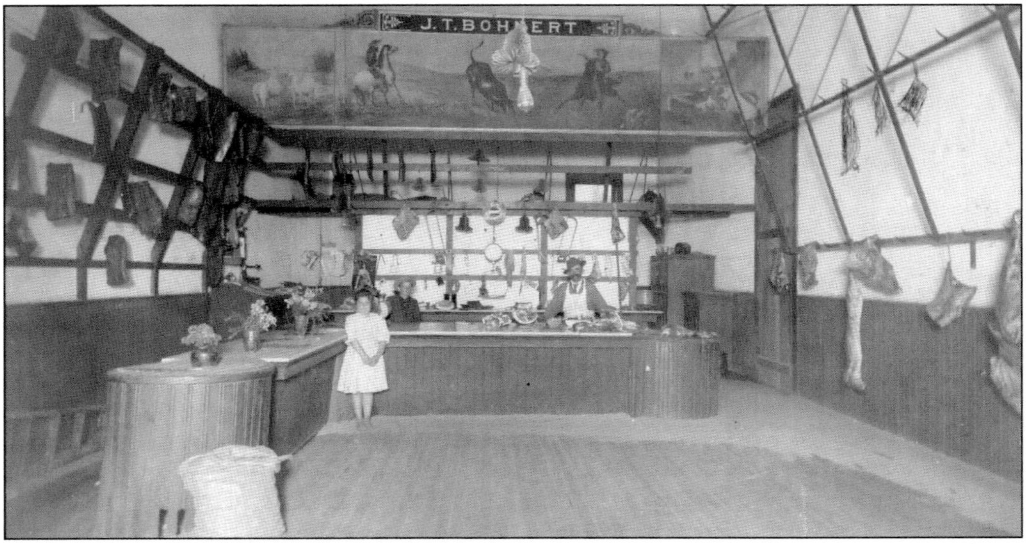

PIONEER MARKET INTERIOR, C. 1910. In a promotional article written in 1913, the *National City News* noted, "Mr. Bohnert conducts a most creditable meat market at 19th Street and McKinley Avenue. He does his own killing and wholesales as well as retails. His market is known to everyone in the city." Bohnert also carried fresh, salted, and smoked meats. At the counter, from left to right, stood Bessie, Karl, and John Bohnert.

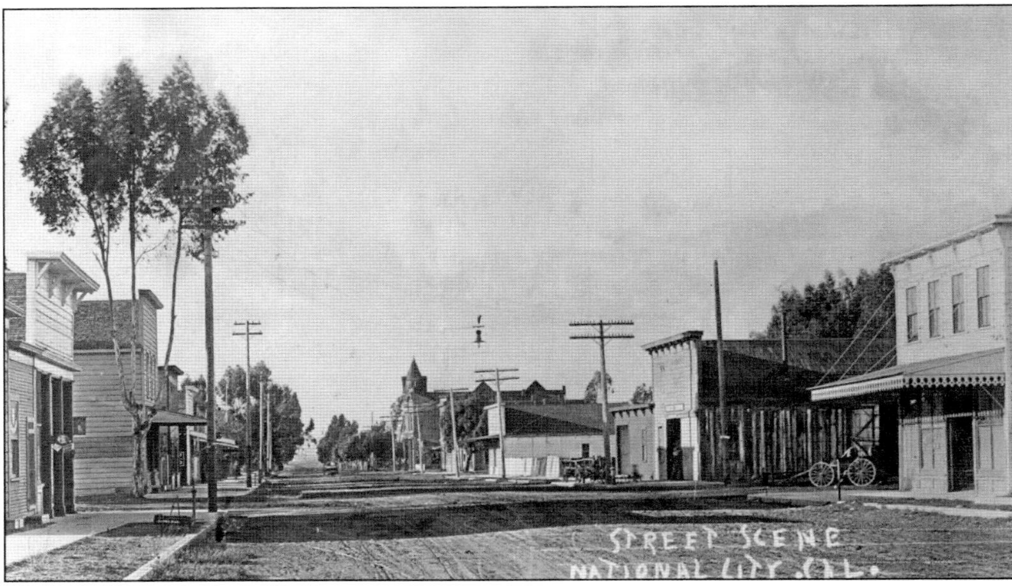

McKinley Avenue, Looking North from Nineteenth Street, c. 1900. In the distance, the building with the tower was the Boyd Building, erected in 1887 at the cost of $20,000. It had a galvanized iron front and a blue granite tower and became the social center of the business district, housing the Boyd Brothers' Drug Store and the post office. The building second from right is Otto Stang's blacksmith shop, on the corner of Eighteenth Street.

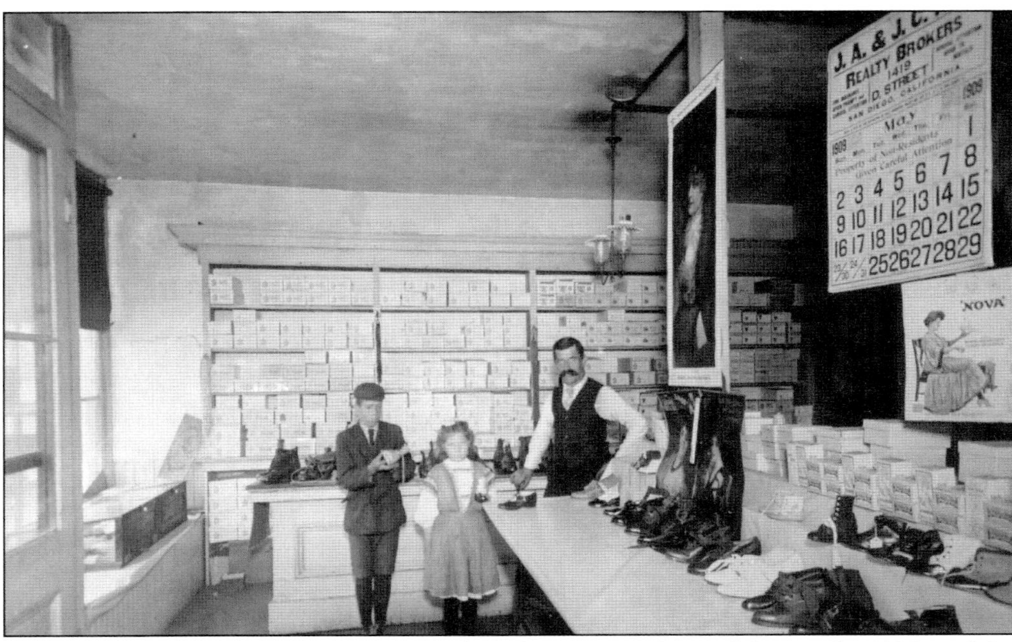

Schwenke Shoe Store, 1906. Gus E. Schwenke came to National City in the 1890s with his wife, Margaret. He opened the first shoe store in National City at 1632 McKinley Avenue, where he sold a line of footwear and did shoe repairing of all kinds.

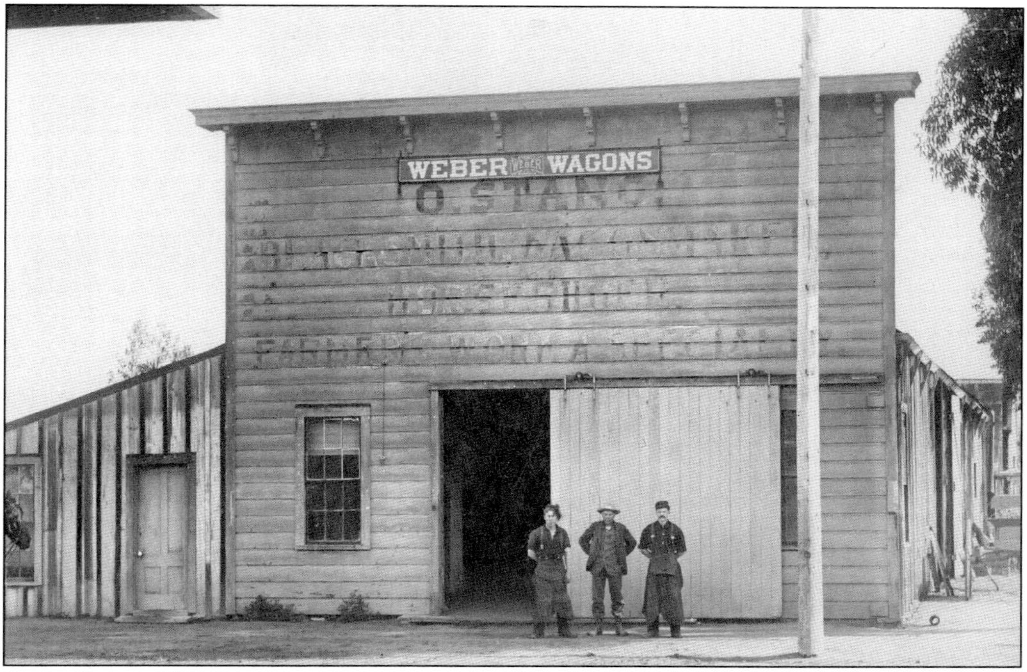

OTTO STANG BLACKSMITH SHOP, C. 1900. Stang opened his blacksmith shop in 1896 on Eighteenth Street and McKinley Avenue, and his business sign went on to hang there for the next 60 years. He was the premier blacksmith in National City. Frank Kimball mentions using Stang's services in his diaries.

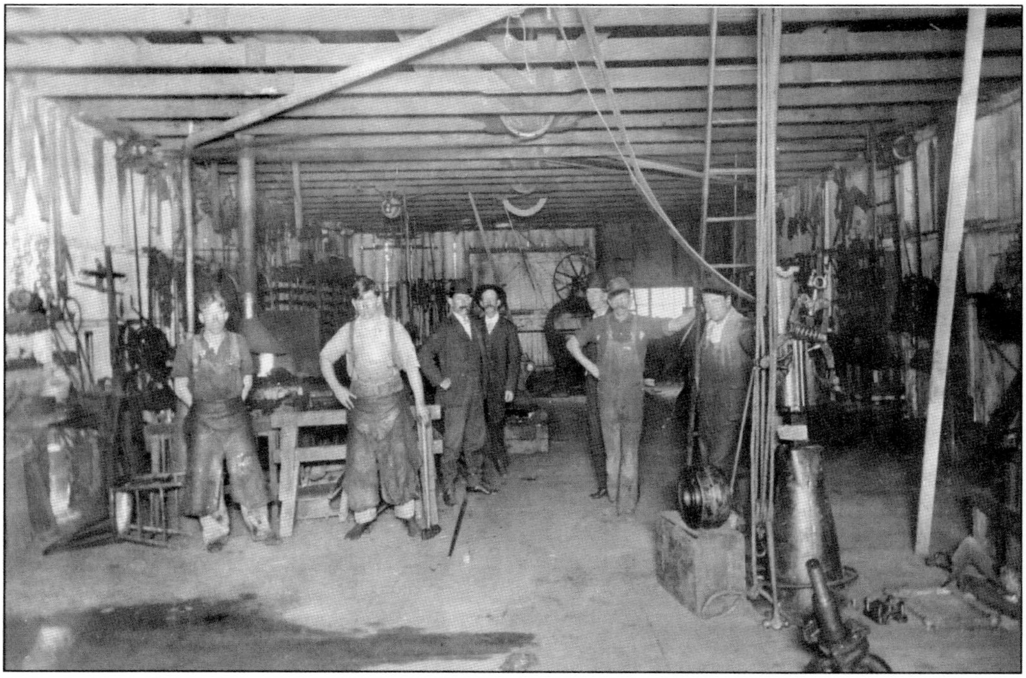

BLACKSMITH SHOP INTERIOR, C. 1906. Otto Stang not only shoed horses, sharpened tools, and constructed wagons, but he was a dealer in vehicles and farm equipment of all kinds. In later years, he built truck bodies in his shop.

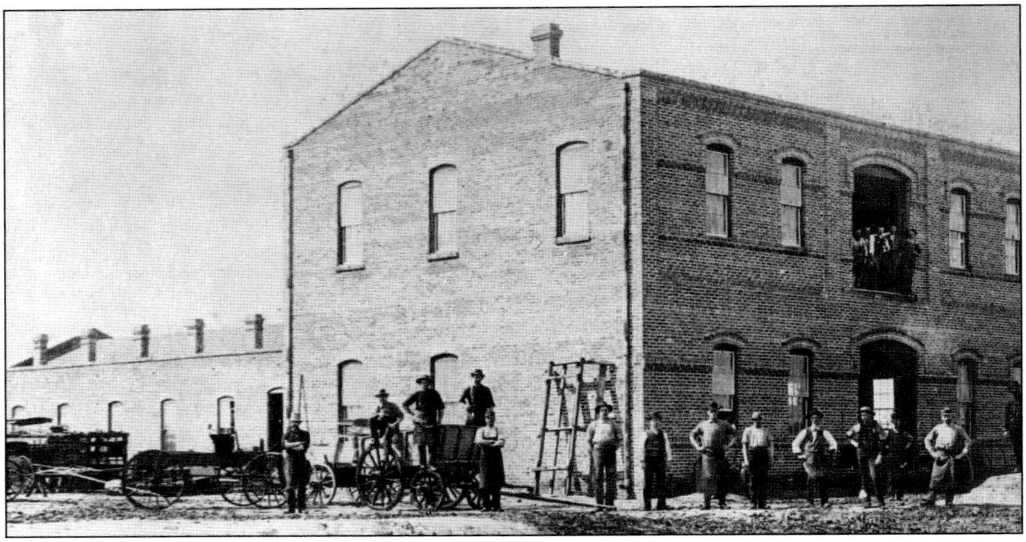

NATIONAL CARRIAGE MANUFACTURING COMPANY, C. 1890. Located at Twenty-third Street and National City Boulevard, this enterprise constructed expensive "road carts." Their vehicles were shipped as far as Los Angeles, Riverside, and even San Francisco. The May 30, 1889, *National Record* notes that the orders for vehicles were given "Not through sentimentalism or prejudice, but upon a thorough comparison of prices, quality of the material, and the workmanship."

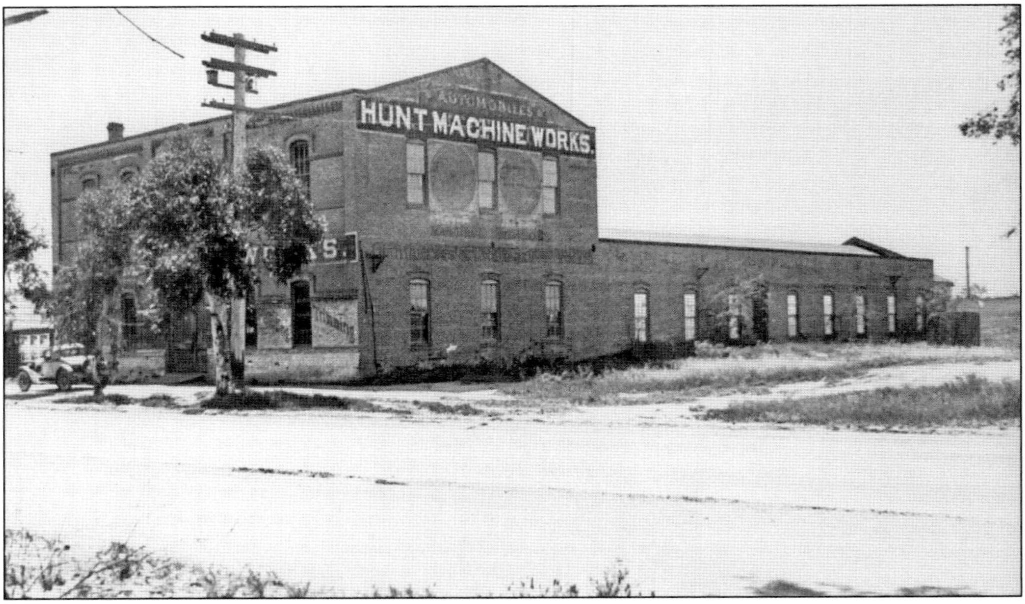

HUNT MACHINE WORKS. In 1904, brothers Clarence and William Hunt chose the empty National Carriage Manufacturing Company building in which to house their machine shop and repair business. At the request of Arnie Babcock, the Hunt brothers built a car—for the exorbitant cost of $16,000—that would be durable enough to transport Babcock on the rough roads between San Diego and his cattle ranch below Ensenada.

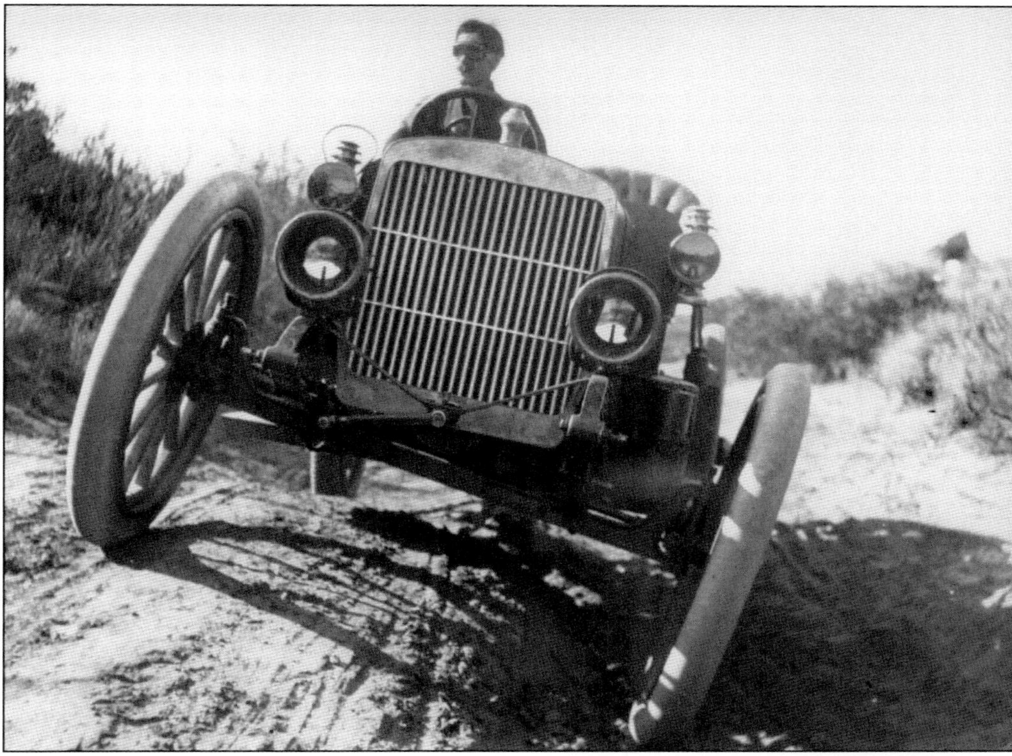

THE HUNT SPECIAL, C. 1910. It took the Hunts several years to complete this 5,000-pound automobile. It was unique in having a double chain drive, a 60-inch tread (which spanned the ruts in the road), and a center clearance of 18 inches. Babcock died soon after the car was completed, leaving the Hunt Special in Mexico. When rediscovered in 1955, it had been encased inside a store, which had to be partly dismantled when the automobile was removed.

RETURN OF THE HUNT SPECIAL, 1971. Joseph Straub restored "Alkali Ike," as the automobile was affectionately called, to its original condition under the supervision of William Hunt. Hunt actually rode in the car in the 1971 National City Western Days parade. The car can be viewed at the San Diego Automotive Museum.

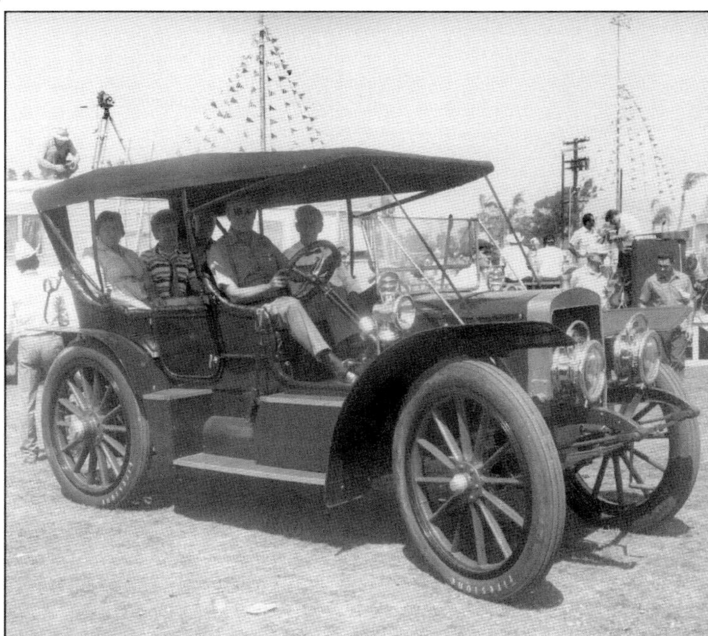

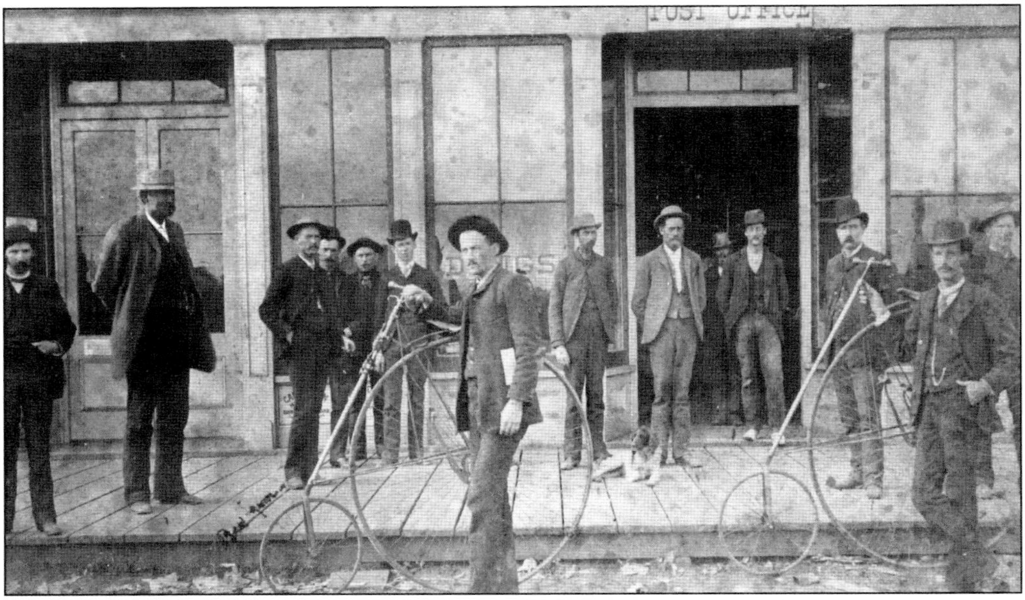

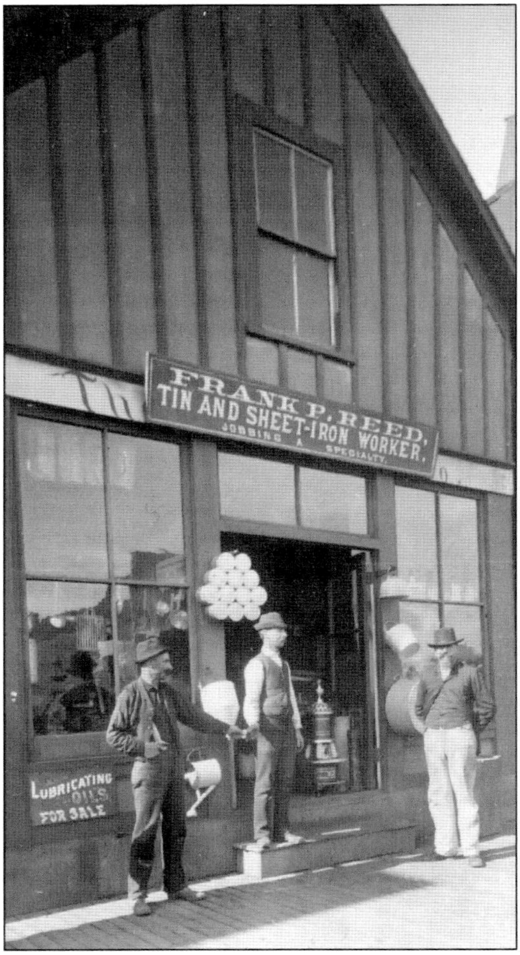

GROUP IN FRONT OF BOYD BUILDING, 1887. The men in this photograph are posing in front of the post office, located in the Boyd Building on the southeast corner of Sixteenth Street and McKinley Avenue. The businessmen included in this group are James D. O'Connell (real estate agent), J. R. Harris (jeweler), Lynn Boyd (postmaster, appointed July 23, 1886), George Chase (real estate agent), Ware Boyd (druggist), and Peter Rouland.

REED HARDWARE. Franklin Pierce Reed arrived in National City in 1883. He managed D. C. Kinsell and Son's Hardware, Stove, and Tin Store on McKinley Avenue between Eighteenth and Nineteenth Streets. He eventually bought and ran the business, changing the name to Frank Reed Hardware.

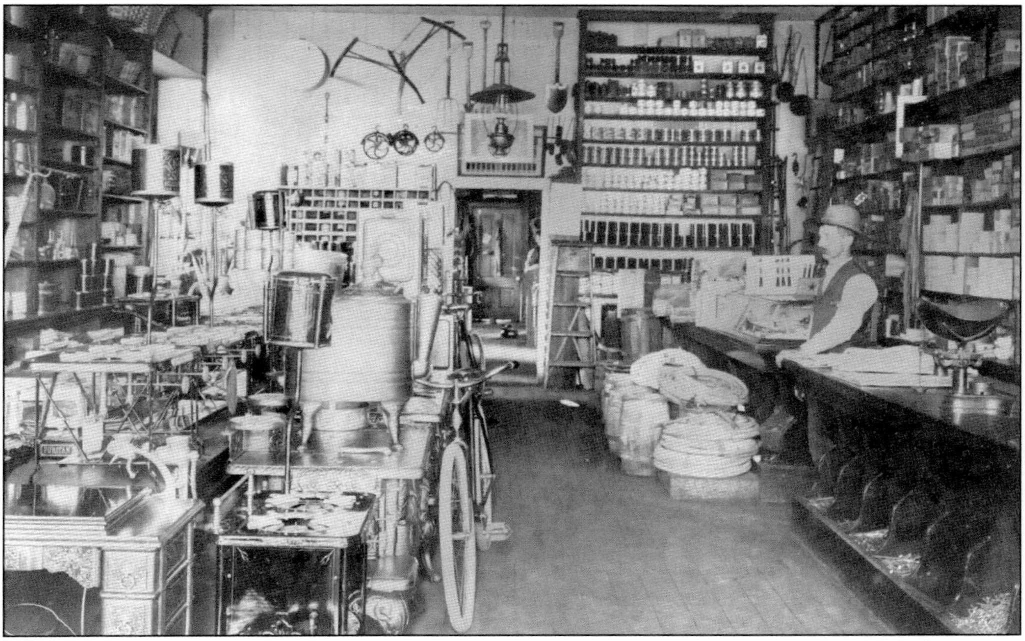

Reed Hardware Interior. Reed worked in the hardware business from 1883 until he retired in 1907. He married Hannah Jane Kimball Barnes, the daughter of George Kimball, and they raised two daughters, Chassie and Hazel. The store sold a wide variety of items needed in a rural community, ranging from hoes, sewing machines, and bicycles to saws and hay pulleys (seen on the back wall).

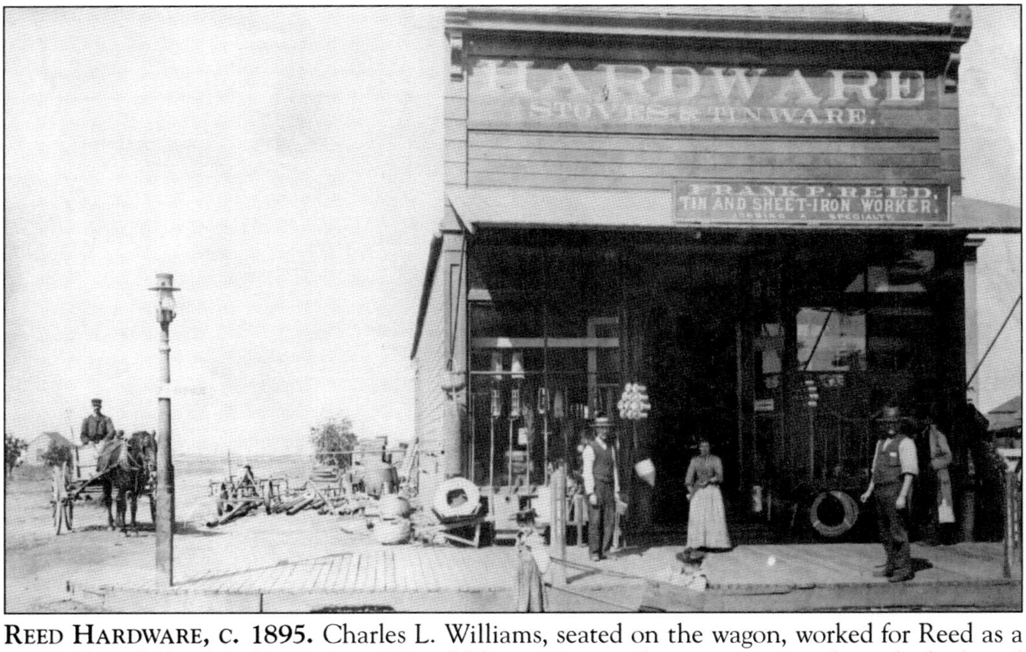

Reed Hardware, c. 1895. Charles L. Williams, seated on the wagon, worked for Reed as a tinsmith and plumber for 18 years. The old horse, Sox, took an active part through thick and thin and stayed with the family for some 23 years until he died August 21, 1907. Franklin and Hannah Reed stand in front of their store, with Nelson T. Chaffin on the right. In the foreground, Chassie Reed takes her sister, Hazel, for a ride in a small wooden cart.

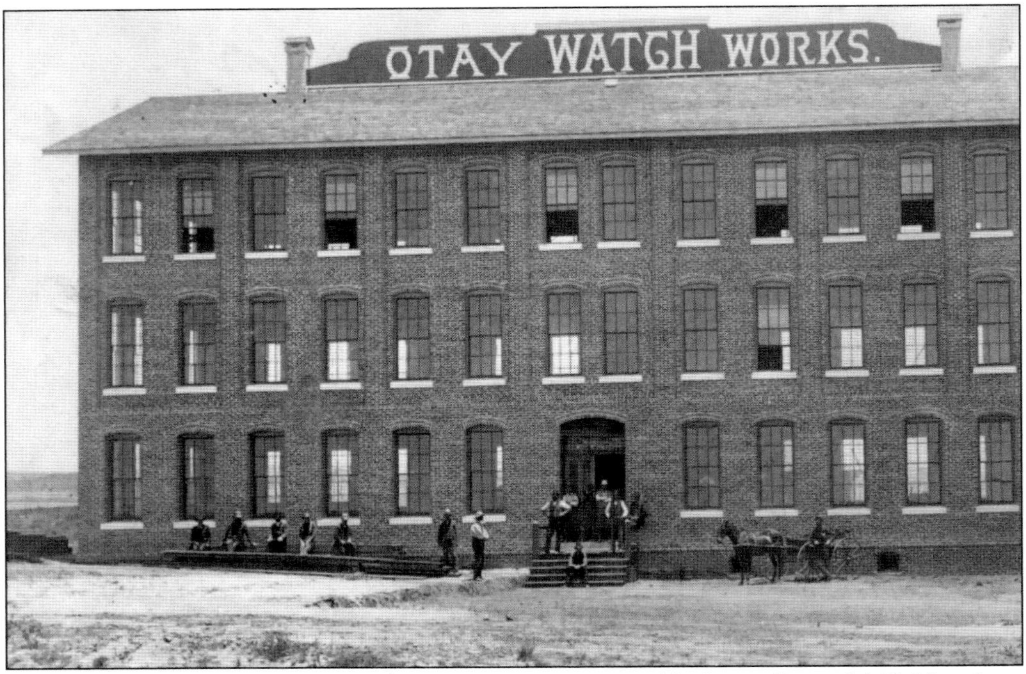

OTAY WATCH FACTORY, C. 1889. The company was organized by James Guion, M. D. Hamilton, and P. H. Wheeler in 1889 and started production in May 1890. At its peak, it employed almost 100 workers and was manufacturing 25 completed watches a day. Yet the factory could not pay for its new machinery or the workers' wages. Frank Kimball invested $70,000 to salvage this industry but to no avail; it closed in November 1890, with Kimball losing all his investment. Approximately 1,200 of these rare watches were produced, with the first edition appropriately named the *Frank Kimball.*

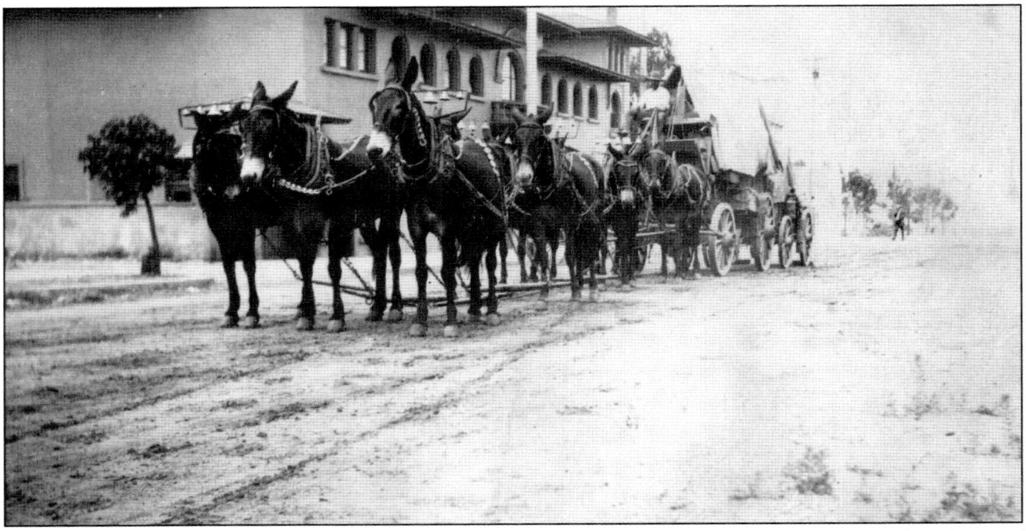

NATIONAL CITY REDUCTION WORKS, C. 1909. The mule-drawn wagons are pictured in front of the Granger Block at Eighth Street and National City Boulevard. The reduction works stood at 2310 Cleveland Avenue, where 10 stamps crushed quartz ore hauled in from Julian, San Bernardino, and Baja California, separating out the gold. On return trips, the wagons carried supplies to the miners. This company operated from 1887 to 1910.

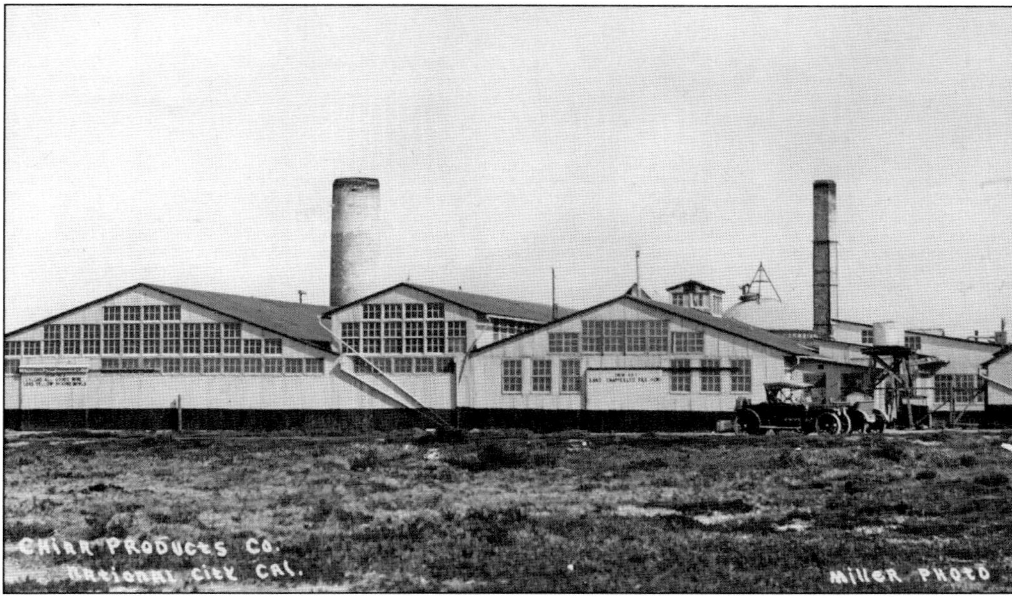

California China Products Company. Walter and Charles B. Nordhoff, father and son, in partnership with mineralogist John F. McKnight established this company in 1911. Located at McKinley Avenue and Twelfth Street, this was the first porcelain factory west of the Mississippi. Its 12,000-square-foot kilns were the largest in the country. The company became known locally for its brilliant, polychromatic Hispano-Moresque faience tiles, which can be seen today at the historic Santa Fe Railroad Station in San Diego (completed in 1914) and on the majestic California State Building rotunda and tower in Balboa Park (completed in 1915). After six brief years of operation, the California China Products Company closed its doors in 1917. With the advent of World War I, Charles Nordhoff enlisted, eventually becoming a fighter pilot in Europe; he is, however, best known for writing *Mutiny on the Bounty*.

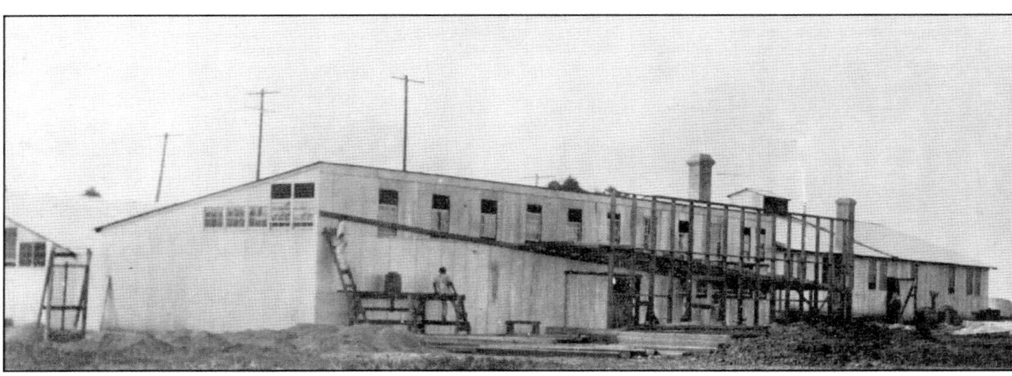

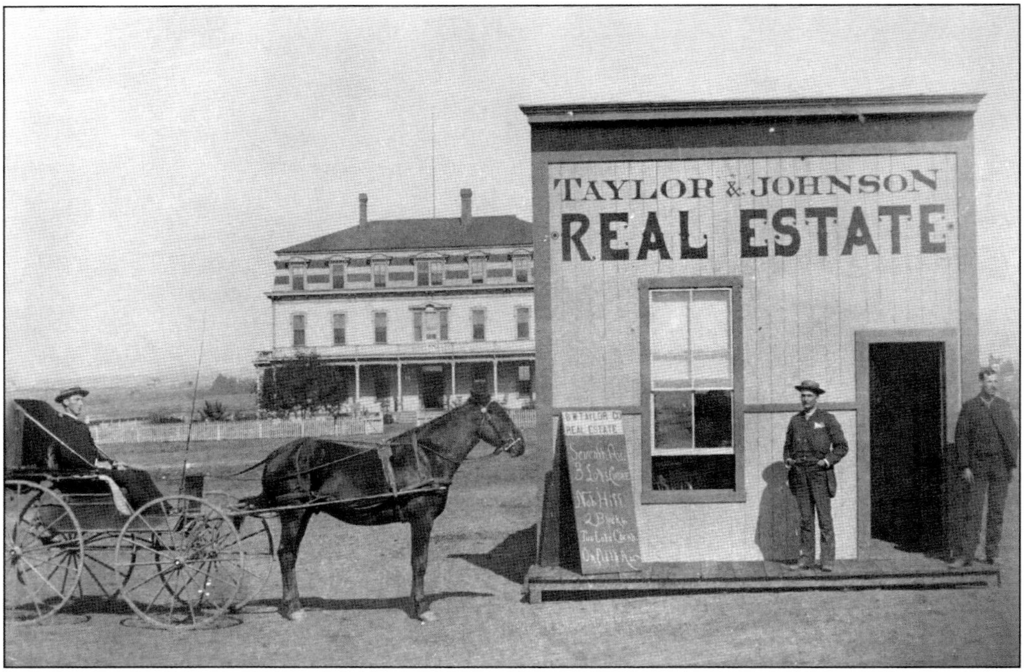

TAYLOR AND JOHNSON REAL ESTATE OFFICE, C. 1887. At the corner of McKinley Avenue and Twenty-third Street, this real estate office stood in an opportune spot directly between the depot and the International Hotel (seen on the left)—a perfect place to capture prospective buyers. During the boom years, many of the city's most prominent citizens delved into the real estate business; noteworthy among them were the Kimball brothers, Frank Reed, Julius A. Rice, and brothers John and Elizur Steele.

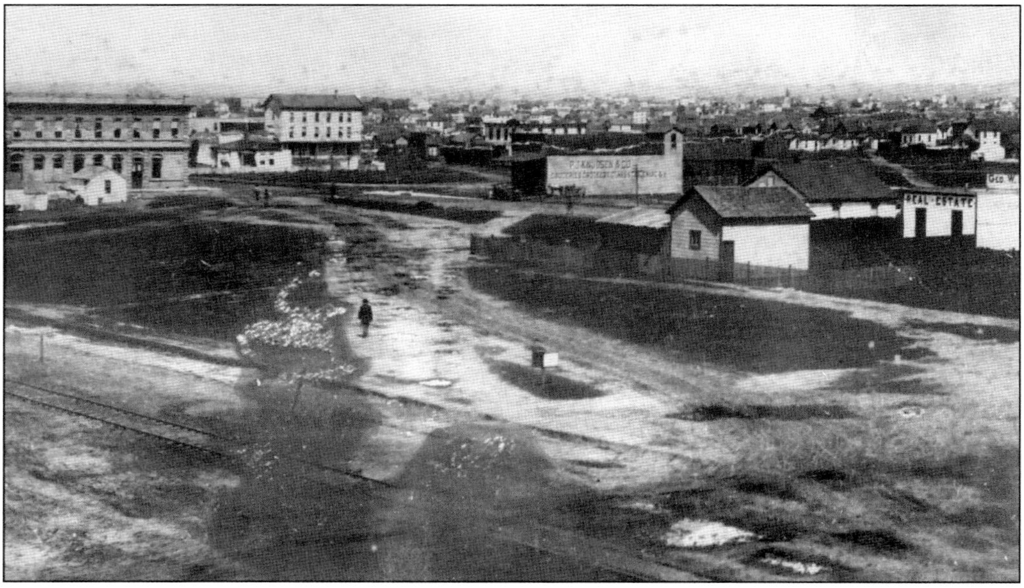

NATIONAL CITY LOOKING NORTHEAST. The Bank of National City, the two-story brick building on the left, opened on June 30, 1887, at Twenty-first Street and McKinley Avenue. Frank Kimball was president, while his brother Warren was vice president. In 1892, the bank had $300,000 in capital. (For another view of the bank, see page 71.)

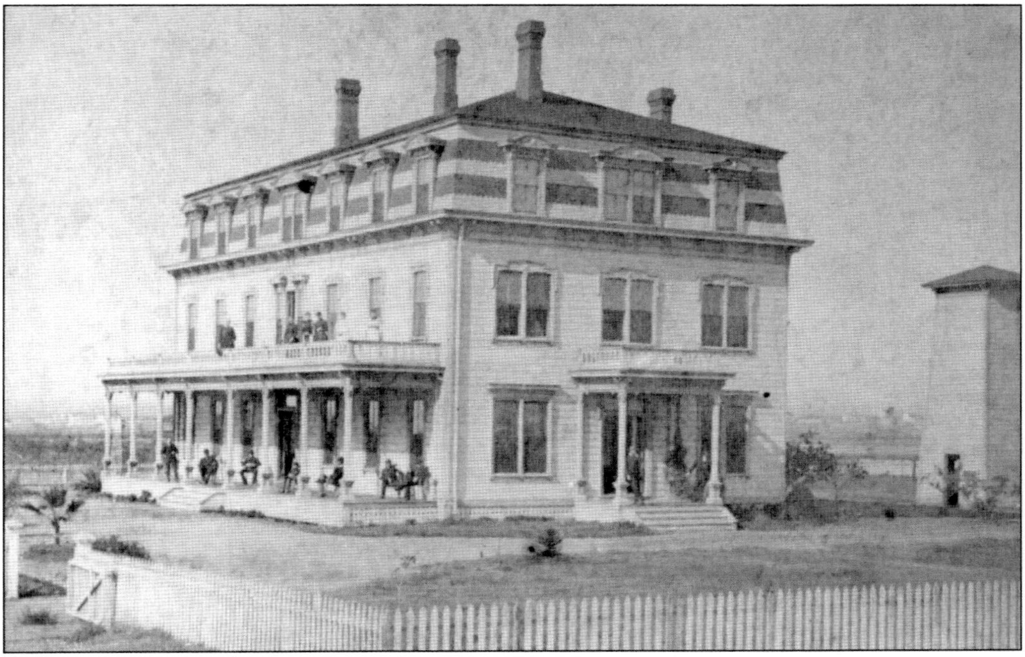

THE INTERNATIONAL HOTEL, C. 1885. The California Southern Railroad built the International Hotel to accommodate the many newcomers who were anticipated after the transcontinental rail line to National City was completed. It was located on Taft Avenue between Twenty-second and Twenty-third Streets. Frank Kimball wrote, "The best families of the country are guests at the International Hotel." The crowds that followed necessitated, at times, the use of cots on the balconies for extra sleeping space. The hotel boasted a beautiful garden with a fishpond and fountain.

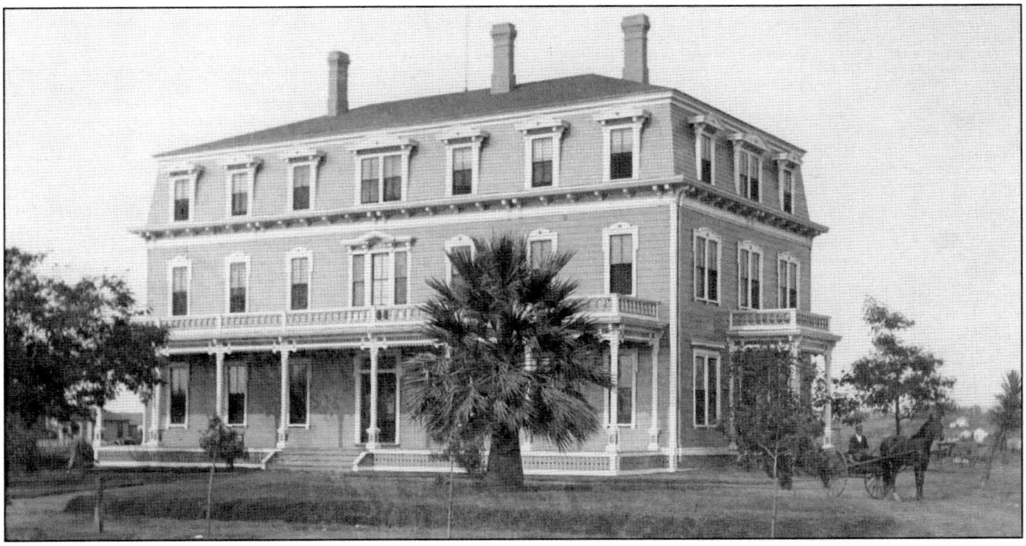

THE HOTEL SAN MIGUEL, C. 1900. The boom period for the International Hotel ended with the opening of the Hotel Del Coronado across the bay. After the start of the 20th century, the hotel's management changed its name to the San Miguel, where it predominately housed the railroad workers on the San Diego and Arizona Eastern Railroad. By 1916, the hotel was only a memory.

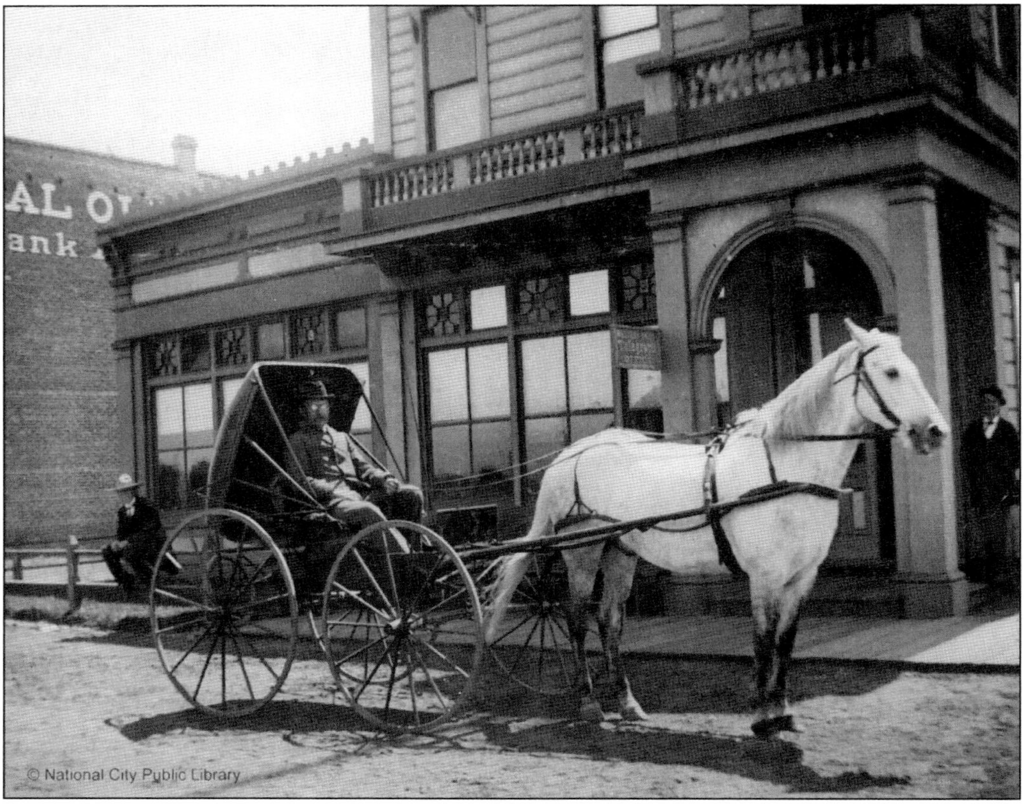

SAN DIEGO LAND AND TOWN COMPANY. California law forbade railroad companies from dealing in real estate, so in 1881, to facilitate the transfer of land and water rights from the Kimballs to the railroad syndicate, the San Diego Land and Town Company was created. Its offices were located on the corner of Cleveland Avenue and Twenty-third Street. John E. Boal (pictured in the buggy) became general manager after his father-in-law William G. Dickinson died.

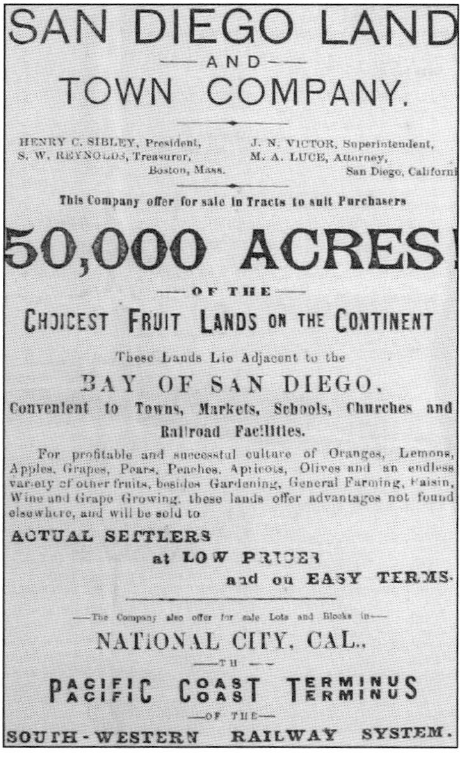

SAN DIEGO LAND AND TOWN COMPANY ADVERTISEMENT, C. 1887. After William Dickinson arrived to manage the San Diego Land And Town Company, advertisements such as this appeared weekly in the *National Record*. A portion of the 50,000 acres offered for sale was part of the land subsidy the Kimball Brothers had signed over to the railroad as an inducement to build the rail line to National City.

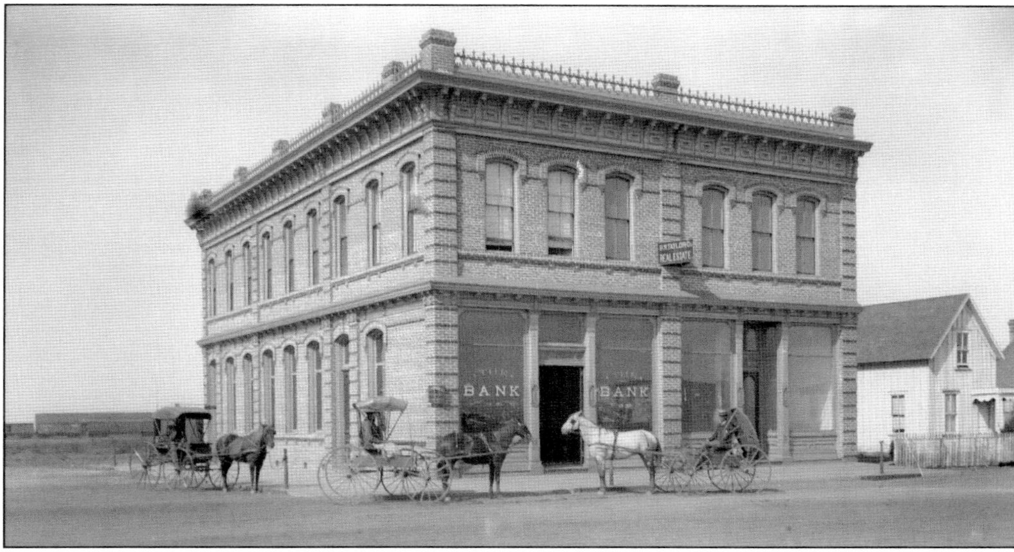

THE BANK OF NATIONAL CITY. Warren Kimball built an impressive two-story brick building at McKinley Avenue and Twenty-first Street in 1887. The Kimball Brothers, Frank and Warren, opened the Bank of National City on June 30 of that year. Sadly the bank closed its doors in 1896, heavily in debt. This building later became home to the Ammex Motion Picture Company from 1911 to 1916, much to the excitement of the surrounding community.

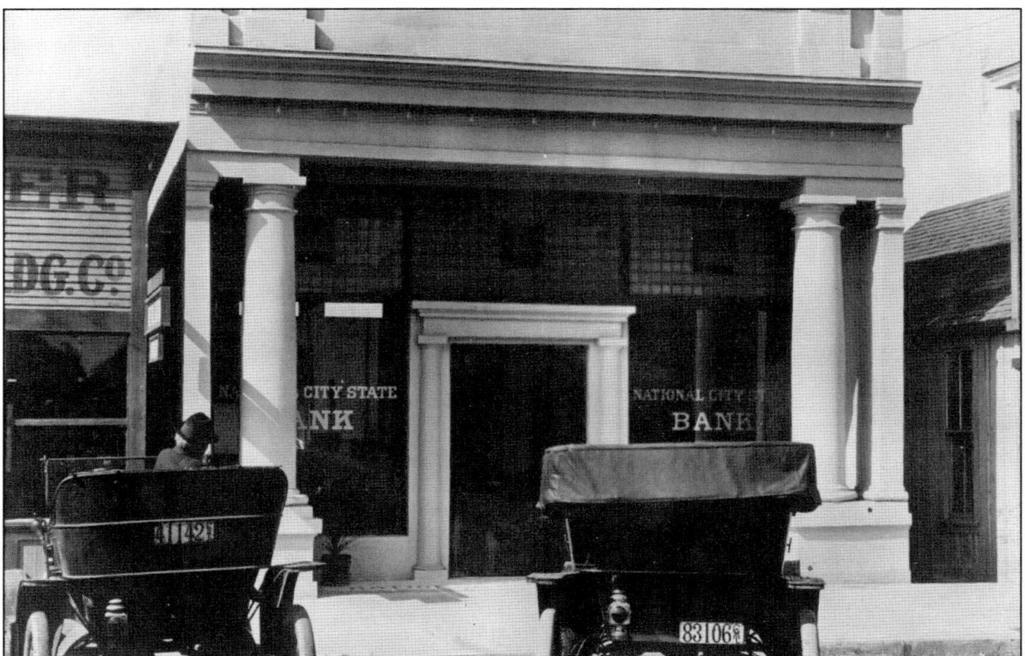

NATIONAL CITY STATE BANK. Located on the west side of National City Boulevard between Eighth and Ninth Streets, the National City State Bank was opened in December 1912. Built of concrete and hollow tiles, the building's classical design included Ionic columns adorning the front entrance. The interior consisted of hardwoods, onyx, glass plates, and mosaic tiling throughout. The bank was an open corporation with over 40 subscribers; unfortunately it closed its doors by 1921.

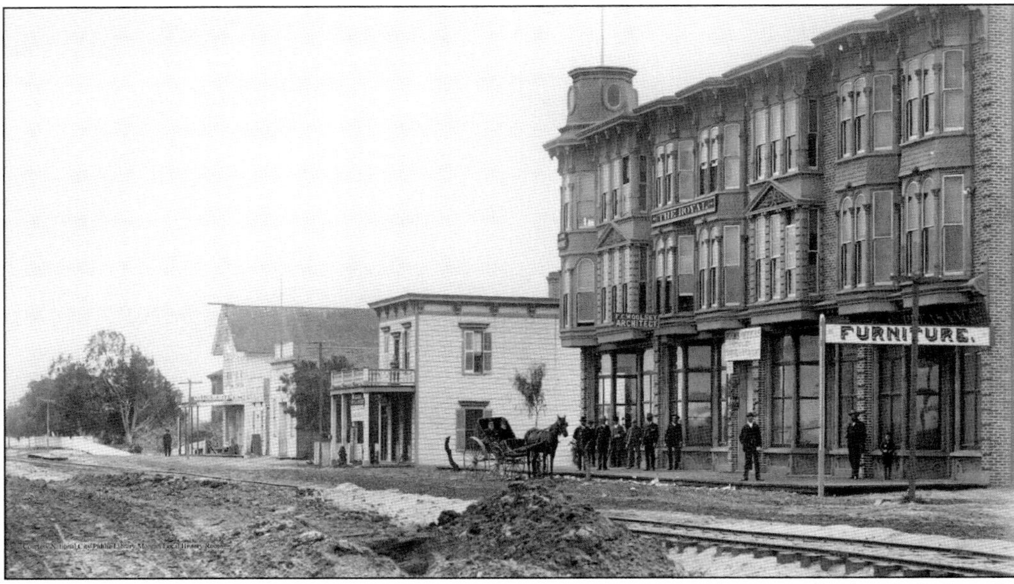

Eighth Street and National City Boulevard, c. 1890. Elizur Steele decided that the center of town should be moved eastward from McKinley Avenue to National City Boulevard. Putting his money where his mouth was, he spent $100,000 to build a three-story brick building on the northwest corner of Eighth Street and National City Boulevard in 1889. Looking south from left to right are trees at the edge of Frank Kimball's property, the two-story Grange Hall, a real estate office, Horticultural Hall, W. R. Johnson's Funeral Home, and the Steele Block.

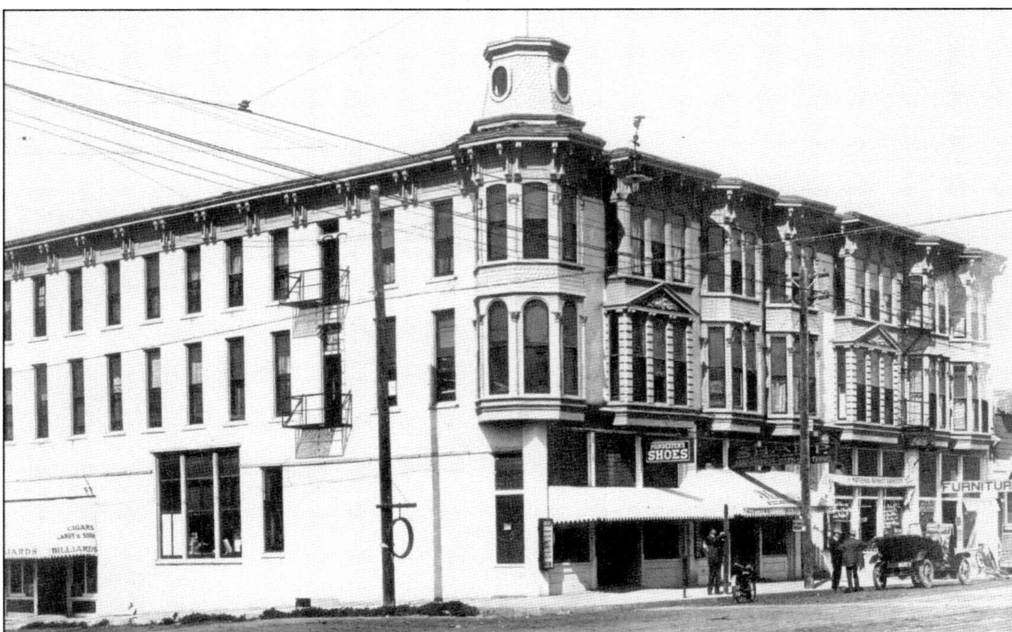

Steele Block. W. S. Hill's drugstore was located for years in this building, as was the People's State Bank, under Pres. Edmund Thelen. The latter was one of the few banks in California able to withstand the Panic of 1893. A locomotive's iron wheel is seen hanging from the light pole; it was used to sound an alarm in case of fires. A red light would burn in the tower until the emergency was over.

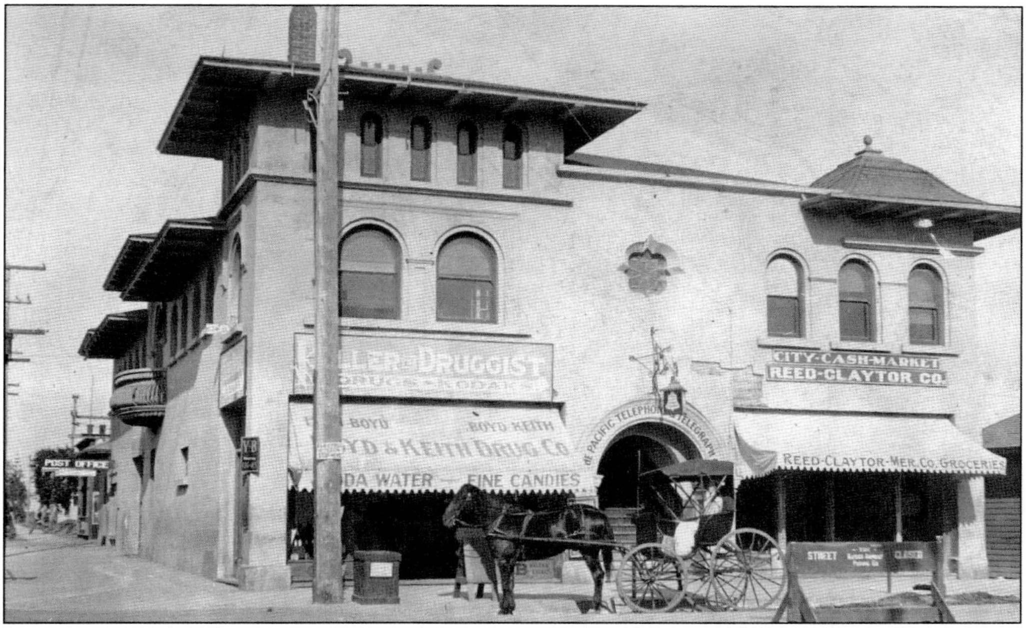

THE GRANGER BLOCK. Ralph Granger built this mission-style building in 1897 on the southeast corner of Eighth Street and National City Boulevard. It housed a variety of businesses, including Joll's Store (which advertised stationery, novelties, candy, and Temperance drinks), the post office, and the People's State Bank. The Knights of Pythias also met here. In 1910, after Ralph Granger moved to San Diego, B. J. Edmonds purchased the building.

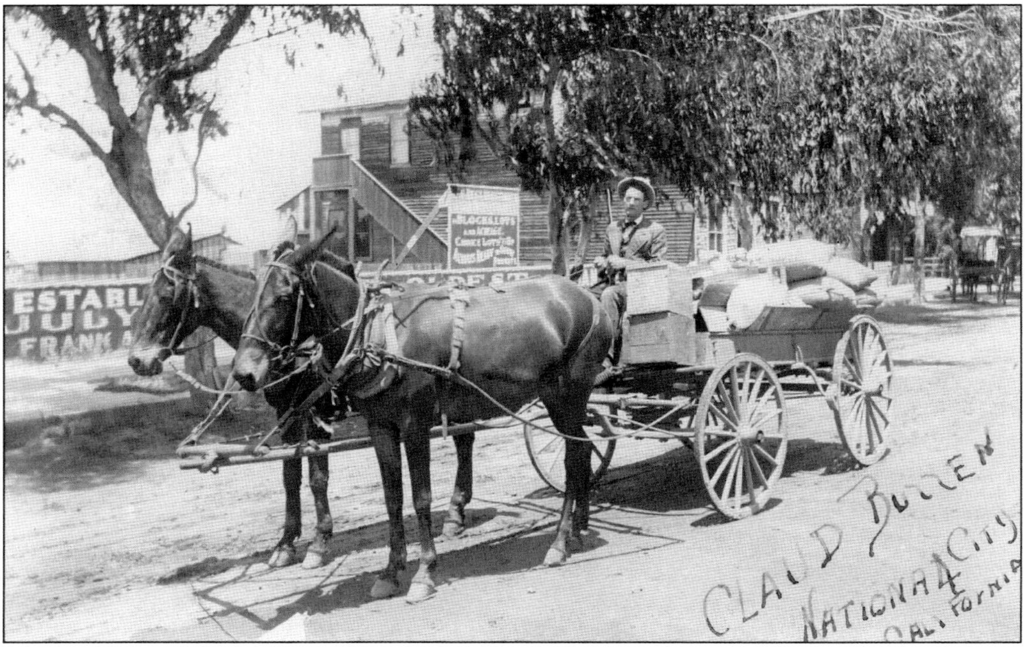

D. E. LOZIER AND COMPANY WAGON, C. 1909. Claude Bullen, clerk for D. E. Lozier and Company, is at the reins of this freight wagon. Bullen ran for city clerk in 1910 and was also an experienced stenographer and bookkeeper. The wagon stands in front of the Grange Hall on National City Boulevard.

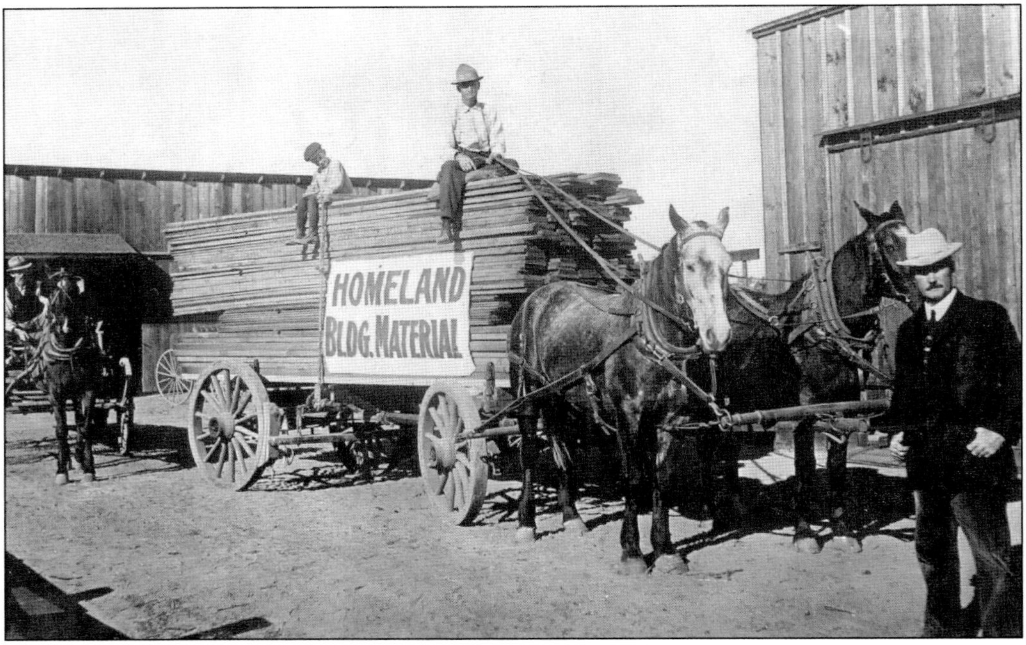

HOMELAND LUMBER COMPANY, C. 1912. The Homeland Lumber Company was formed in 1905, supplanting the former Russ Lumber and Mill Company, which had supplied redwood from Humboldt County and pine from Astoria for area homes as early as 1881. D. E. Lozier was the president of this business for many years.

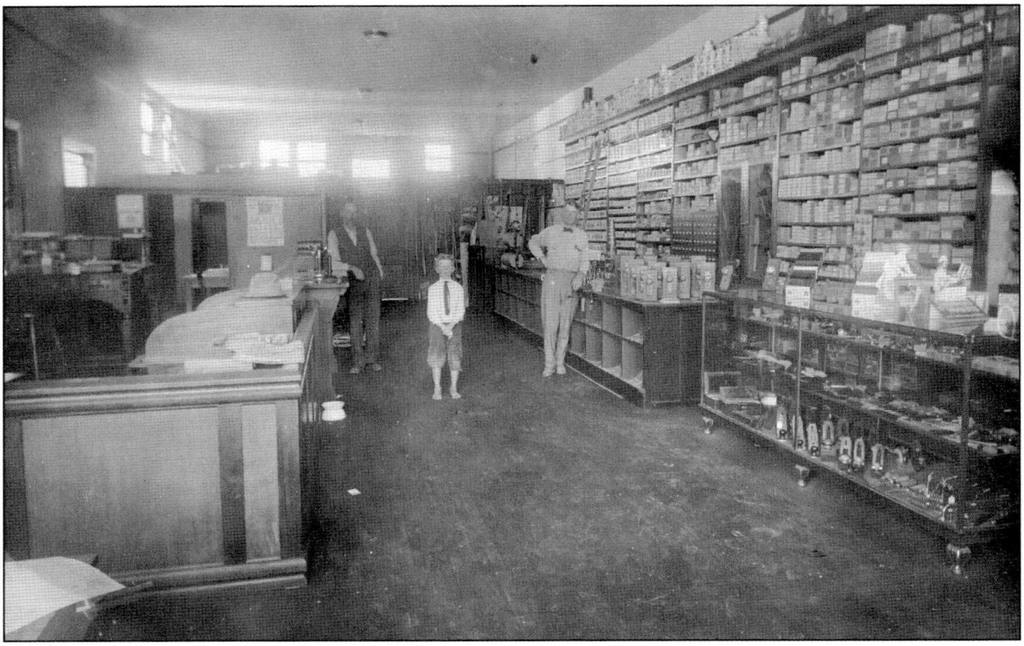

HOMELAND LUMBER COMPANY INTERIOR. In 1912, the Homeland Lumber Company moved from its original location on the corner of Coolidge Avenue and Eighth Street to a new 30-by-80-foot store built on the north side of Eighth Street, between National City Boulevard and A Avenue. The new store cost $5,000 to build; it supplied the National City construction industry for over 40 years.

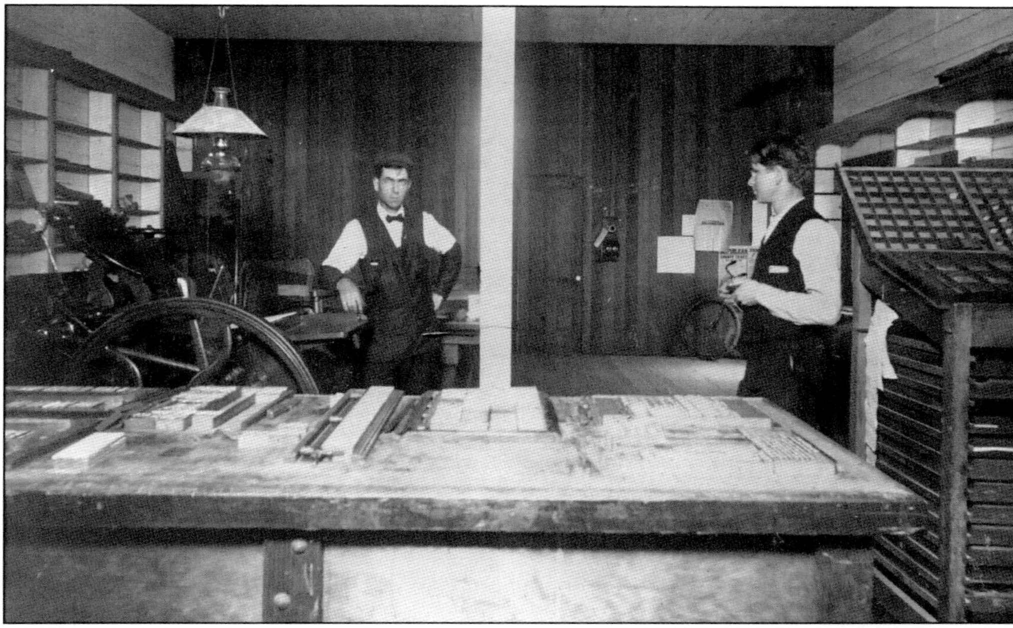

NATIONAL CITY NEWS, c. 1905. Located in a rear room of the old Grange Hall, under the editorship of William Burgess, the first edition was published on September 28, 1882. In 1903, at the urging of his uncle Frank Kimball, Augustus Kimball bought the local newspaper, becoming the new owner and editor. This photograph shows Augustus (left) with his assistant Kyle Alexander.

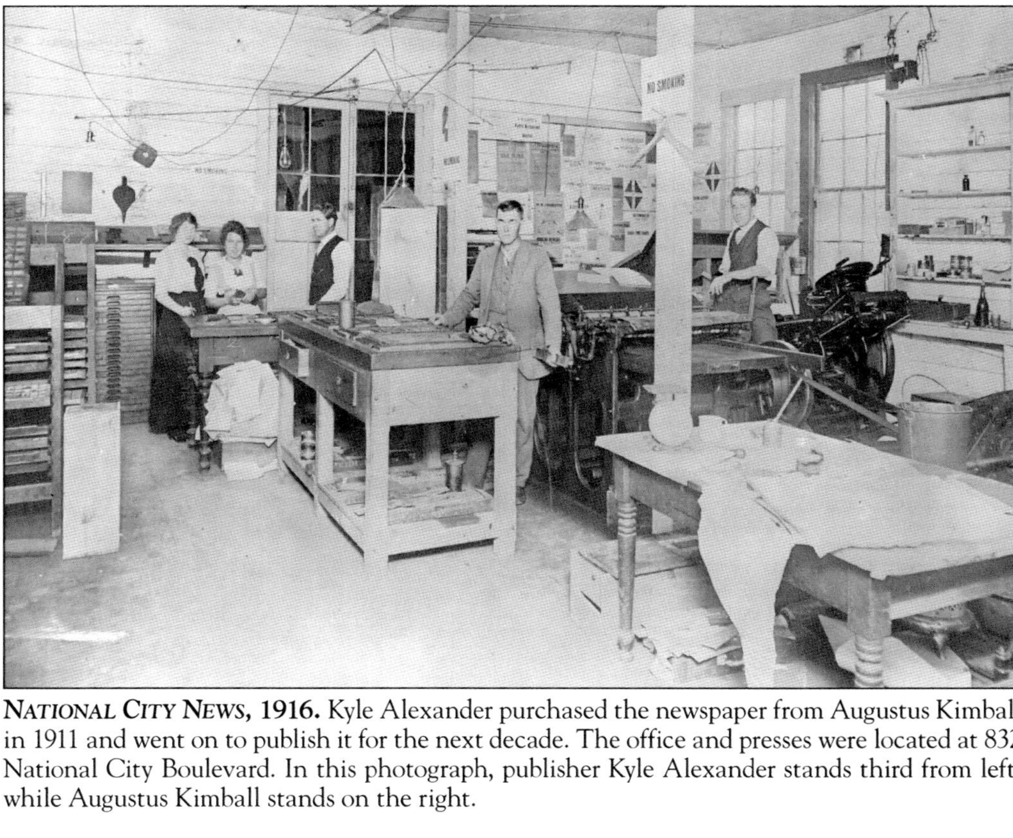

NATIONAL CITY NEWS, 1916. Kyle Alexander purchased the newspaper from Augustus Kimball in 1911 and went on to publish it for the next decade. The office and presses were located at 832 National City Boulevard. In this photograph, publisher Kyle Alexander stands third from left, while Augustus Kimball stands on the right.

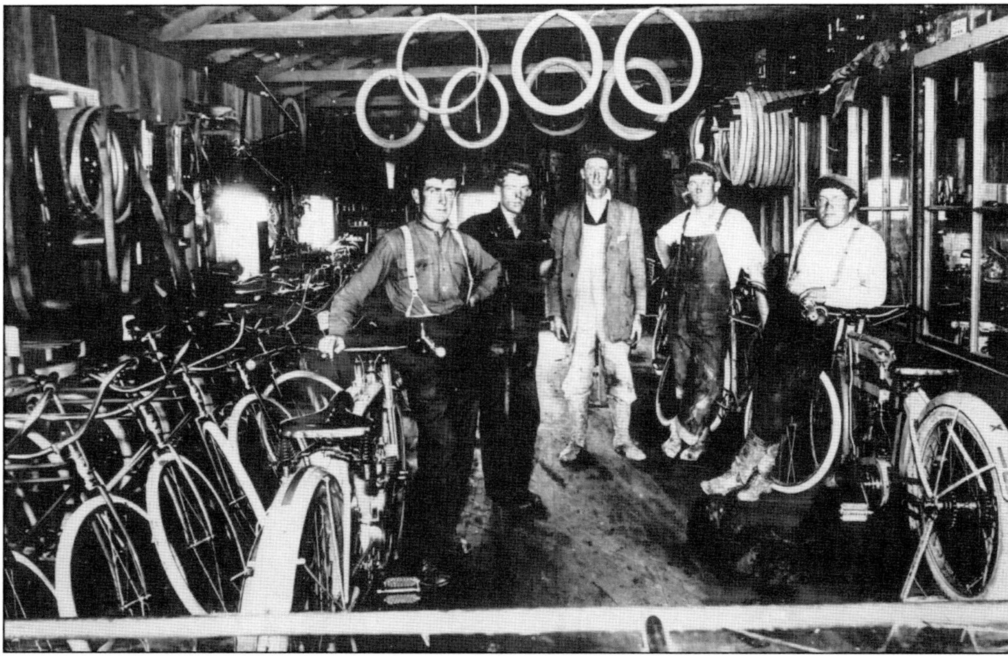

JULIUS WEISSER'S BICYCLE SHOP, C. 1911. In 1910, Julius Weisser worked as a mechanic and lived with his brother Lawrence Weisser, owner of the National Auto and Machine Shop. By the following year, Julius had his own bicycle shop on National City Boulevard near Tenth Street. This photograph shows Julius Weisser (with his hand on a bicycle), William Mordhorst (near the showcase), and Alfred Fernberg (in overalls).

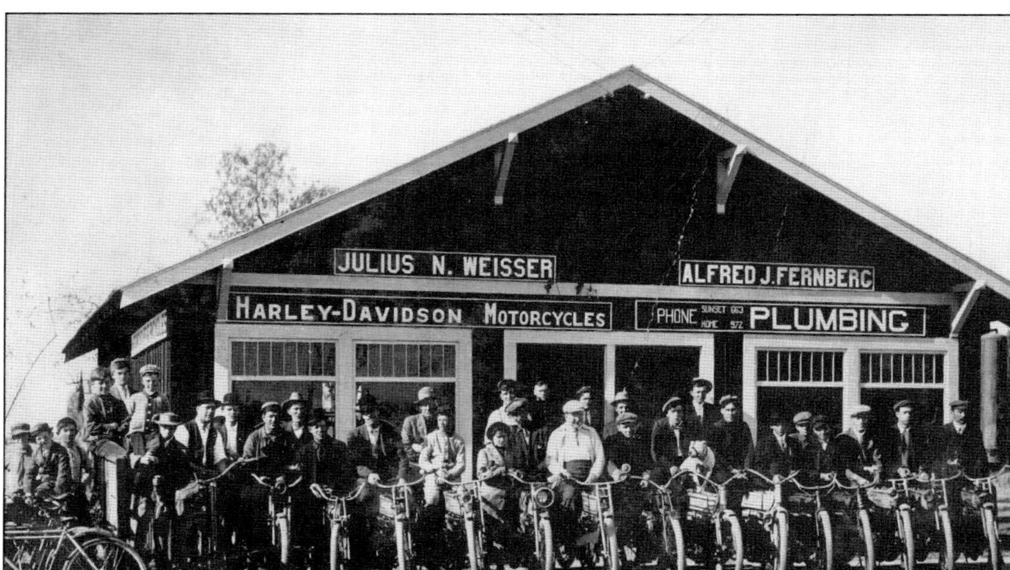

JULIUS WEISSER'S BICYCLE SHOP, C. 1917. By 1917, Weisser's Bicycle Shop expanded to include motorcycles. In 1925, Julius's shop finally evolved into Weisser's Sporting Goods, which continued until the 1990s—National City's longest running business.

Five

Forming a Community

Schools, Churches, Post Office, and Fire Department

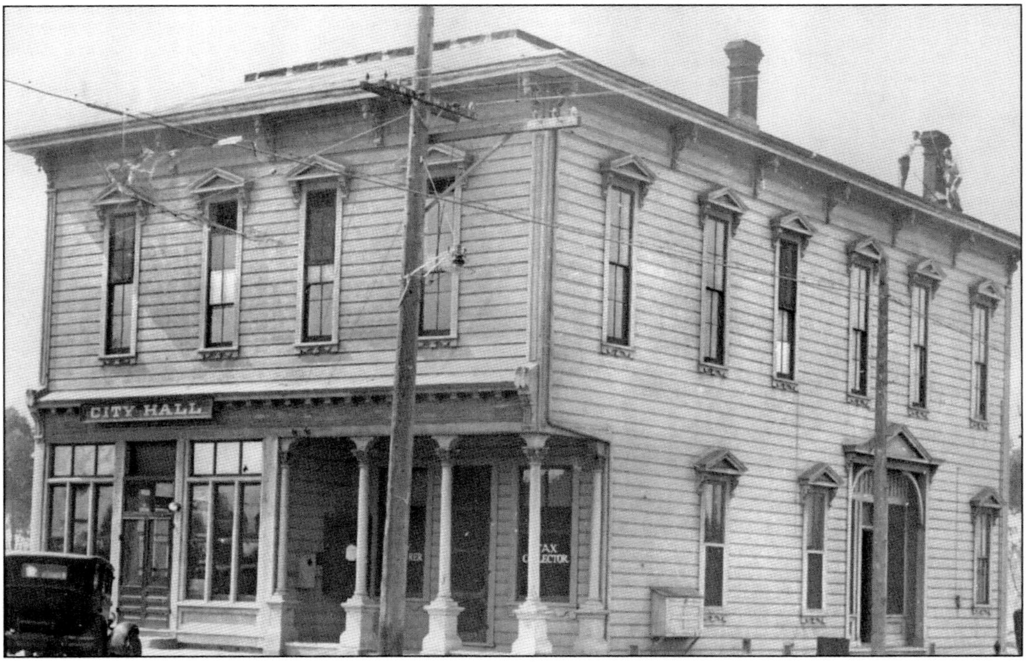

Ayleworth Hall. Built in 1887 for the sum of $6,000, Ayleworth Hall stood at 1408 Harding Avenue. When the Women's Christian Temperance Union struggled to find a hall in which to meet, as the men's groups seemed to take precedence, Elizabeth Ayleworth built this hall dedicated as a meeting place for women. Later it housed the library, the city hall, and finally a community health center, Casa de Salud.

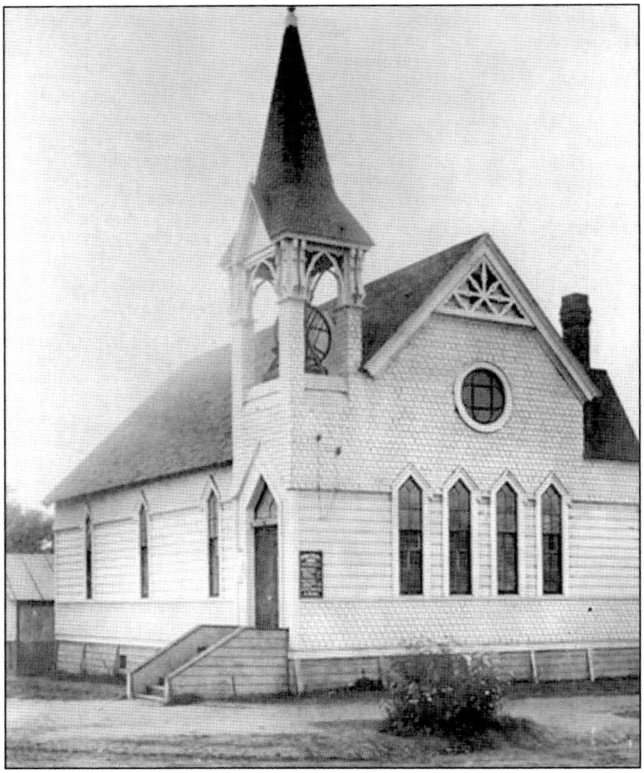

FIRST METHODIST CHURCH. The Methodists first held a meeting to organize their new church on October 1, 1886, in Dranga Hall, with Rev. S. H. Todd officiating. The San Diego Land and Town Company donated four lots on the corner of Roosevelt Avenue and Thirteenth Street at the urging of Frank Kimball. His diary records, "I have given my subscription towards building the Methodist Church, $100." The congregation dedicated the new church on July 31, 1887.

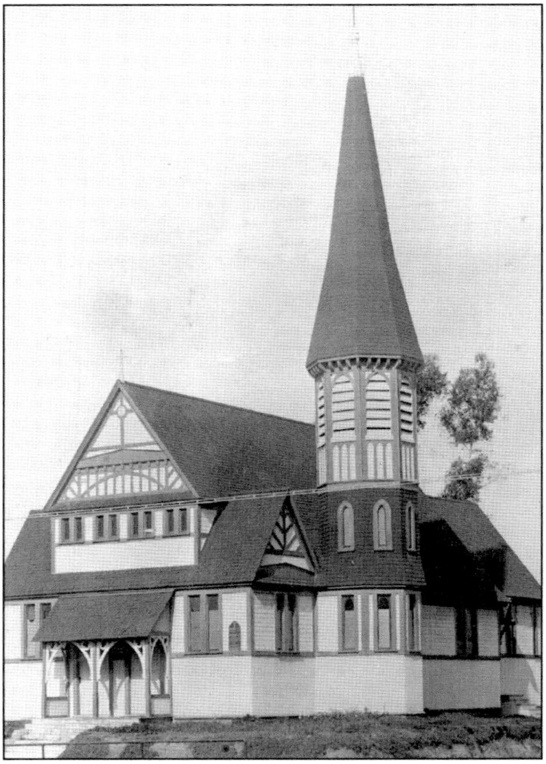

ST. MATTHEW'S EPISCOPAL CHURCH. Elizur Steele and Frank Kimball contributed large sums to the building fund for St. Matthew's Episcopal Church, which was constructed in 1887. Chula Vista architect William Herman designed the Tudor-style church to resemble an English countryside chapel. St. Matthew's steeple was a landmark, as it could be seen for miles. The building is listed on the National Register of Historic Places.

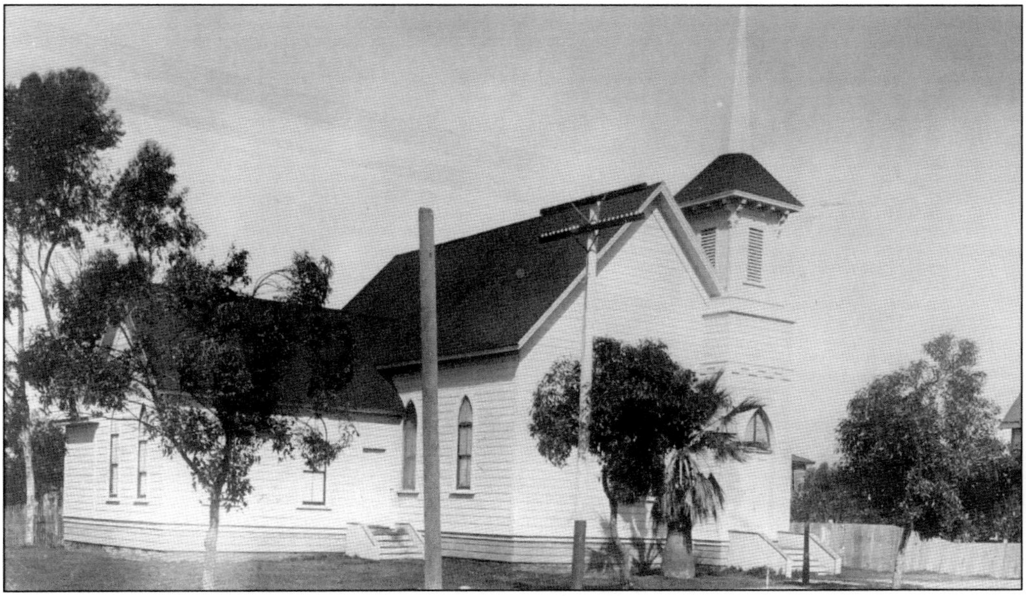

CONGREGATIONAL CHURCH. On November 21, 1869, Theron Parsons wrote in his diary of a meeting at his house for the purpose of organizing an independent Congregational Church. Eleven people were present. Parsons gave land for the church on the northeast corner of Eighth Street and A Avenue, but a decade passed before the church was built and dedicated for worship in December 1882. Rev. F. A. Field was the first pastor of the little flock.

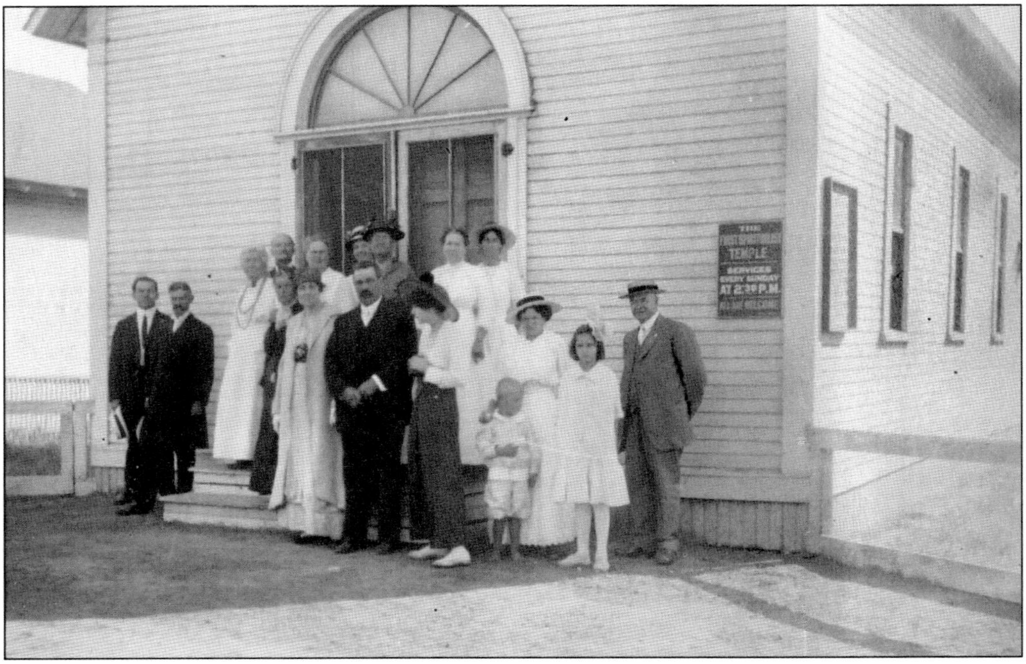

FIRST SPIRITUALIST CHURCH. The congregation of First Spiritualist Church first met on April 23, 1883, and Frank Kimball noted in his diary, "Attended Spiritualist meeting in Grange Hall." After they met in rented halls for six years, the widow of Silas Field donated land on the southwest corner of Twelfth Street and Coolidge Avenue. It was another 10 years, however, before enough money was raised to build a sanctuary.

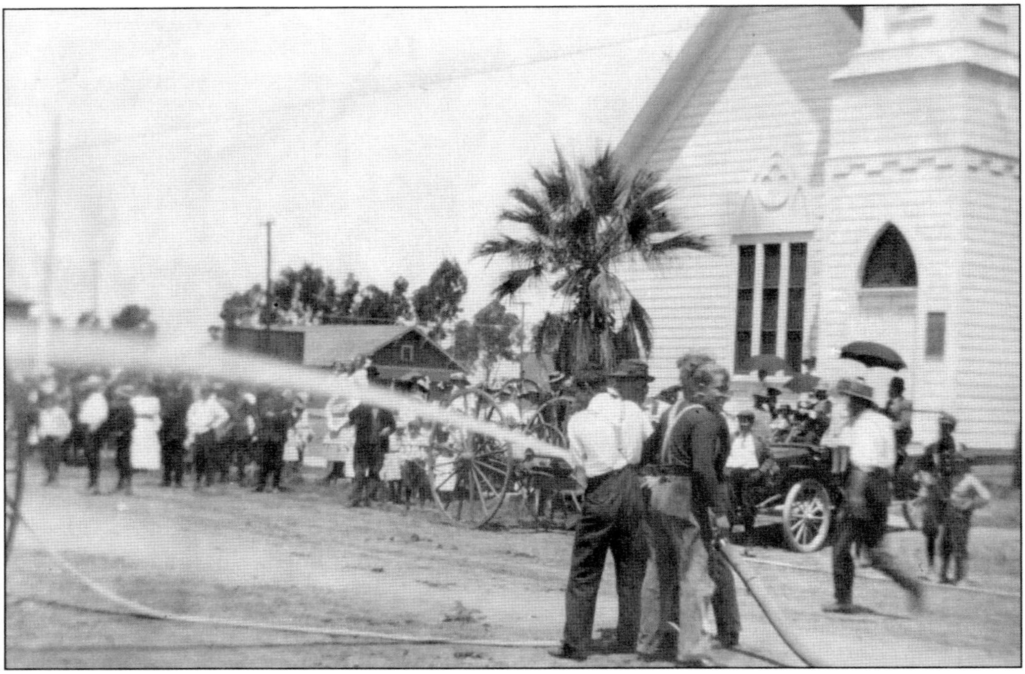

FIREMEN CELEBRATE FOURTH OF JULY, 1911. The National City volunteer fire brigade celebrated with a hose demonstration in front of the Congregational Church, thrilling onlookers with the power of the water and the skill of their volunteer firemen. This was before the fire department had a gas-powered fire truck, and the hose carts had to be pulled to the scene of a fire. The volunteer fire department was organized on August 23, 1888.

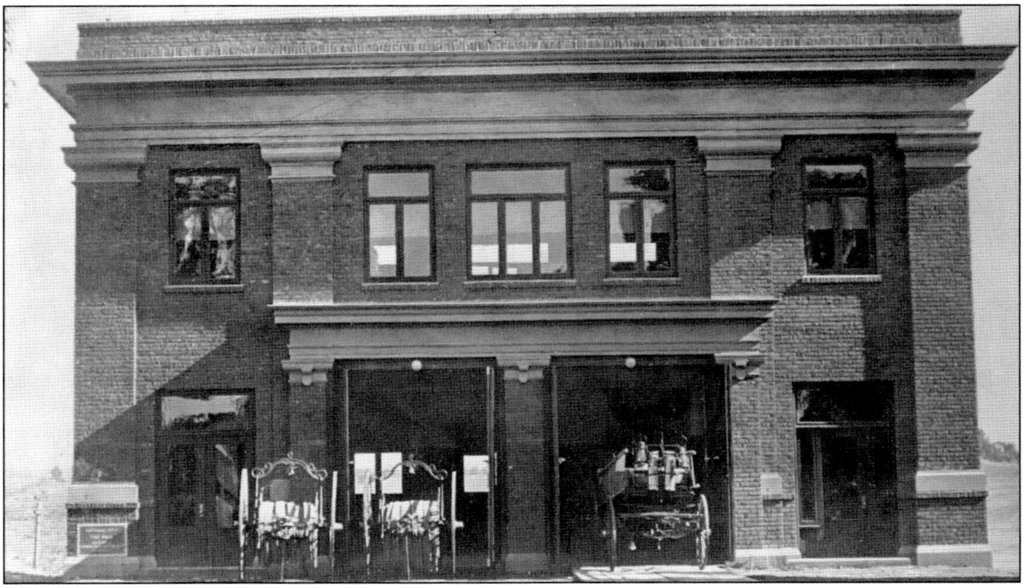

FIRE STATION NO. 1, 1910. This handsome fire station, built in 1910, stood on National City Boulevard where the city hall is now located. The hose carts and hook and ladder (on right) originally had to be pulled to fires either by hand or horse. The *National City News* noted, "Doctors Owens and Fly are old standbys at a fire. When they hear the whistle from the Santa Fe shops they rush towards the blaze and their autos pull the cart at top speed."

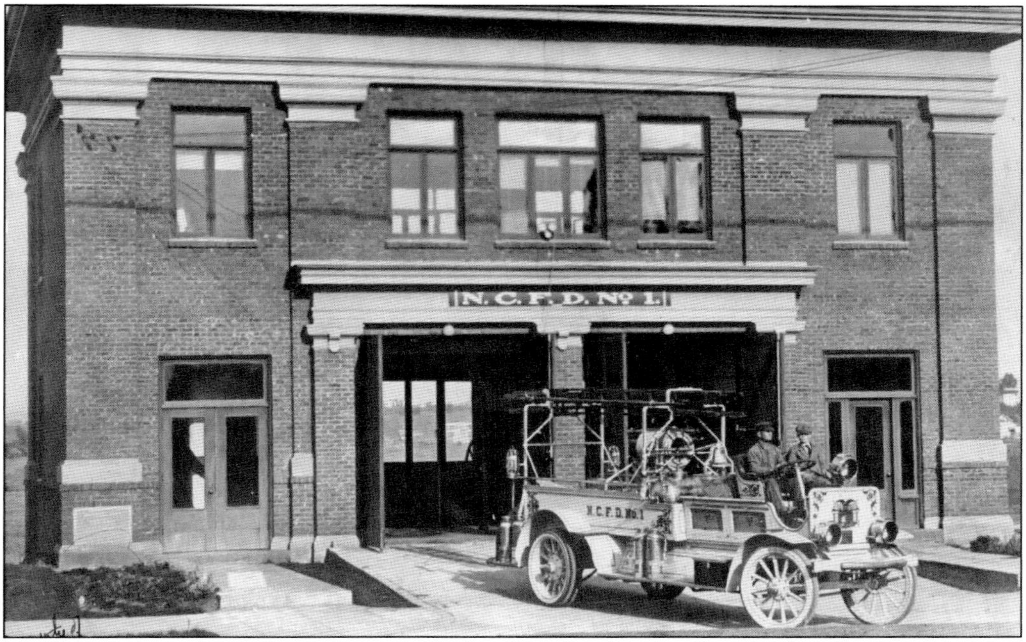

Fire Department's New Seagrave Engine. A shiny new Seagrave fire truck is displayed outside Fire Station No. 1 at Thirteenth Street and National City Boulevard by the volunteer fire brigade. It supplanted the hose carts and included such modern features as an aerial ladder with an 85-foot extension. Fire chief George Miner (wearing a cap) sits in the Seagrave engine with his men.

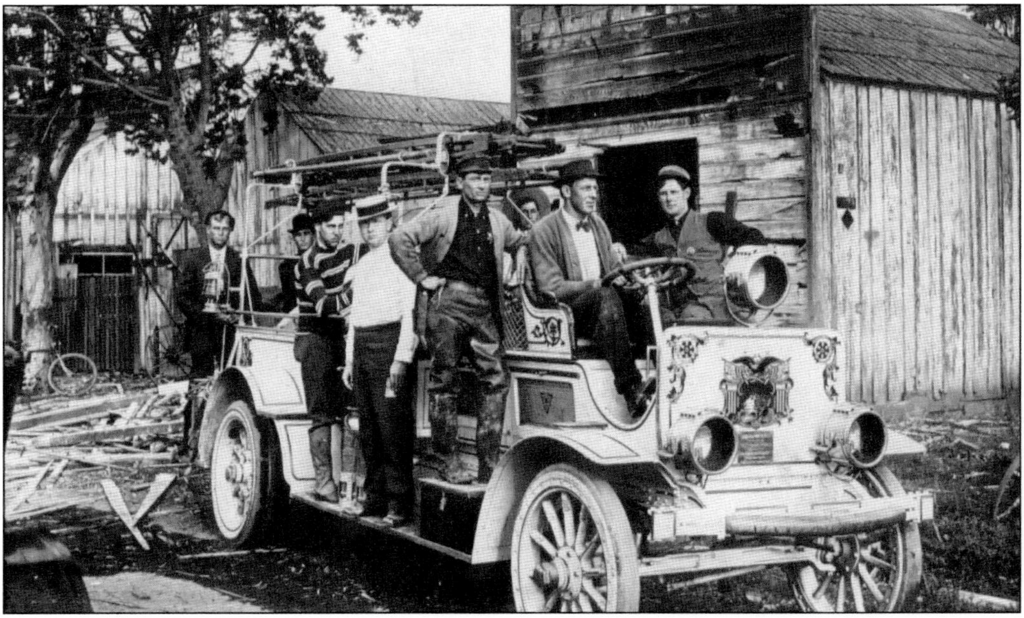

Explosion at the Italian National Macaroni Factory. On September 1, 1912, the alarm went out—the macaroni factory was burning. The new Seagrave fire truck hurried to the scene of the explosion on the south side of Eighteenth Street near McKinley Avenue. Included in the photograph are Lawrence Weisser, Robert Milligan, Kyle Alexander, Harry Lindner, Fred Patterson, and George Miner (fire chief).

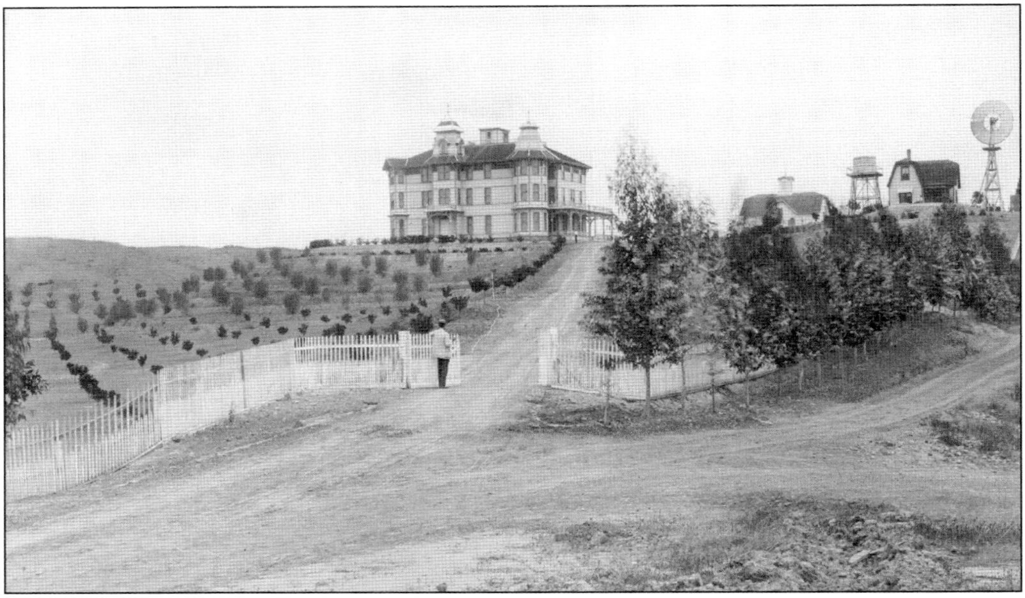

POTTS' SANITARIUM IN PARADISE VALLEY. Impressed with the healthful climate of the National Ranch, Dr. Anna Mae Longshore Potts purchased property in Paradise Valley on which to build a sanitarium. The *National Record* announced on September 28, 1882, the improvements being made on Mount Paradise; in 1888, a large reception was held for the dedication of the enterprise. Dr. Potts went on many extended lecture tours, leaving the sanitarium in the hands of managers during her absence. By 1897, the sanitarium was abandoned and the property up for sale. Ellen G. White, a founder of the Seventh-day Adventist Church and health advocate, purchased the sanitarium. After she refurbished the building and located an adequate source of water from a well drilled near the corner of Eighth Street and Euclid Avenue, Paradise Valley Sanitarium opened its doors and patients began to stream in.

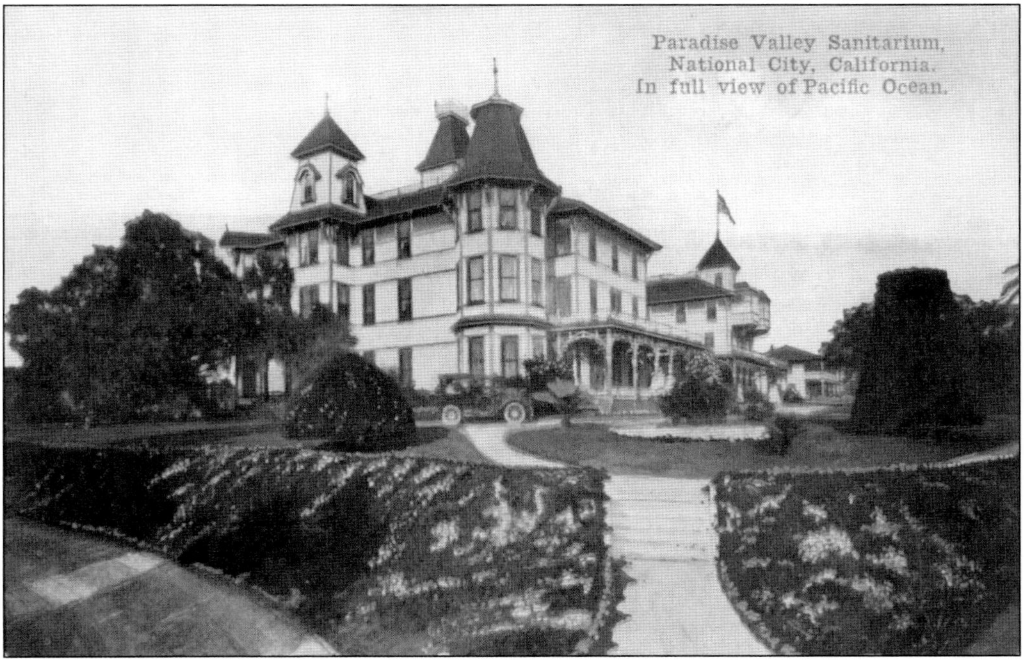

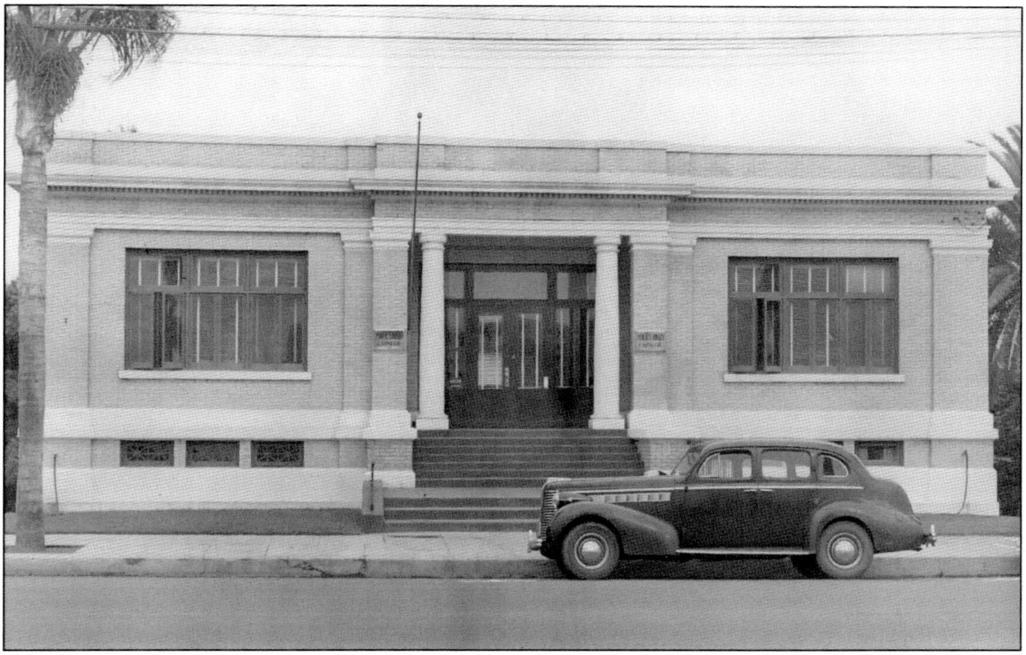

CARNEGIE LIBRARY. Dedicated January 13, 1911, National City built its Carnegie Library on National City Boulevard at Twelfth Street. Architect William Sterling Hebbard designed the building in the Classical Revival style with lots of light—the interior had over 20 windows, with a skylight above the lobby. One story with a full basement, it was made of brick and had two Doric columns in front and six windows, three on each side of the door.

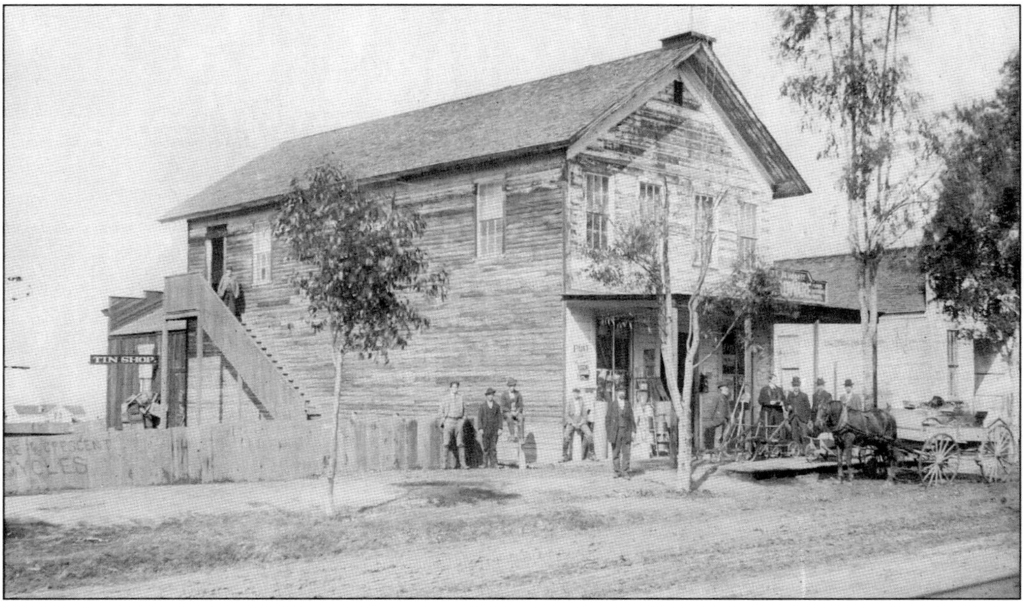

GRANGE HALL, 1903. The National Ranch Grange No. 235 was organized in November 1874, with Frank Kimball serving as its first master. Completed in July 1875, the hall at 828 National City Boulevard was used for many community events as well as the library for a short while. The first floor housed a furniture store in the front and a tin and plumbing shop in the rear, run by J. L. Mudgett. On the second floor was the lodge meeting hall.

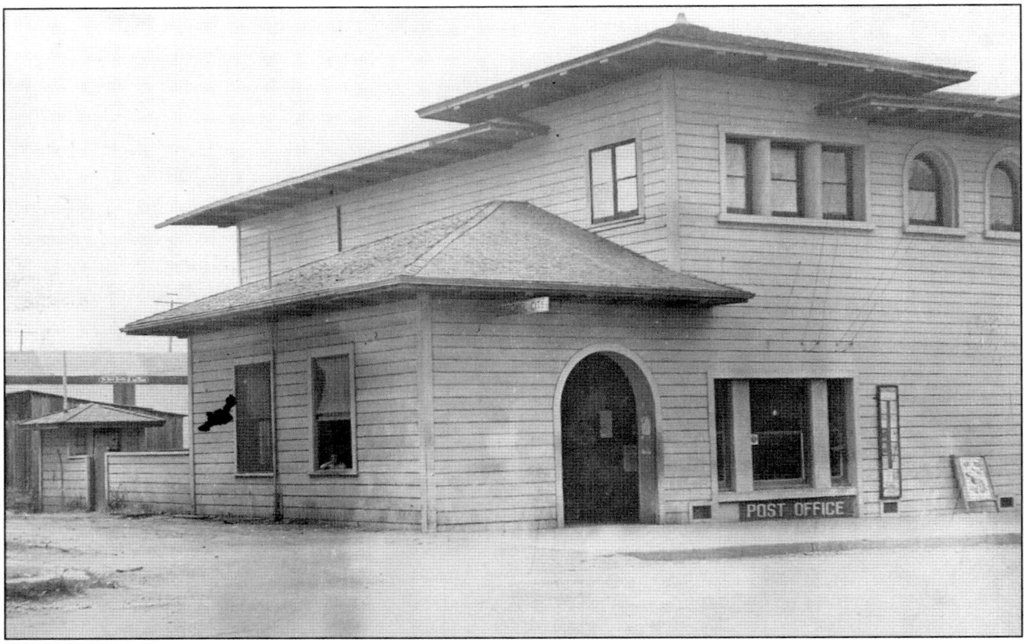

The Granger Block. With the appointment of Samuel S. Johnston to postmaster on April 30, 1898, the post office moved from the west side of town (on McKinley Avenue) eastward to National City Boulevard and was situated in the Granger block at the southeast corner of Eighth Street. Many citizens passionately protested this move, as the center of town was originally along McKinley Avenue.

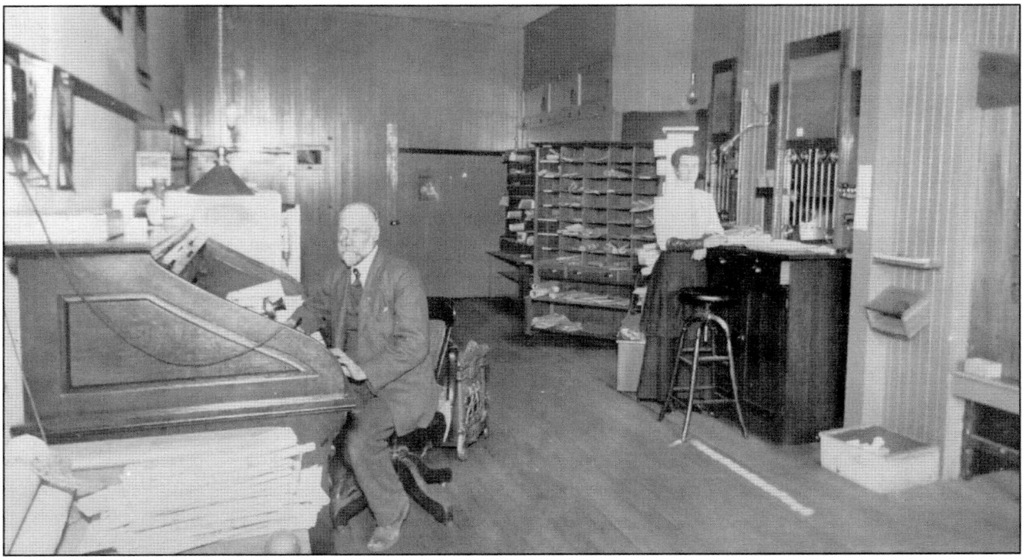

National City Post Office, c. 1912. Postmaster Samuel S. Johnston works alongside his assistant, Mary Copeland. George Kimball's daughter Laura described the first post office established in 1869 thus: "It was in the front room of my father's house, and consisted of a dry-goods box with a green shawl spread over the top and a set of pigeon-holes underneath, one for every letter of the alphabet."

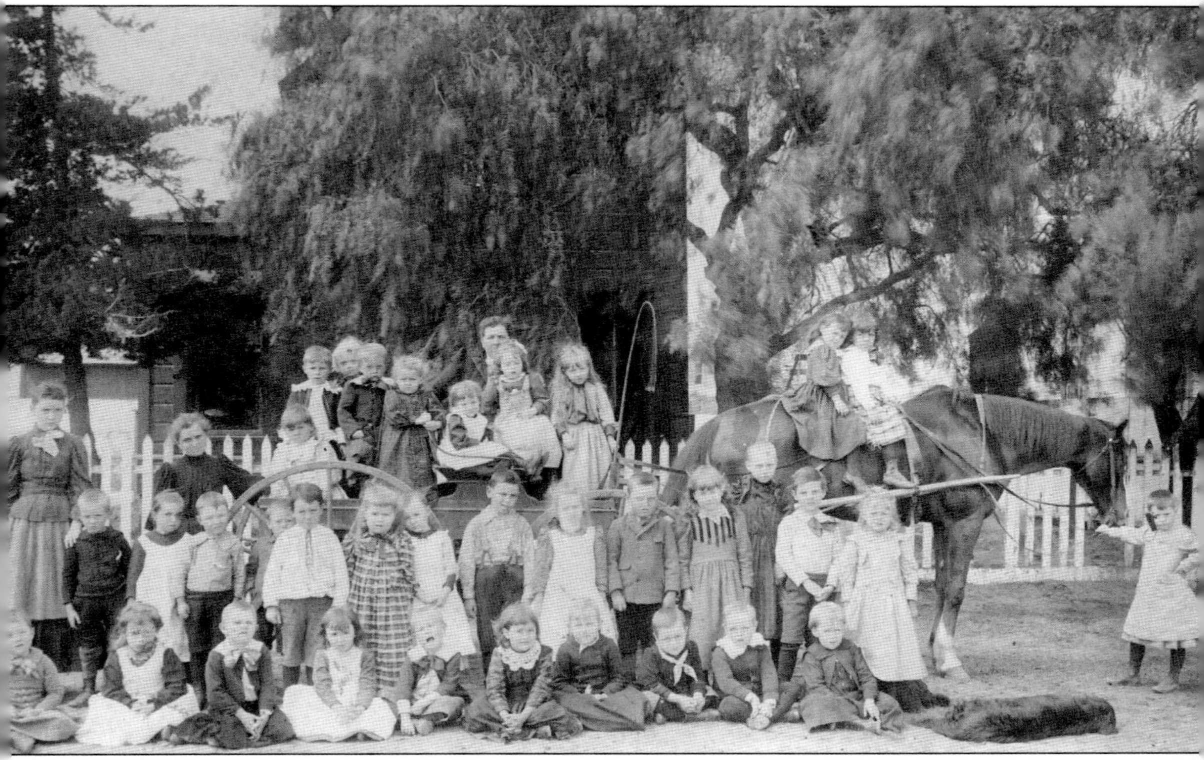

National City Kindergarten, c. 1893. Prompted by Friedrich Froebel, a German educator who started the first kindergarten in 1837, a movement in San Francisco arose to establish free kindergartens. While living in the Bay Area, Sarah Kimball undoubtedly became familiar with the kindergarten concept. When a student of Froebel's, Prudence Brown, came to San Diego, Sarah Kimball persuaded her to start a kindergarten in National City; it was her intention to back this endeavor for one year to see if it had merit. With Sarah Kimball's support, the first free kindergarten in San Diego County began in March 1889. Thirty children responded to the announcement of the free kindergarten, but soon the numbers swelled to 60. The rooms at the rear of Frank Kimball's real estate office quickly became inadequate, and a larger space was found in Elizabeth Ayleworth's new hall. At the end of the year, the *National City Record* announced, "The Public of National City does not need to be told that Mrs. Frank Kimball established and largely maintained the National City Kindergarten." In this photograph, one of the teachers, Mary O'Hara, carries Hazel Reed, while Chassie Reed holds the lines on the dashboard of the wagon used to convey the children to and from school.

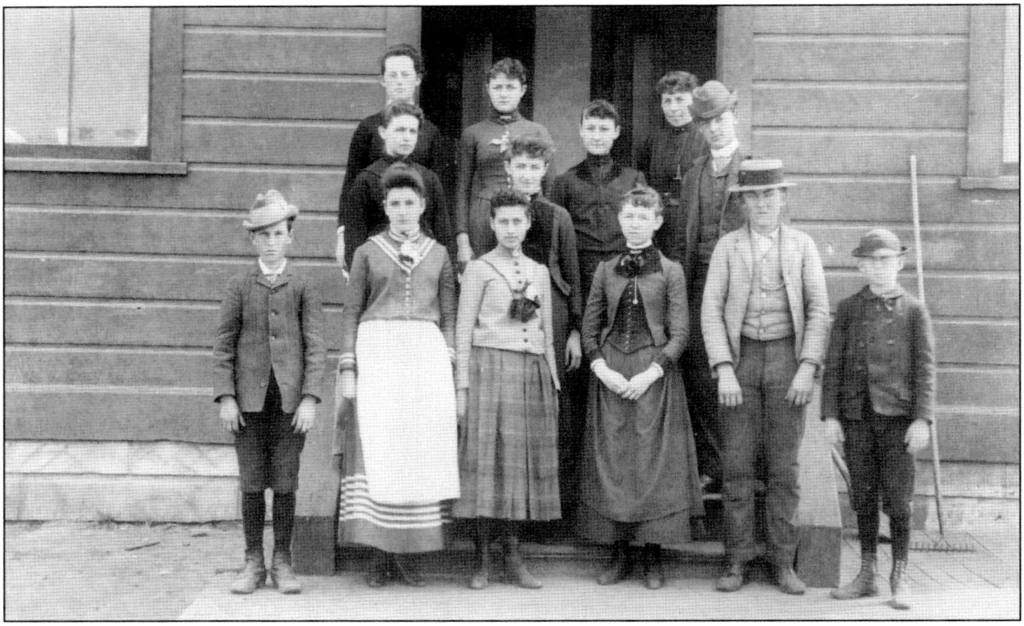

NATIONAL CITY HIGH SCHOOL, 1885. Due to expanding enrollment in 1882, the school board secured a block of land at Ninth Street and E Avenue (the current site of Central Elementary School). They built a plain, two-story building with square cupola and two classrooms on the first floor. The second floor space was originally unfinished and used as a public hall. When built, the school cost $8,167.02, which included $50 for a bell and $125 for an organ.

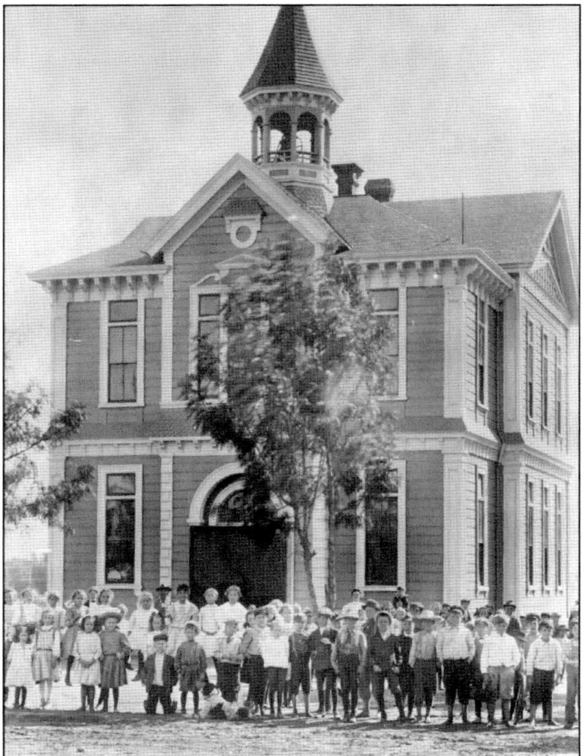

SIXTEENTH STREET SCHOOL, 1892. In 1887, as the student body expanded with the economic boom, the voters approved a $20,000 school. Sixteenth Street School was built the following year at the corner of Hoover Avenue. A reflection of the prevailing economy, it was a much more attractive building than its predecessor, complete with bell tower. By 1888, the principal's salary was $110 a month. By 1889, the city schools enrolled 450 children.

HIGH SCHOOL PLAY, 1893. The Shakespearean Players posed for a formal portrait before their play at the high school. Pictured from left to right are (first row) unidentified, Sallie Stevens, and Daisy Sholl; (second row) Mary Boyd, unidentified, Helen H. Blossom, Guy Blossom, and unidentified. In 1893, the downturn in the economy stretched the budget in the school district so much that principal Julius A. Rice suggested the students perform the janitorial work.

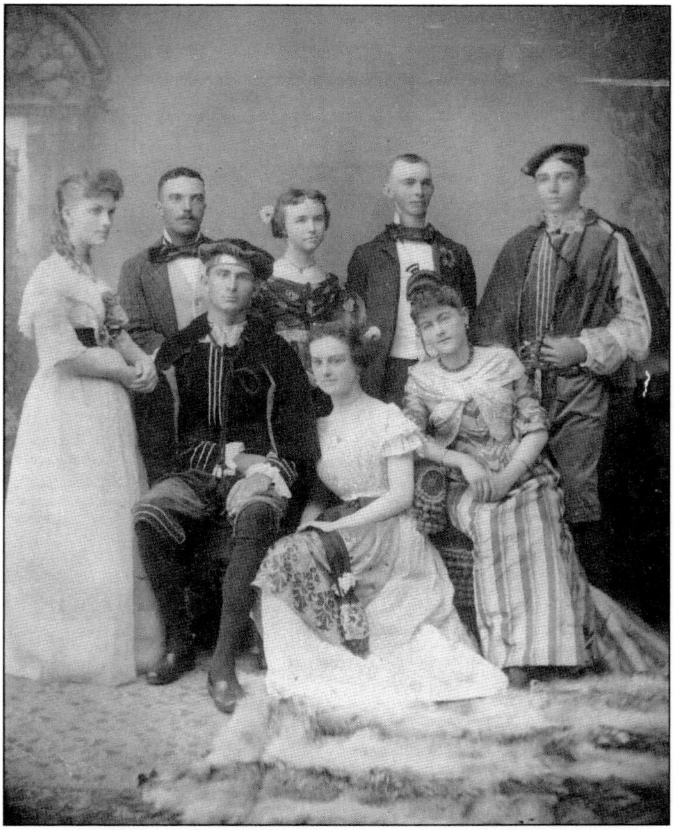

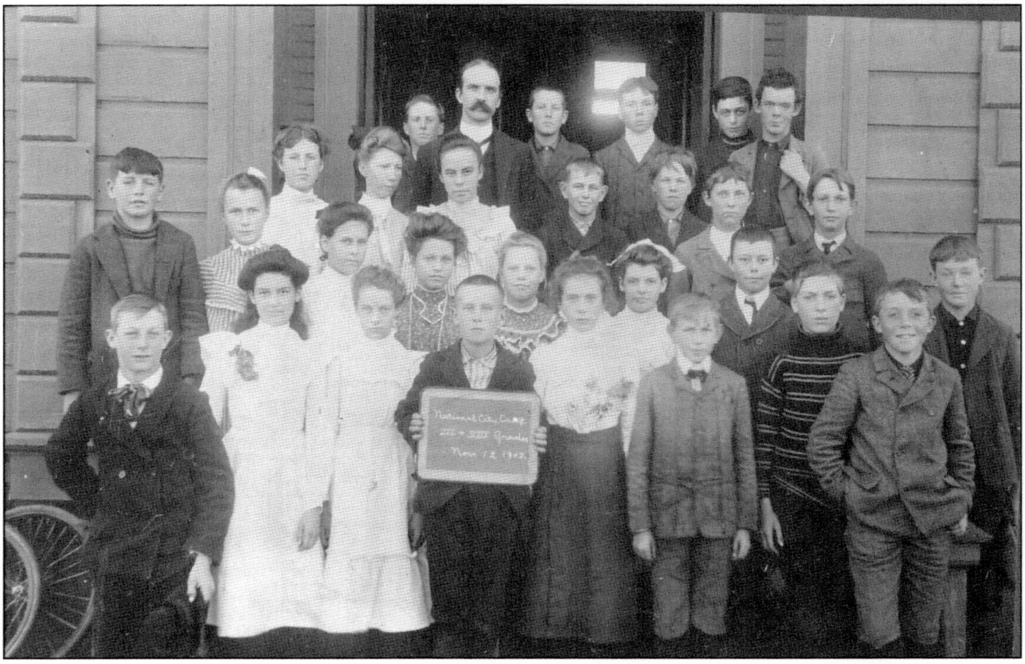

SIXTEENTH STREET SCHOOL, 1903. The seventh- and eighth-grade classes pose in front of the school doors for their group portrait on November 12, 1903.

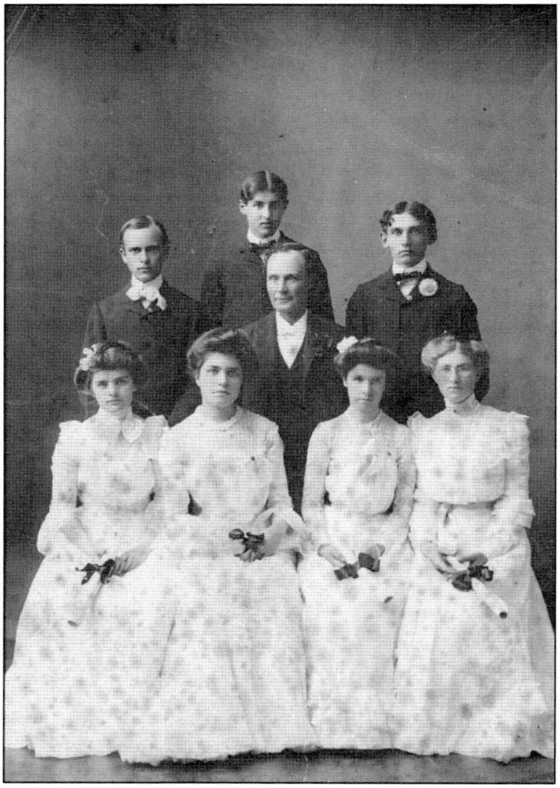

National City High School Graduating Class. The class of 1904 poses for a formal graduation photograph. Principal Cicero P. Evans is in the second row, center. At the turn of the 20th century, the *City Directory* stated that "many of the county's most enterprising and wealthy citizens" resided in National City. At this time, the Southern California Railway, the headquarters of the San Diego Land and Town Company, and the National City and Otay Railroad all called National City home.

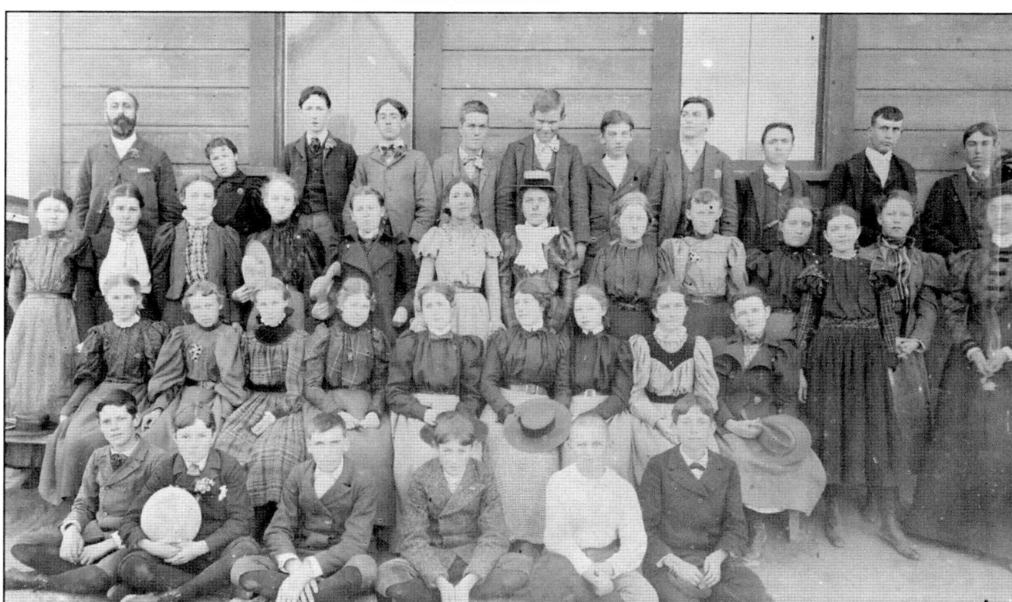

National City High School, 1898. Pictured in front of the high school at Tenth Street and E Avenue are grades 9 through 12. Prof. G. S. Trowbridge, their principal, joined them for this photograph. In 1900, Frank Kimball set up a new flagpole, and the junior class immediately ran up their standard—an olive flag with an orange owl—and cut the rope. It was three weeks before it could be removed.

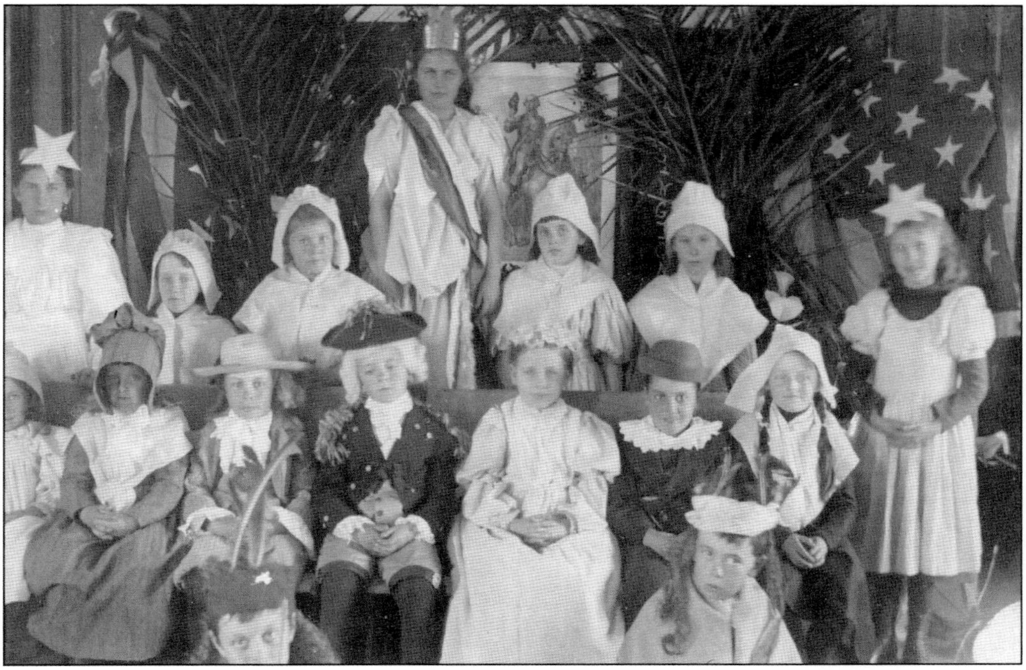

GEORGE WASHINGTON'S BIRTHDAY, 1895. National City schools celebrated George Washington's birthday every year. When Flora Kimball was elected to the school board in 1889, she helped to see that flags flew over all schoolhouses and that Arbor Day was celebrated on February 22. This photograph includes, in the first row, Hazel Reed (second from left), Halbert Johnson (third from left), Lilian Rice (fifth from left), and Percy Copeland.

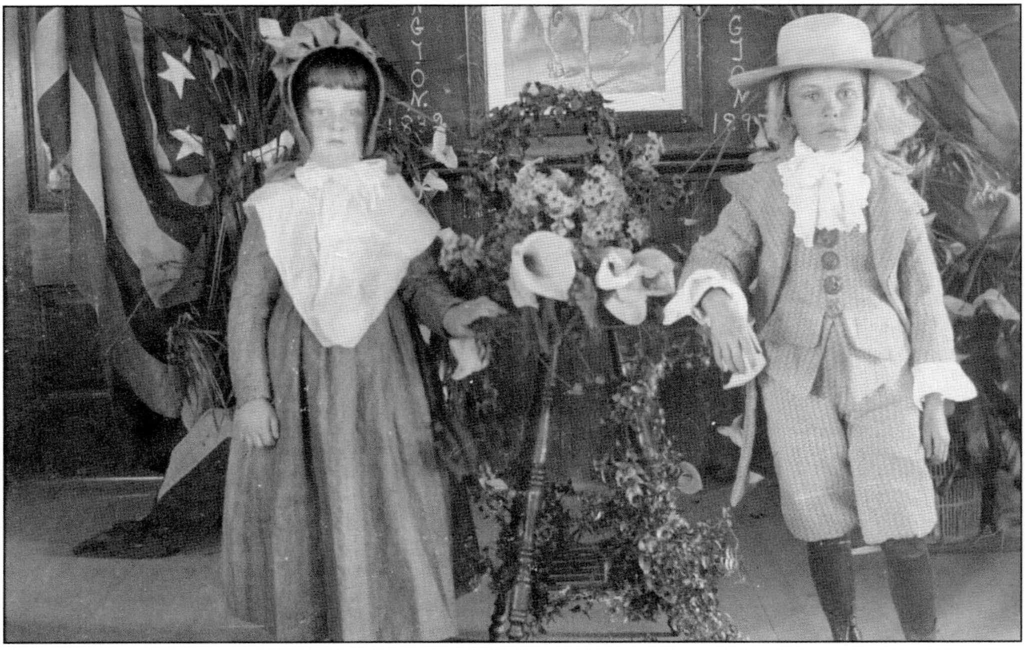

GEORGE AND MARTHA, 1895. Hazel Reed and Halbert Johnson dressed for their school's celebration of Washington's birthday as George and Martha. Note the elaborate floral decorations that were very common in National City celebrations.

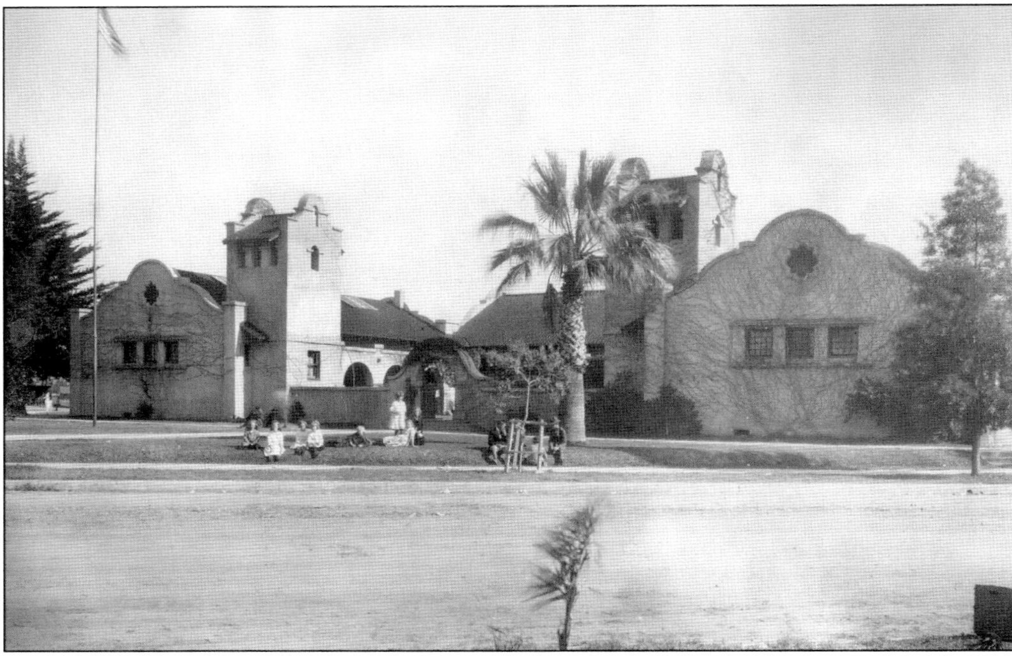

NATIONAL CITY HIGH SCHOOL. As the population increased, the number of schoolchildren once again outpaced the existing educational facilities. On September 25, 1906, a $23,000 bond passed to build a new school building. On March 13, 1908, Frank Kimball wrote that about 400 people attended the dedication of the new high school building at Ninth Street and E Avenue. Designed in the popular mission style, it stood where Central Elementary now stands.

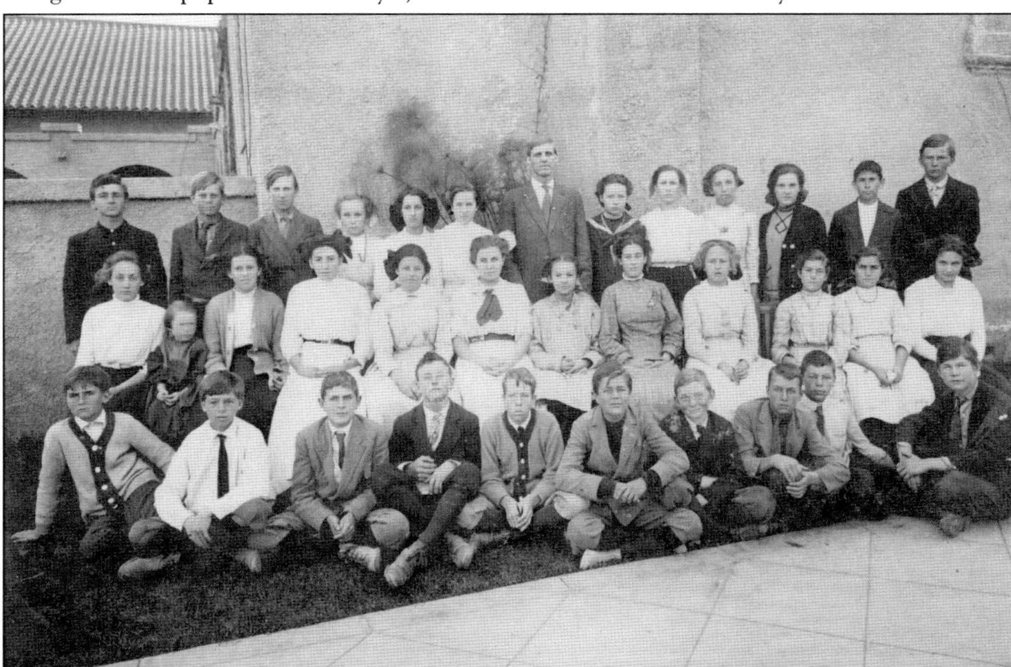

EIGHTH-GRADE CLASS, 1911. The class posed in front of the new National City High School at Ninth Street and E Avenue.

Six

THE RAILROAD

TIES TO COMMERCE

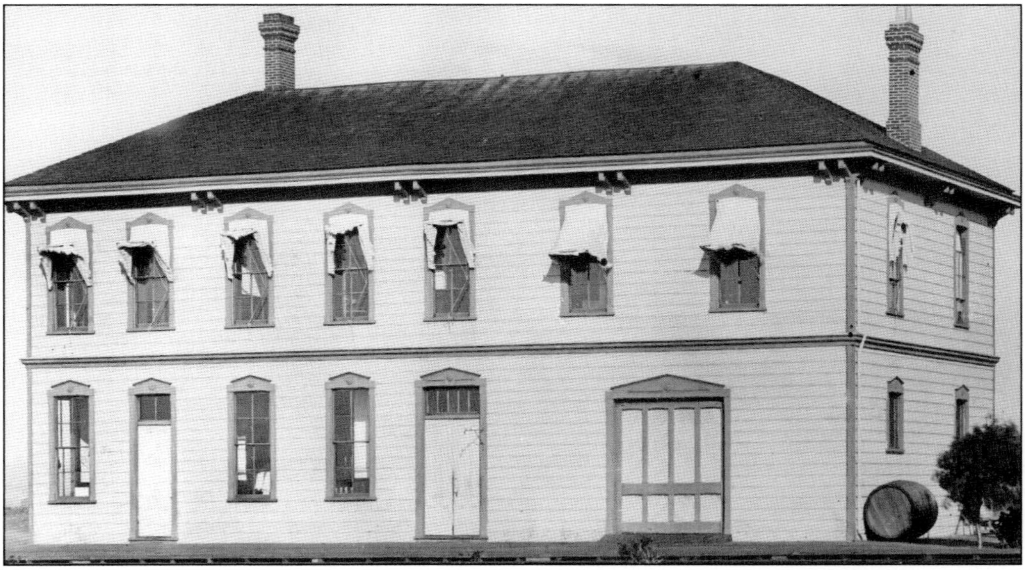

CALIFORNIA SOUTHERN RAILROAD DEPOT. On October 5, 1882, the *National Record* announced, "The work on the new depot and R. R. headquarters building is progressing finely, the painting and the plastering now rapidly nearing completion." Great excitement filled the city as the dream of a local railroad was finally coming to fulfillment. No one had worked harder in this pursuit than Frank Kimball, who had made numerous trips east, often at his own expense, to negotiate with various railroad companies. He finally achieved a successful end in this endeavor to negotiate a contract with a syndicate of men associated with the Santa Fe Railroad. The contract with the railroad stipulated that 10,000 acres of the National Ranch and one half of the unsold lots in National City would be given as a subsidy to the railroad company, in trade for the terminus and shops to be located in National City. This was a tremendous price for the Kimball Brothers to pay, but it was deemed necessary in order that the growing agricultural industry could ship produce to market in a timely manner.

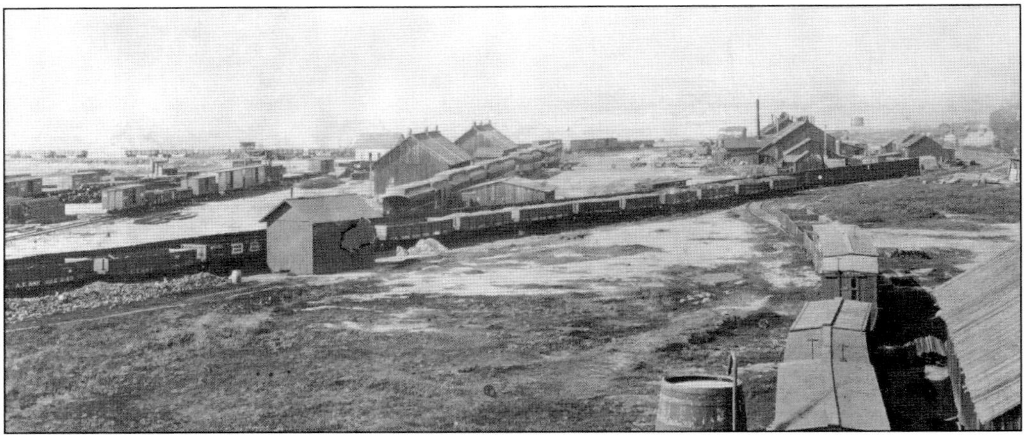

RAILROAD SHOPS. The California Southern rail yards sprawled over 225 acres abutting the bay. The facilities included a roundhouse, blacksmith and mechanic shops, water tanks, and a creosote plant for treating wood. Here the line maintained its engines. During the boom, 1886 to 1888, the National City rail yard had 27 tracks and built and furnished over 500 railcars, including mail, express, and boxcars.

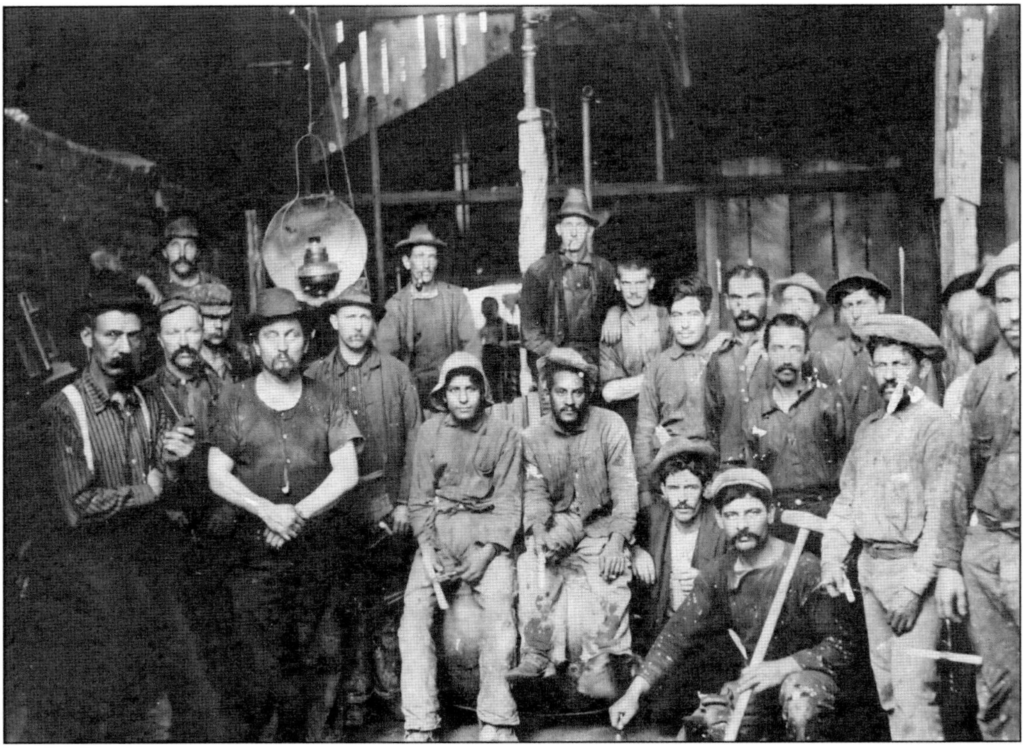

ROUNDHOUSE INTERIOR. The extensive railroad shops created many jobs for the citizens of National City. This rare photograph gives a glimpse of the men who maintained the rolling stock. Unfortunately, in 1889, the shops relocated to San Bernardino. Some said it was the Central Pacific's attempt to maintain control of the railroad, while others believed the railroad wanted to avoid the high cost of transporting vehicles so far south.

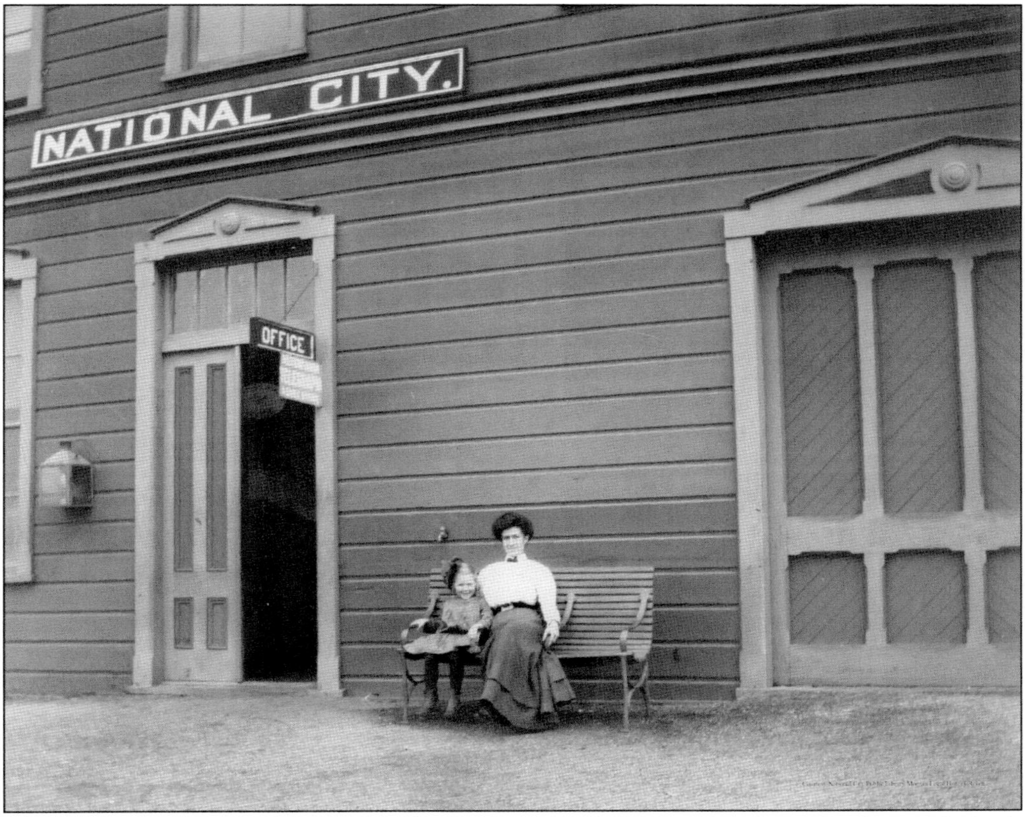

WAITING AT THE SANTA FE DEPOT. The railroad provided a convenient means of travel for both people and trade. An advertisement in the *National Record* of October 1882, announced, "The only all rail line between San Diego Bay and San Francisco, Los Angeles and all the Eastern Cities. The road is well built, well equipped, and runs through some of the grandest scenery on the American Continent."

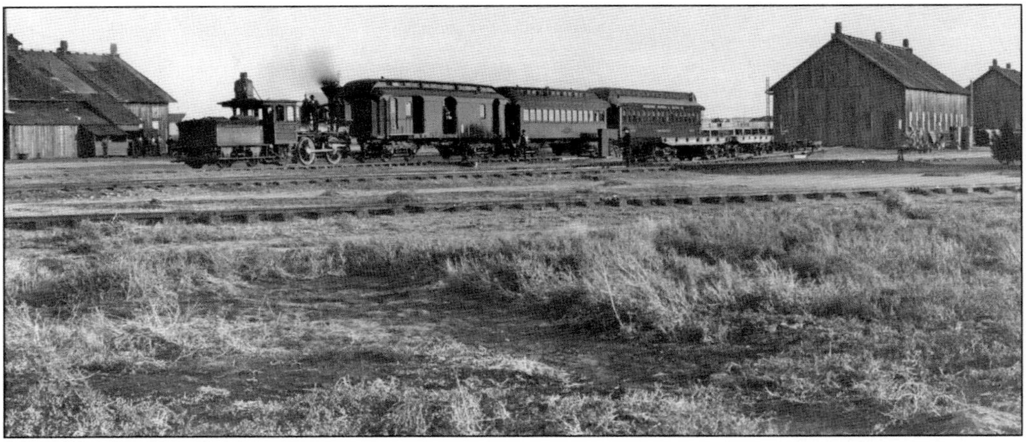

CALIFORNIA SOUTHERN RAILROAD. National City's relationship with the California Southern Railroad was a struggle fraught with legal troubles and many disappointments. Though the depot remained, the closing of the machine shops ended the dream of National City becoming the hub of Southern California's commerce as was initially hoped. In October 1882, the local newspaper announced that the fare from National City to Colton was $6.

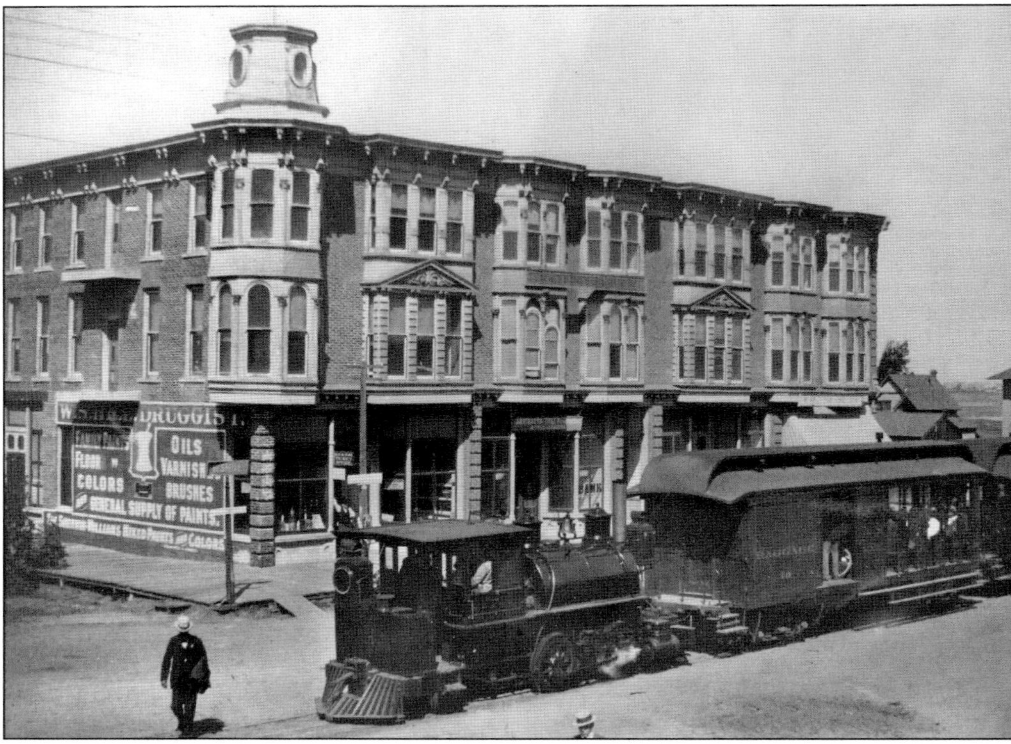

NATIONAL CITY AND OTAY RAILROAD ON NATIONAL CITY BOULEVARD. On December 28, 1886, Frank Kimball wrote in his diary that he had organized the National City and Otay Railway Company with William Dickinson, subscribed to its capital stock with $3,000, and was elected its vice president. Starting on June 15, 1887, the National City and Otay Railroad ran three round-trip trains a day, with the last leaving San Diego about 5:30 p.m.

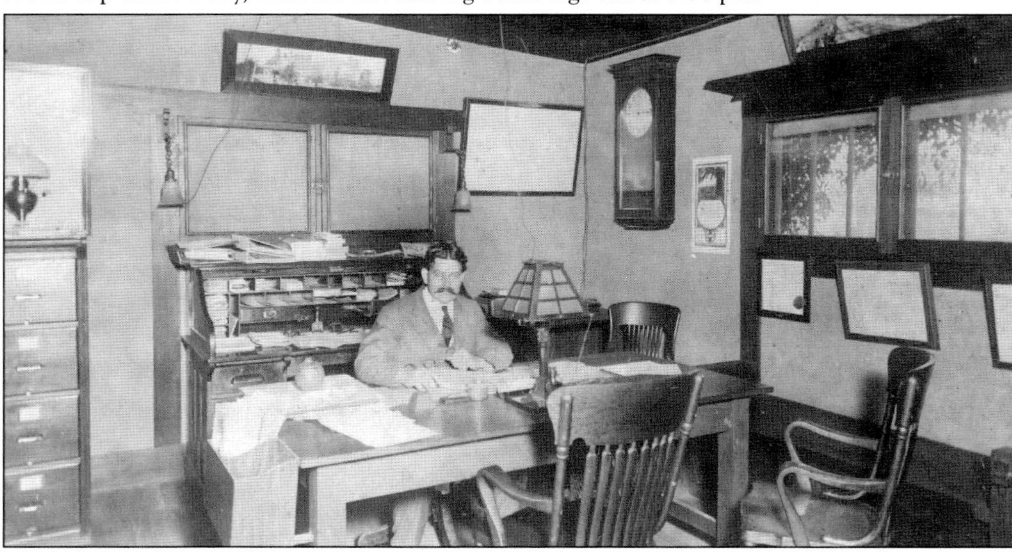

NATIONAL CITY AND OTAY RAILROAD, C. 1910. Henry P. Snow, agent for the National City and Otay Railroad, is pictured in his office on Cleveland Avenue at Twenty-third Street. The Boston headquarters of the San Diego Land and Town Company knew successful colonization required ease of transportation throughout the South Bay.

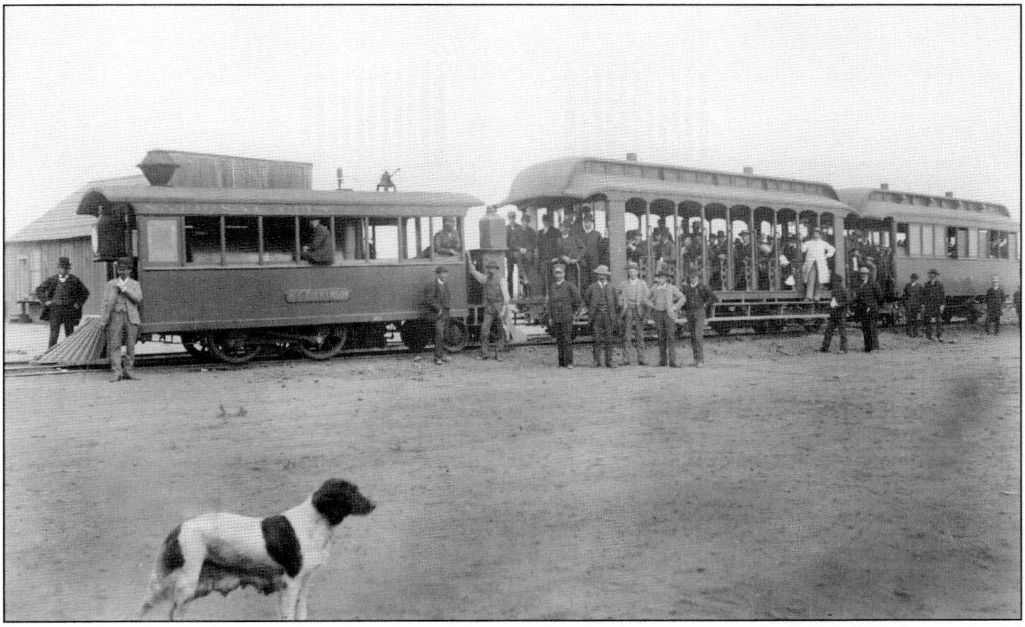

NATIONAL CITY AND OTAY RAILROAD, C. 1890. Frank Kimball and William Dickinson had envisioned a rail line that would transport prospective buyers to show off the available acreage of National City and what was to become Chula Vista, thus encouraging land sales. The little railroad did more than that; it became a vital link between growing communities for transportation and commerce. The car pictured on the left was named the *W. G. Dickinson*.

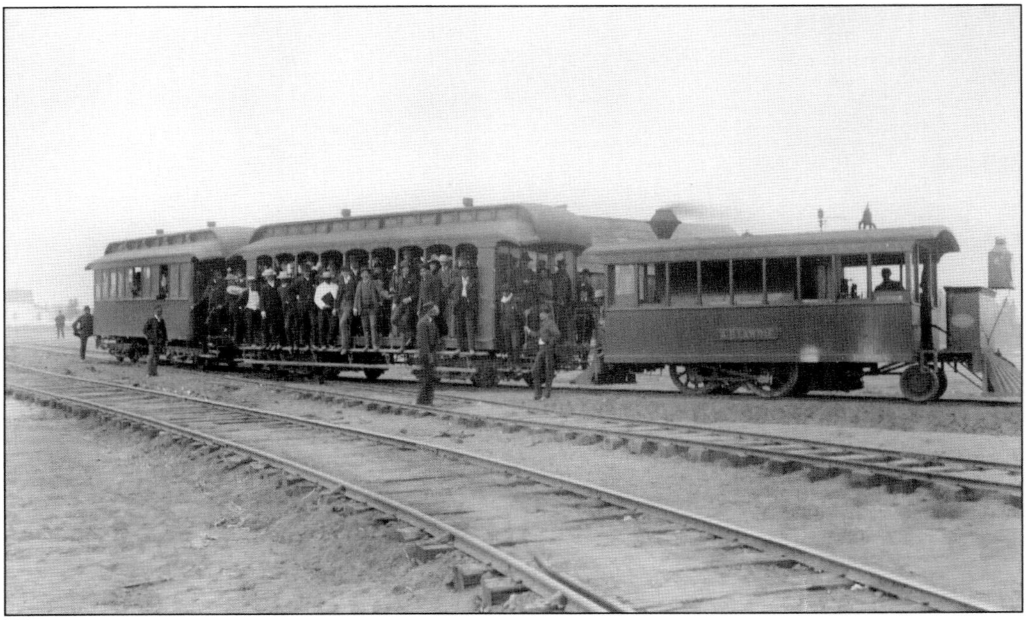

NATIONAL CITY AND OTAY RAILROAD AT SWEETWATER JUNCTION. Built to run on a standard-gauge track, some of the sturdy little Porter engines were boxed in with metal sheets to prevent them from appearing like locomotives and thereby scaring livestock. While some of the passenger cars were enclosed, many were open-sided. By the end of the first year, the train had carried over 240,500 passengers as well as agricultural products to market.

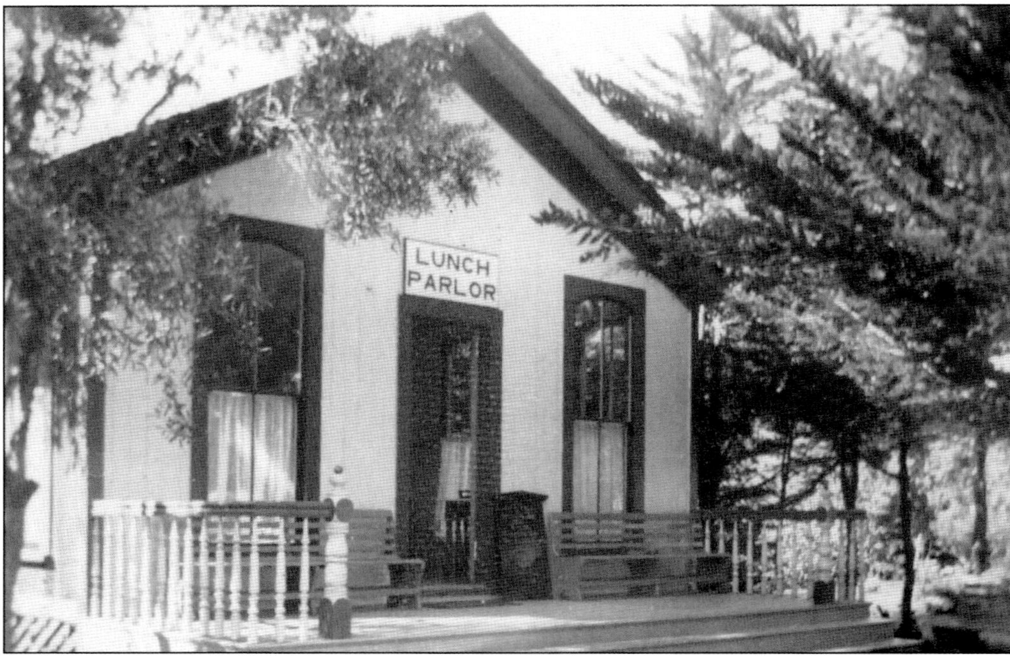

OLIVEWOOD LUNCH PARLOR. A popular tourist stop on the National City and Otay Railroad, the lunch parlor sat on the grounds of Olivewood, the estate of Warren and Flora Kimball. An Olivewood Lunch Parlor promotional brochure stated, "On the return from Old Mexico, at 1 o'clock p.m. lunch will be served to tourists at this ideal California home."

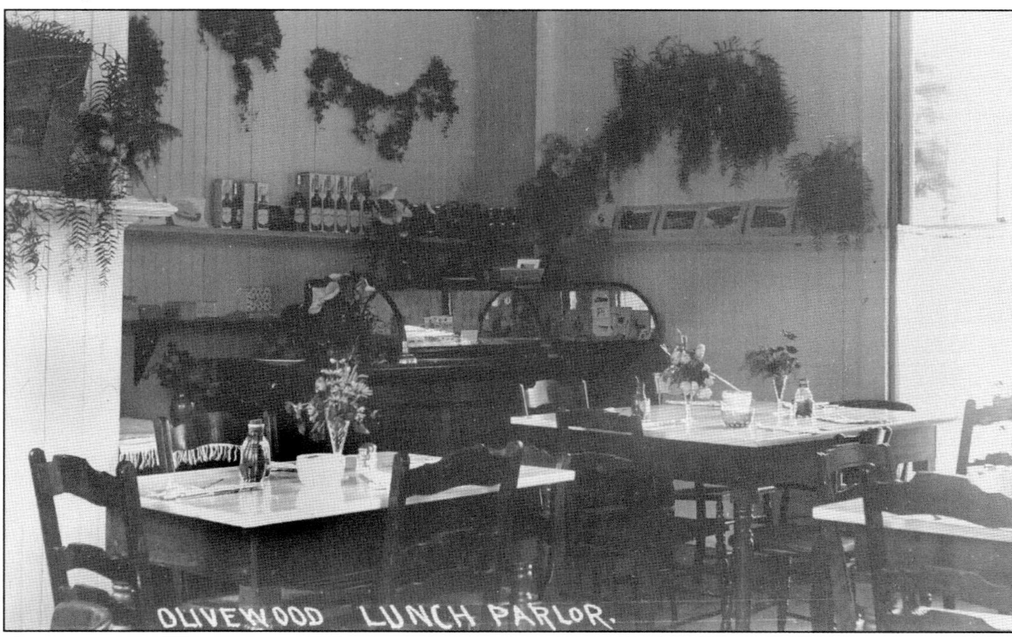

OLIVEWOOD LUNCH ROOM INTERIOR. Tourists on the National City and Otay Railroad had one hour and 10 minutes at Olivewood—time to be served a first-class, home-cooked meal and to rest in the shade of the olive trees. The train left for the Sweetwater Dam at 2:20 p.m. A plain lunch cost 25¢. Tourists could also bring their own lunch basket and enjoy the hospitality of the gardens.

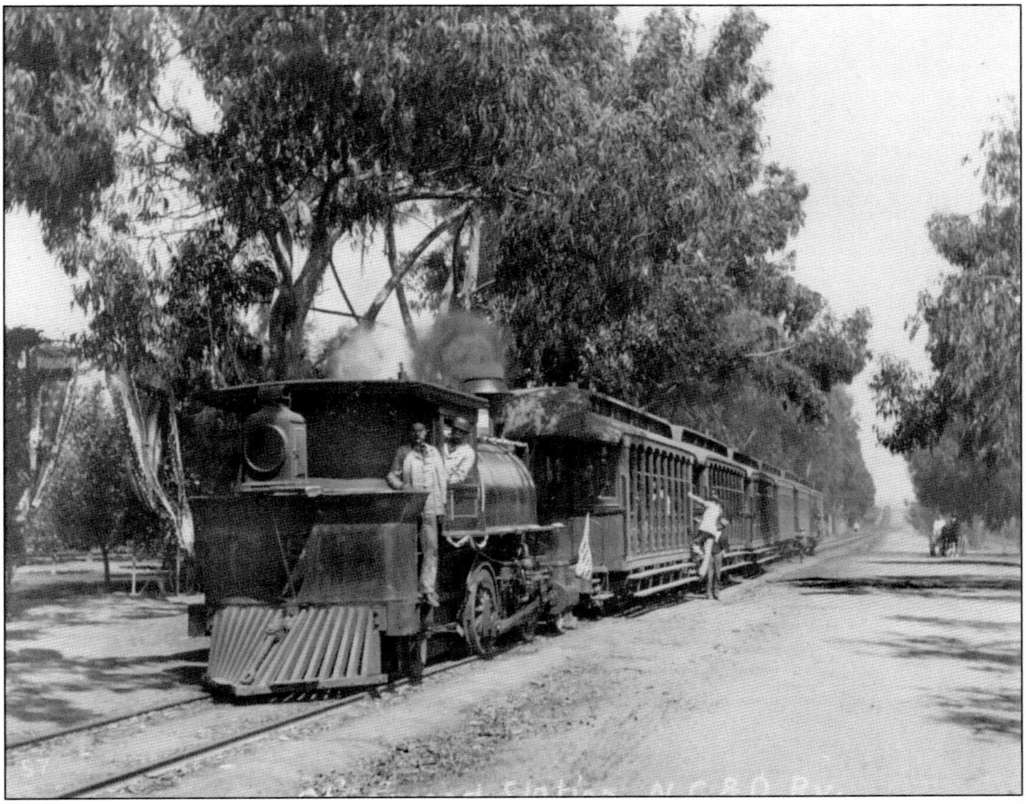

National City and Otay Railroad on Twenty-fourth Street Grade. The National City and Otay Railroad tracks ran up Twenty-fourth Street to L Avenue, then south into the Sweetwater Valley. This photograph was taken looking eastward. The eucalyptus trees that Flora Kimball planted along the street, and watered by hand, had grown quickly and made Twenty-fourth Street very picturesque.

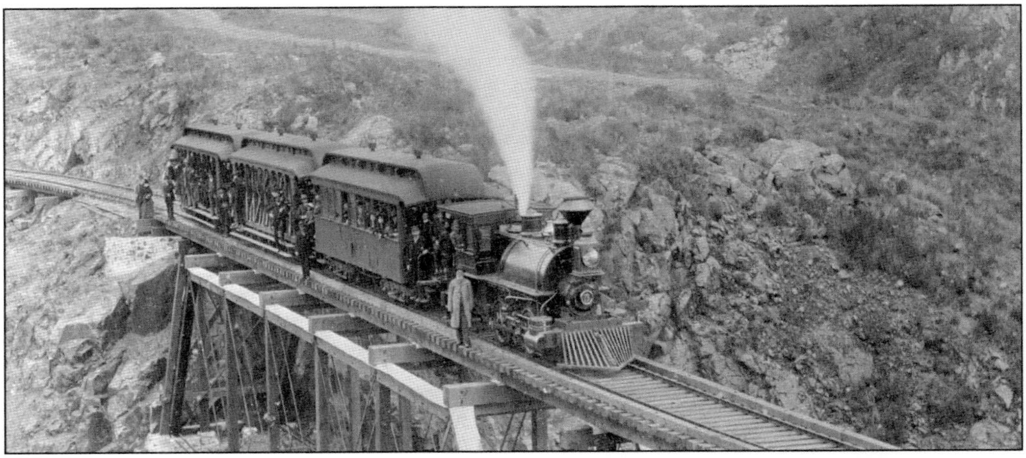

National City and Otay Railroad Trestle, c. 1888. Shown on High Bridge, near the Sweetwater Dam, engine No. 5 of the National City and Otay Railroad delivers tourists to the dam site. Built by the San Diego Land and Town Company, the train was loved by National City residents because it provided convenience and necessary transportation throughout the South Bay. The line also provided a means to bring produce into town from outlying areas.

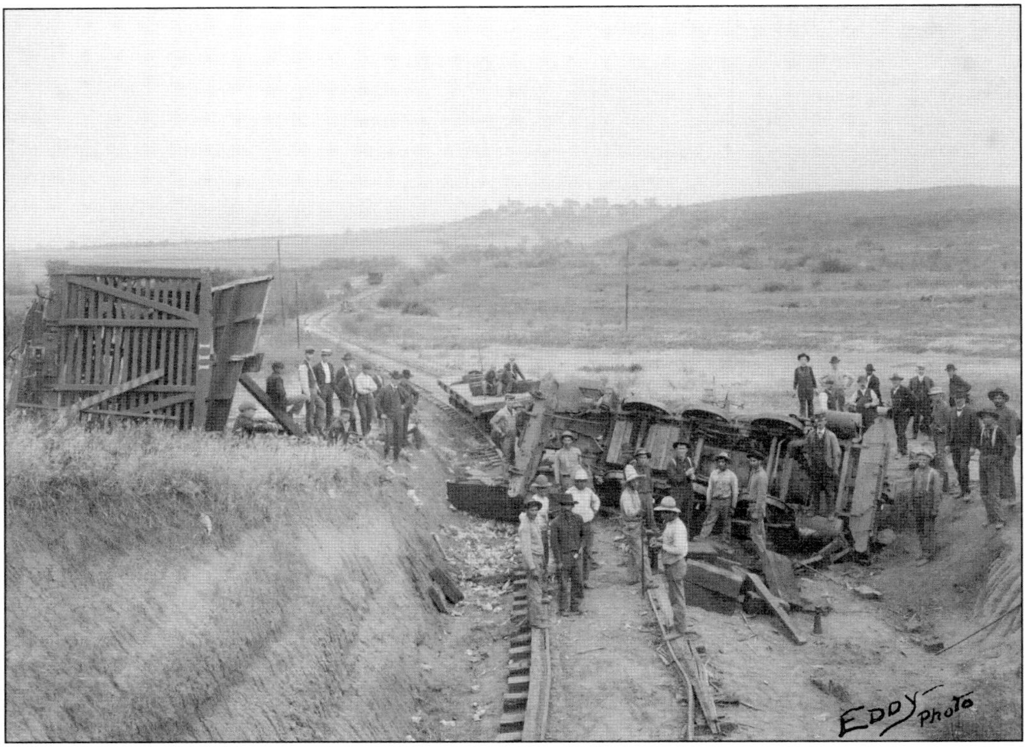

WRECK ON THE NATIONAL CITY AND OTAY LINE, MAY 20, 1905. Engineer Mark Baird died when his engine ran off the track and overturned, tearing up the line. This occurred at the junction located at the foot of Chula Vista Hill, in the Sweetwater River Valley. Baird came to National City with his family in 1880 and lived at 1114 East Eighth Street, overlooking Paradise Valley. Frank Kimball's diary mentions that the sermon given at his funeral was heart-breaking.

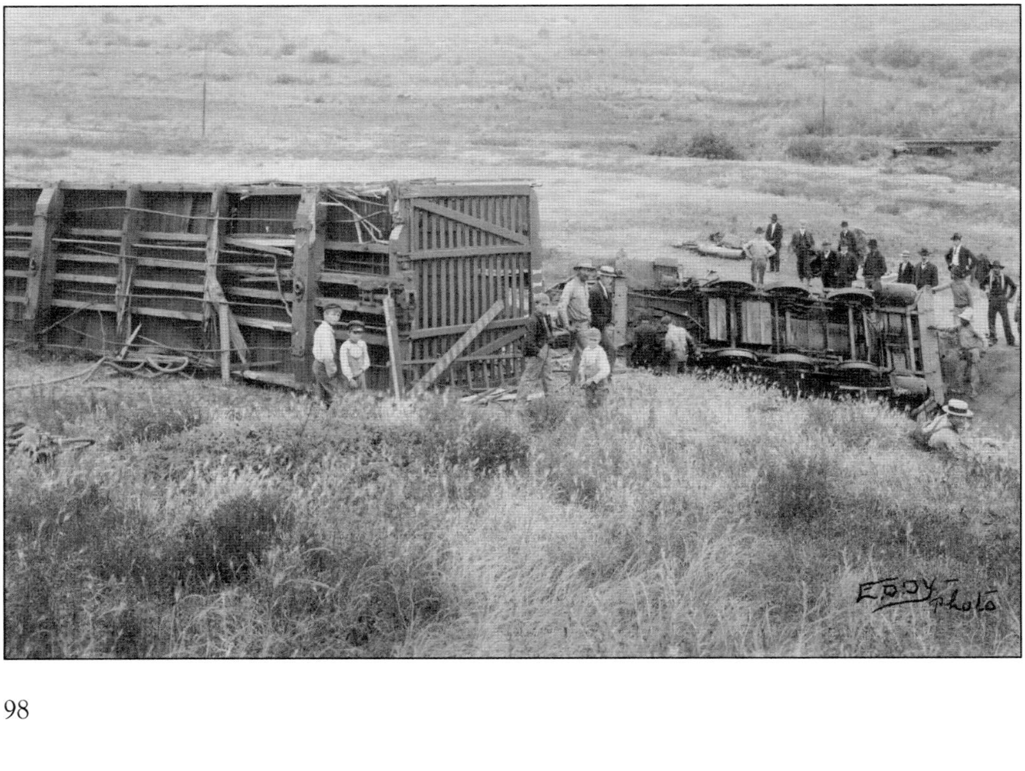

Seven

SWEETWATER DAM

WATER FOR A DRY LAND

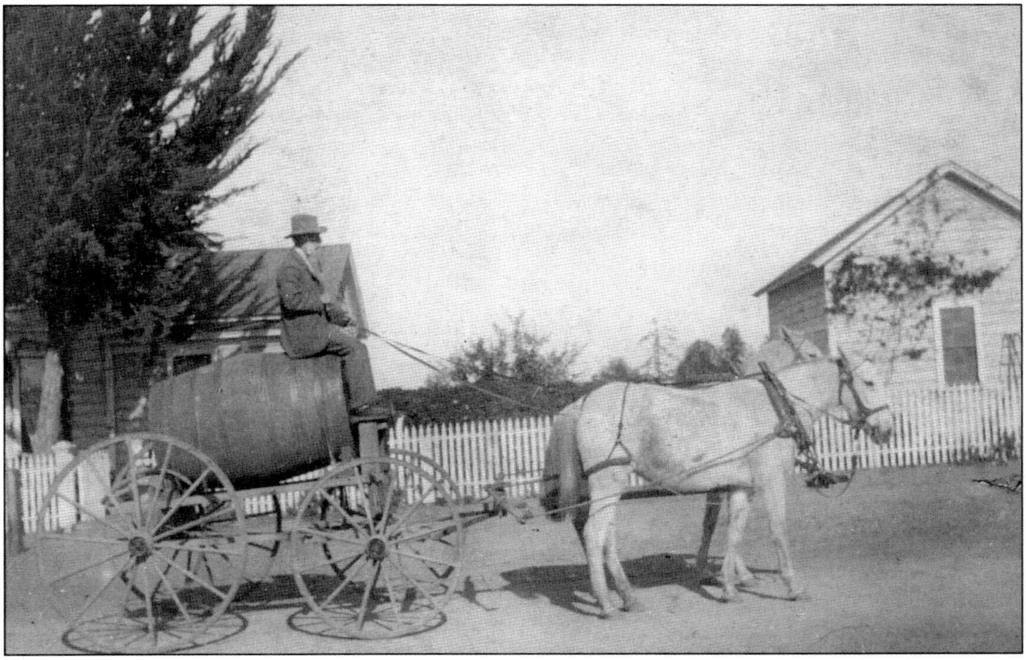

CAPT. F. T. MOORE DELIVERING WATER. The *National City Record* noted, "Captain F. T. Moore defies the drought. Found good water at 50 feet." Moore peddled water in a former wine barrel, but it was said that no one objected to the unusual taste from the well at 620 Fifth Street. Before the completion of the Sweetwater Dam, people of the South Bay feared drought. Many folks had wells on their property, but during dry years, it was necessary for most people to buy water. In Frank Kimball's diary on July 8, 1873, he mentions that he bought water at 75¢ for 10 gallons. Later, in April 1879, he writes, "Have hauled about 70 barrels of water and put it around the olive trees, a barrel to each tree." On September 2, 1886, Frank Kimball met with Elijah S. Babcock at the San Diego Land and Town Company's office and discussed the water question. Two days later, he rode over to Jamacha Canyon with William Dickinson, and the men spent several days examining all the reservoir sites for 25 miles, starting at the headwaters of the Sweetwater River.

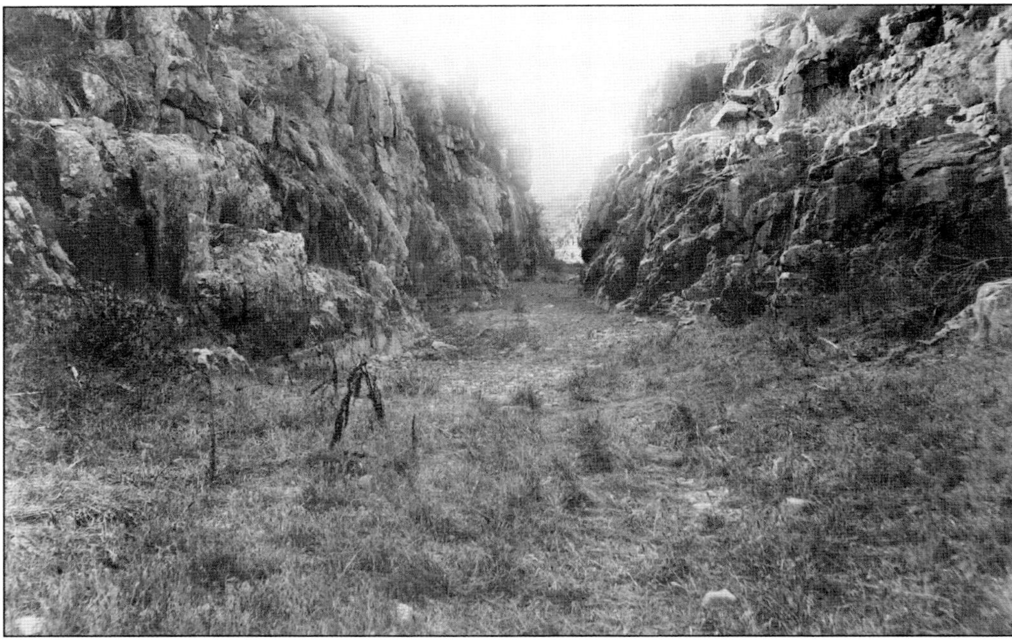

Dam Site, c. 1880. Frank Kimball had long been aware of the great natural resource the northeastern edge of the National Ranch offered—an ideal configuration of hills and river in which to build a dam that would hold an adequate supply of water for the growing area. Before Kimball purchased Rancho de la Nacion, he wrote in his diary, June 3, 1868, "Today I have seen the finest water power site on the National Ranch."

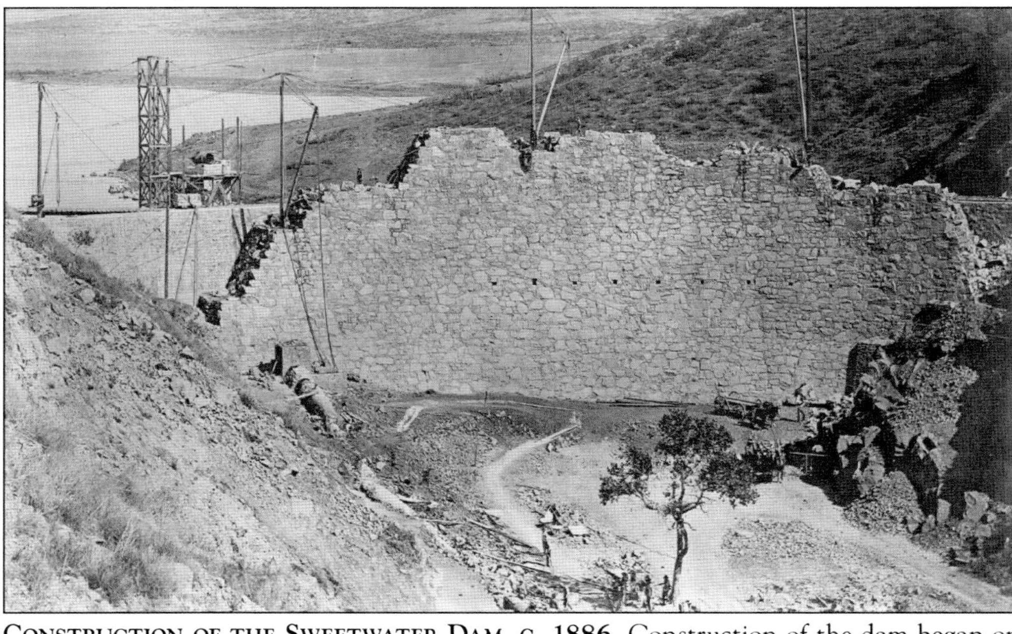

Construction of the Sweetwater Dam, c. 1886. Construction of the dam began on November 17, 1886, with F. E. Brown in charge. Brown had previously supervised the building of a small rock dam in the San Bernardino Mountains, and he was quickly engaged to supervise the project on the Sweetwater River. Brown hired the many laborers needed for work on the dam at $1 a day. (Courtesy of the Sweetwater Authority.)

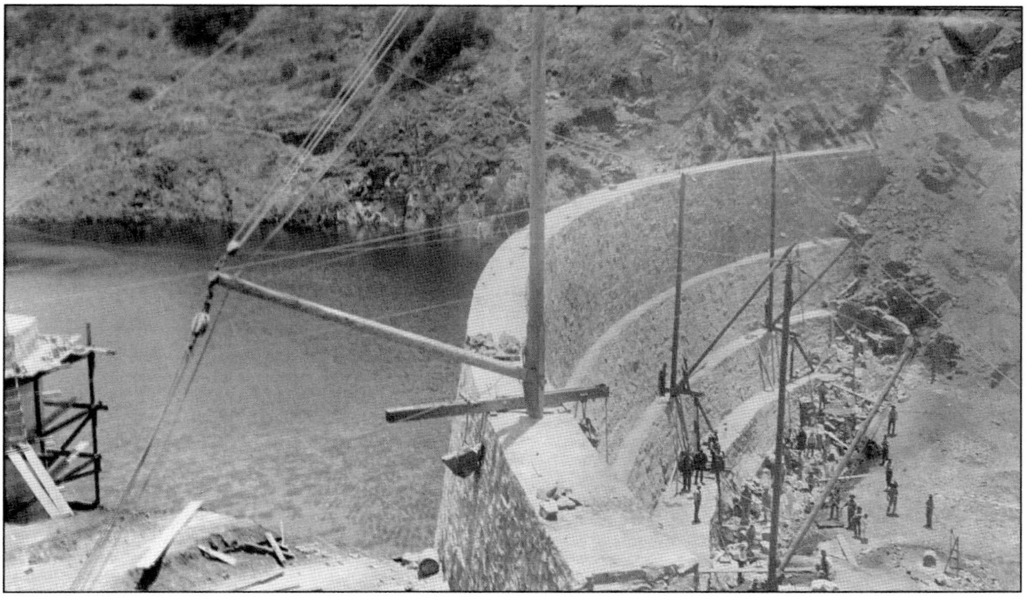

SWEETWATER DAM CONSTRUCTION, C. 1887. The leadership of the San Diego Land and Town Company felt an urgency in constructing the dam; the sooner plentiful water was available, the sooner the company could sell its thousands of acres of land. Dickinson's first choice of an engineer proved not to be a good one, and he was soon fired. When James Dix Schuyler was appointed supervising engineer, he set the course for the dam to become the engineering marvel of its time. (Courtesy of the Sweetwater Authority.)

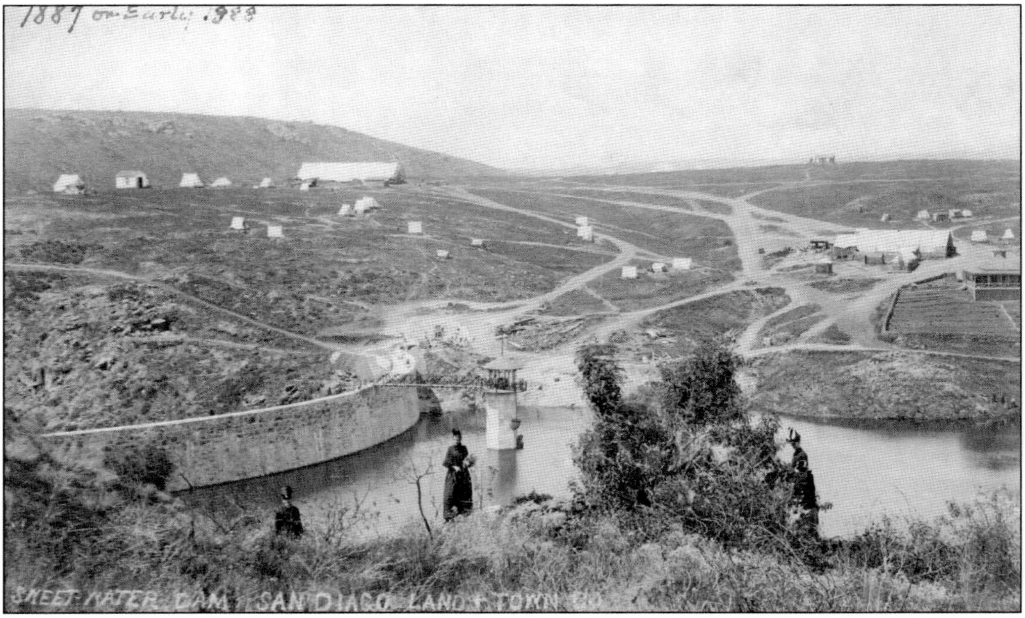

SWEETWATER DAM, C. 1887. Supervising engineer James Schuyler changed the original plans, calling for a 50-foot masonry wall with a base only 10 feet thick into a 60-foot wall with a base 35 feet thick. In the spring of 1887, he decided that by adding 30 additional feet in height to the dam wall, the reservoir would hold five times more water and would irrigate an additional 10,000 acres of land. Permission was granted, and the dam soared to a height of 90 feet.

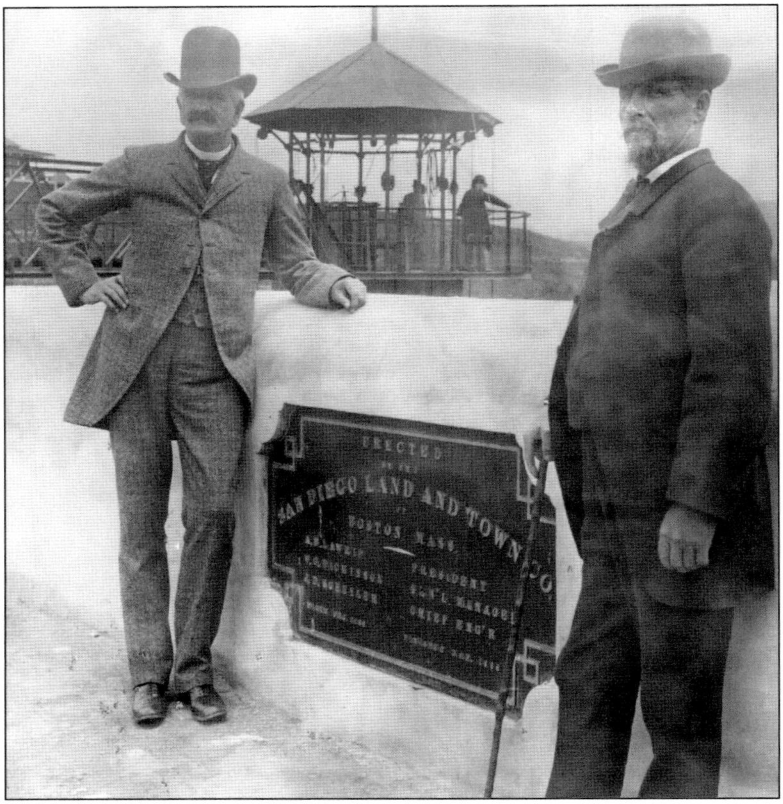

DICKINSON AND KIMBALL AT DAM, 1888. William Green Dickinson (left), general manager of the San Diego Land and Town Company, and Frank Augustus Kimball stand at the completed dam next to a bronze plaque that reads, "Erected by the San Diego Land and Town Company, Boston, Mass." The dam for which Kimball had begun purchasing the water rights as early as 1869 was finally completed through the financial backing of Dickinson.

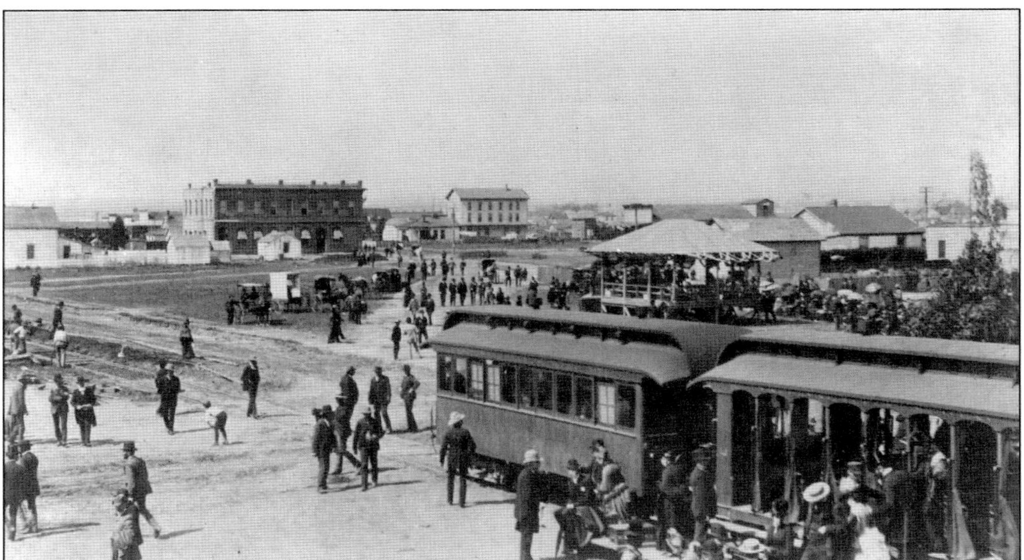

ARRIVING AT THE WATERWORKS CELEBRATION. On April 19, 1888, trains along the newly opened National City and Otay Railroad poured passengers into National City to celebrate the completion of "National City's Great Water System," as the newspaper heralded. The newspaper went on to say that 6,000 people participated in the great event. The festivities were held at Cleveland Avenue and Twenty-third Street.

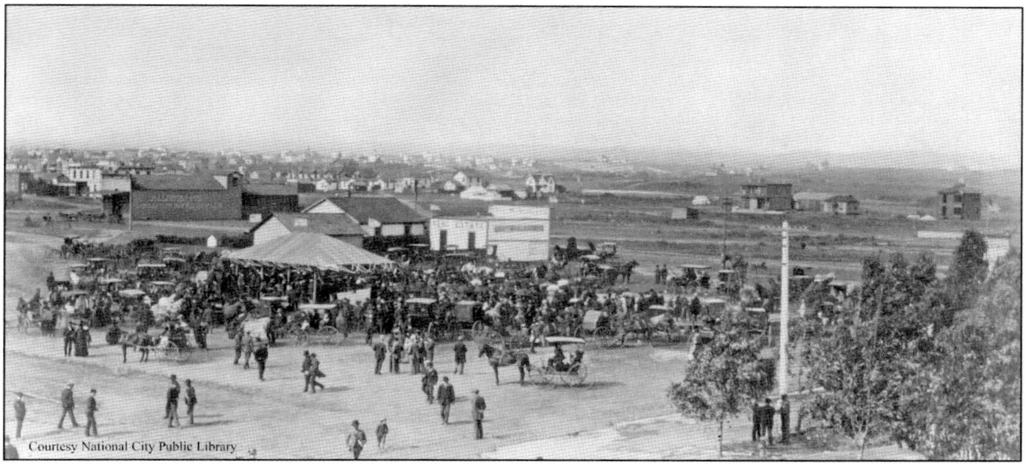

Courtesy National City Public Library

CELEBRATION OF THE WATER WORKS, APRIL 19, 1888. Instead of fireworks, it was waterworks that marked the celebration of the city's new water system. Using two 2.5-inch hoses with 1-inch nozzles, streams of water were shot 70 feet into the air in front of the International Hotel, "just to prove there was plenty of it," according to the local newspaper. A parade with a band heralded the joy felt by everyone on this occasion. Many speeches marked the celebration of the city's new water system, the first appropriately being from Frank Kimball. An unfinished warehouse became a display hall laden with the fruits and vegetables representing the coming bounty predicted for the farms of the South Bay. The day's events ended with a banquet in the International Hotel and finally a ball held in Horticultural Hall.

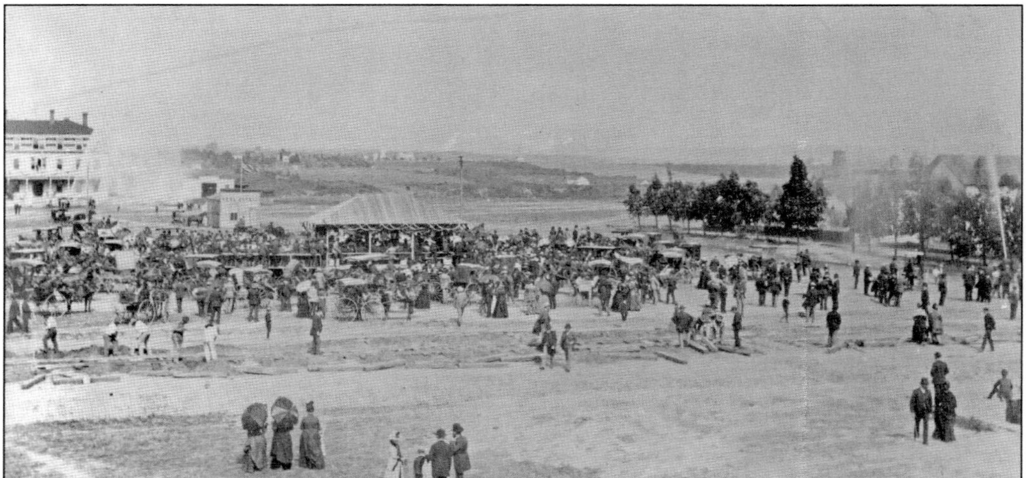

Courtesy National City Public Library

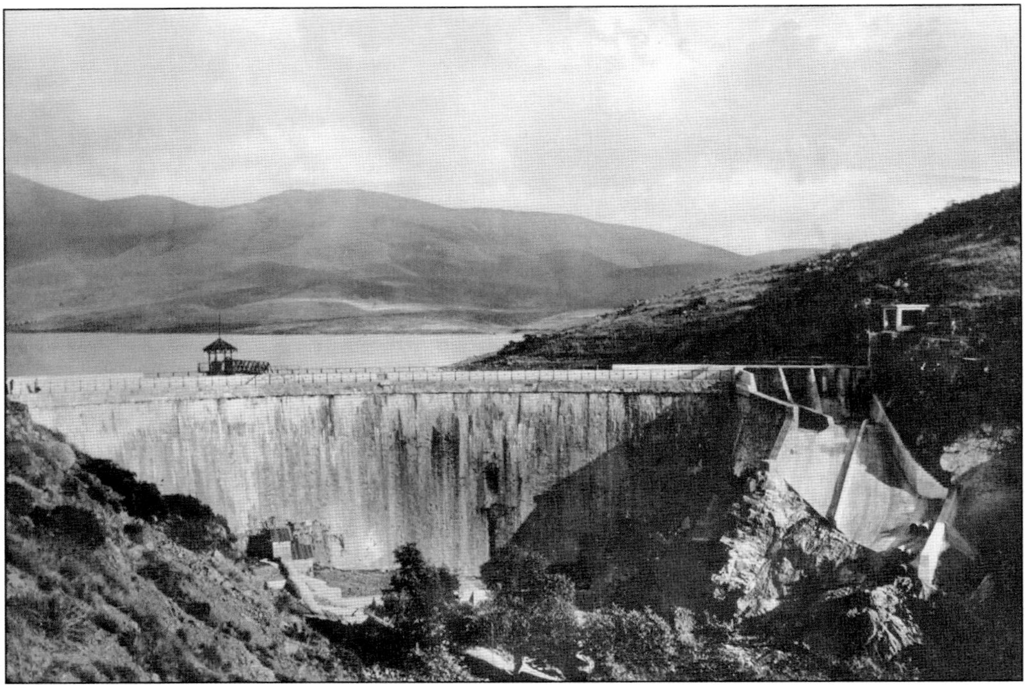

SWEETWATER DAM, 1890. After its completion in 1888, at the cost of $234,174.11, the Sweetwater Dam stood 20 feet higher than any other masonry arch dam in the United States. The dam's water distribution system included more than 65 miles of pipeline. Starting at the reservoir, the pipes ran five miles to Chula Vista. At Fourth Avenue and E Street, the main split, with one line heading south supplying Chula Vista and the other heading north for National City. Supervising engineer James Dix Schuyler reported that the reservoir and its distribution system added "a value of $1,500,000 to the principle tract of five thousand acres [Chula Vista] . . . and another million to the value of the town property in National City, and lands in the immediate vicinity."

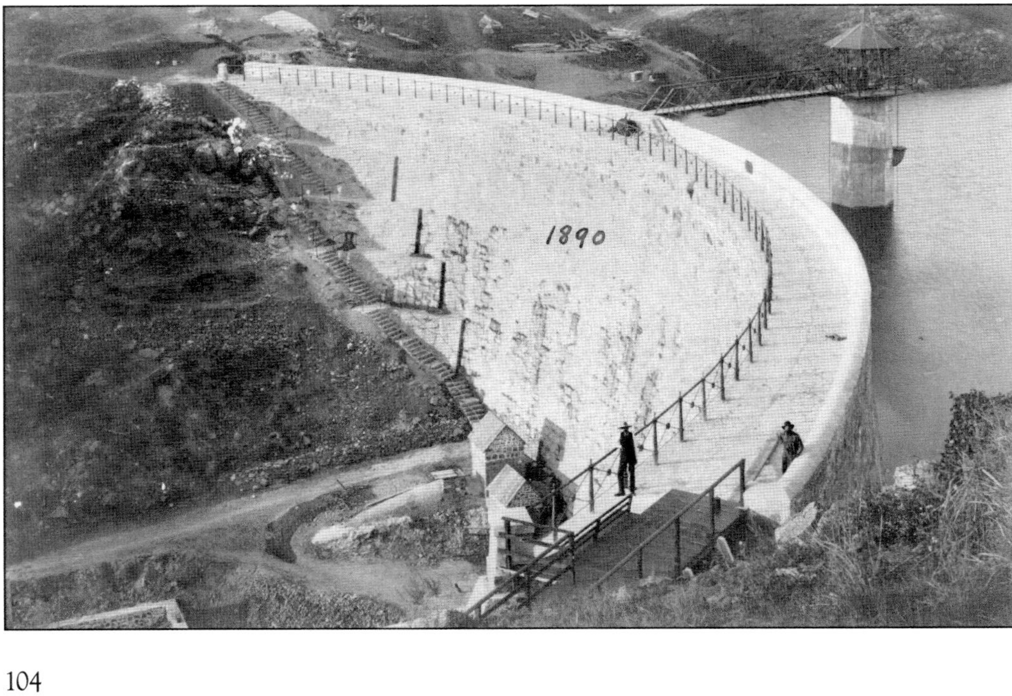

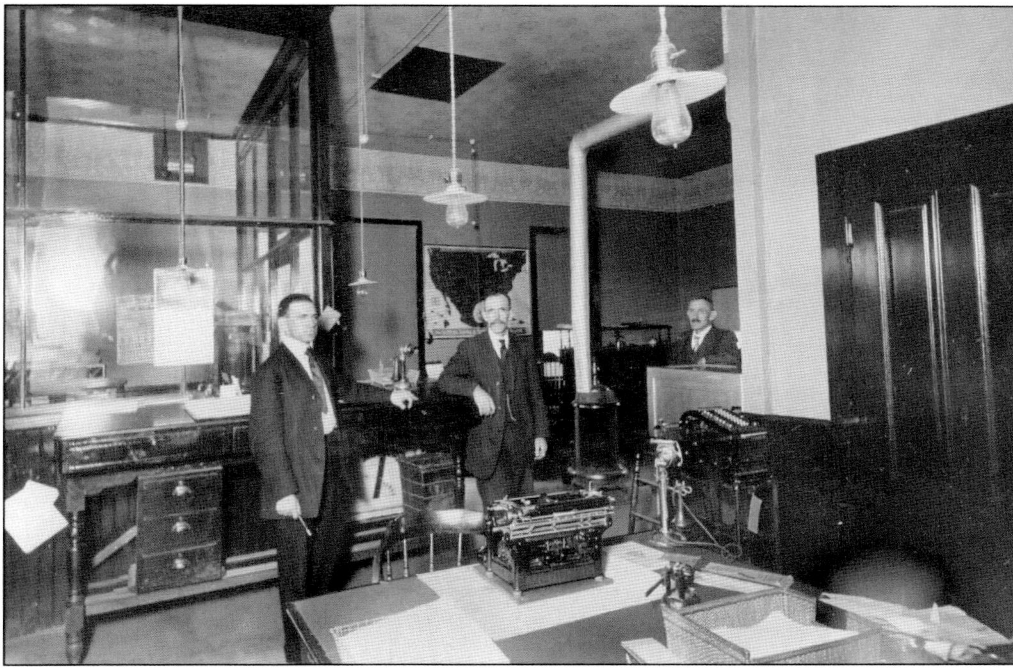

SWEETWATER WATER COMPANY INTERIOR, 1907. On March 31, 1902, the water company separated from the San Diego Land and Town Company under the name Sweetwater Water Company. The water company retained control of the dam, water supply, and water rights. John Boal continued as general manager of the San Diego Land and Town Company. Pictured are, left to right, employees Charles Tingley, Edward Hamilton, and John Gould.

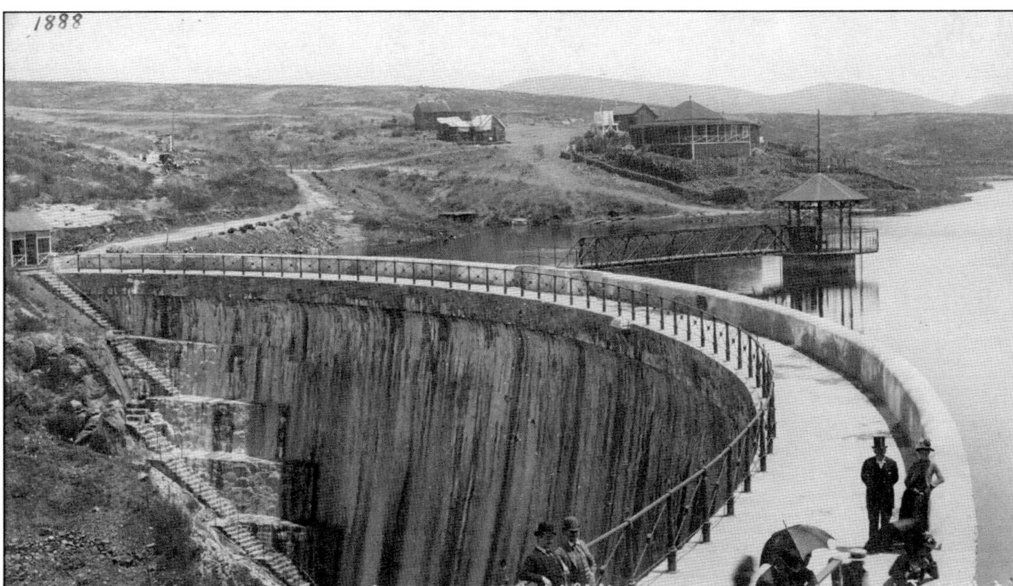

SWEETWATER DAM IS TOURIST DESTINATION. The National City and Otay Railroad brought many tourists out to view the dam. It was a landmark worthy of a visit, as it was the highest masonry arch dam in the whole country. Located in the shadow of Mount Miguel, it made for a very scenic place to enjoy a family outing.

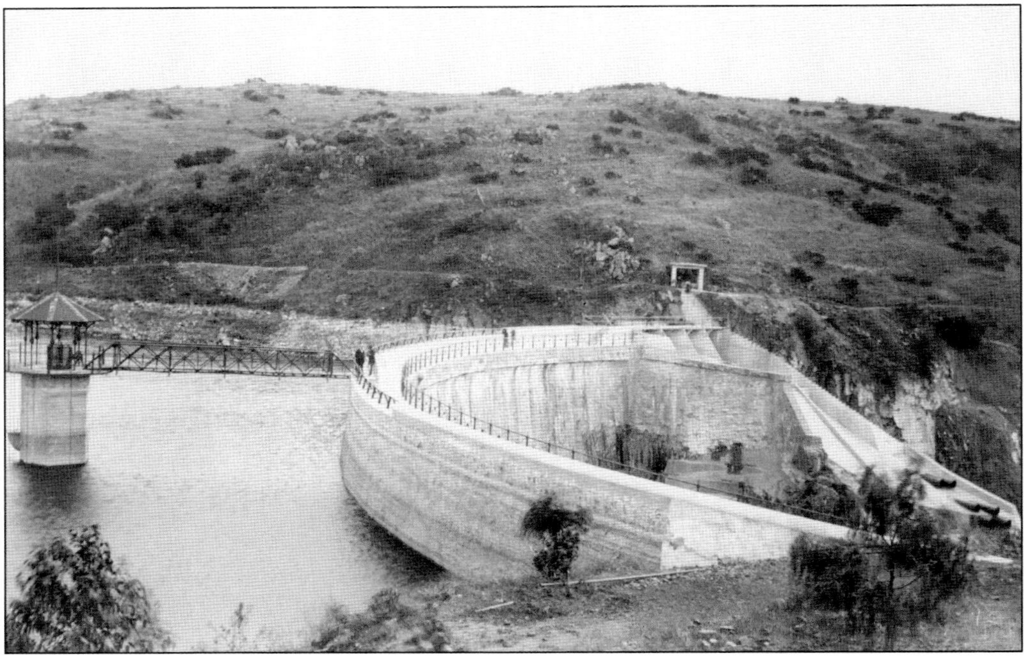

YEARS OF DROUGHT. The drought of 1897–1904, and the drying up of the Sweetwater Reservoir, forced the San Diego Land and Town Company to install 17 pumping plants to draw water from over 200 wells along the riverbed. But the water belied the standard set by the Sweetwater name; one resident complained, "What water there was contained so much sulfur and alkali that the orchards and all other vegetation were injured or completely ruined."

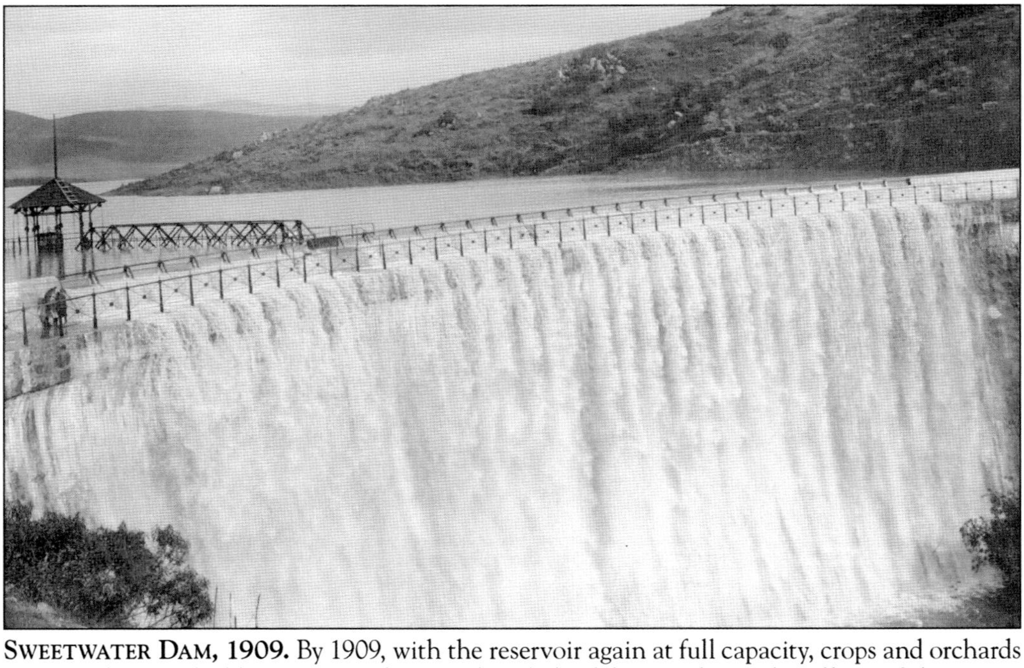

SWEETWATER DAM, 1909. By 1909, with the reservoir again at full capacity, crops and orchards flourished. A profitable return on their produce helped farmers forget the effects of the seven-year drought.

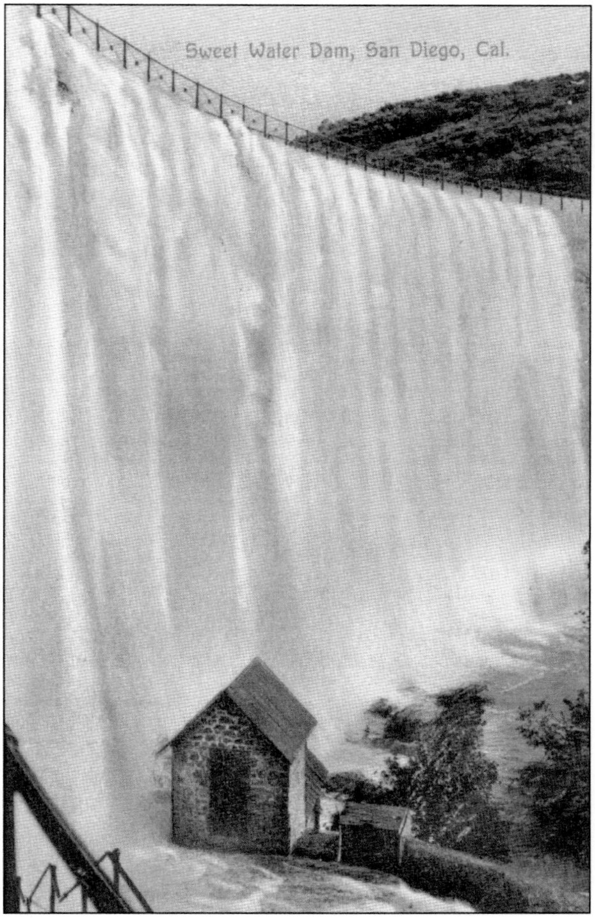

SWEETWATER DAM SPILLWAY, 1909. The first 20 years of the dam's existence had witnessed several challenges. When waters flooded George Neale's land, the result of an increase in the height of the dam, he filed suit, and the reservoir had to be partially drained. Citizens also sued over increased water rates. When the seven-year drought finally ended in 1904, the filling dam brought a general feeling of well-being. At this time, many postcards were produced of the dam.

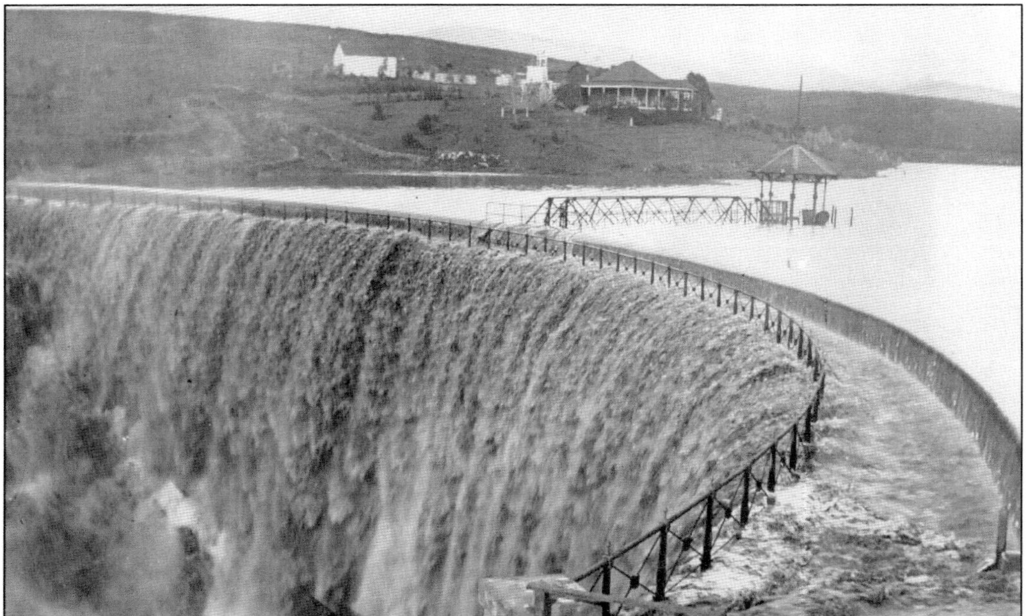

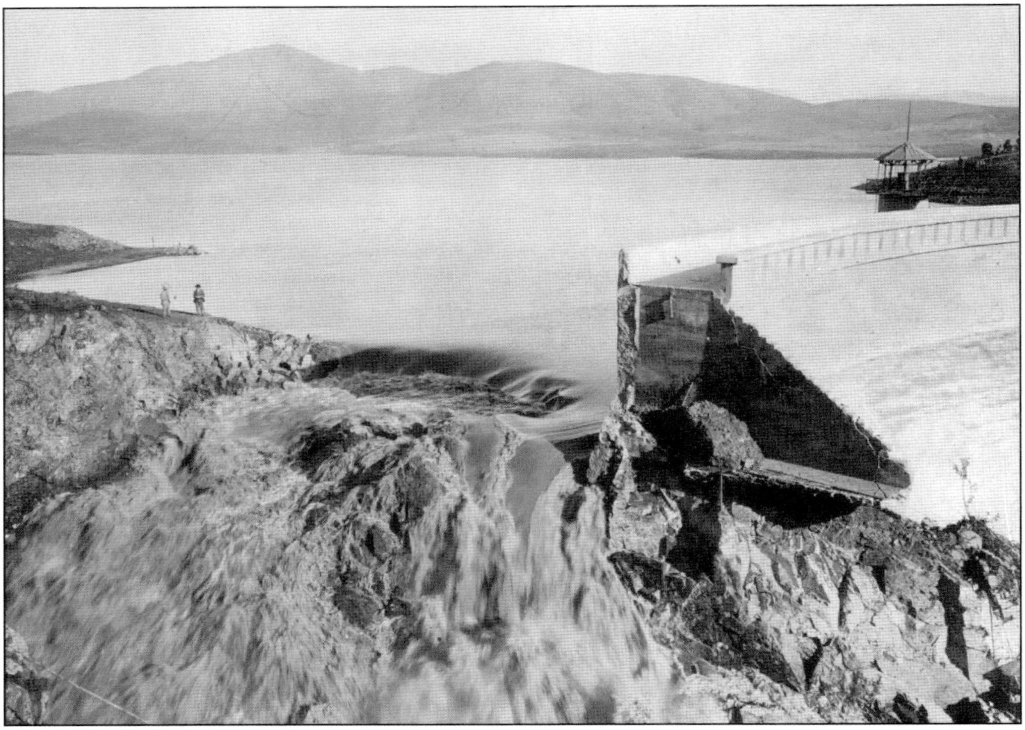

The Sweetwater Dam Breaks, 1916. After the region experienced another bout with lack of rain, the San Diego city council hired "rainmaker" Charles Hatfield to fill Morena Reservoir. The results were more than anyone bargained for. While the dam itself held, the torrent of water that overflowed its top washed out its abutments and tore down the valley, taking everything in its path out to sea. In the bay, the remnants of houses, trees, and railroad ties could be seen. (Below courtesy of the Sweetwater Authority.)

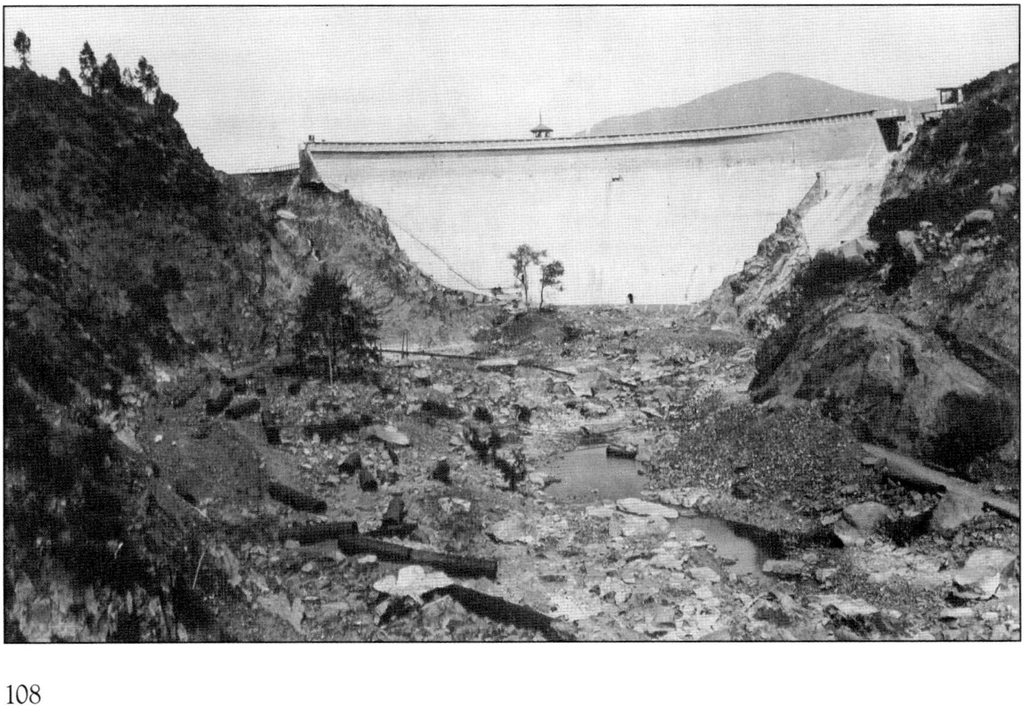

Eight

AGRICULTURE

THE BASIS FOR GROWTH

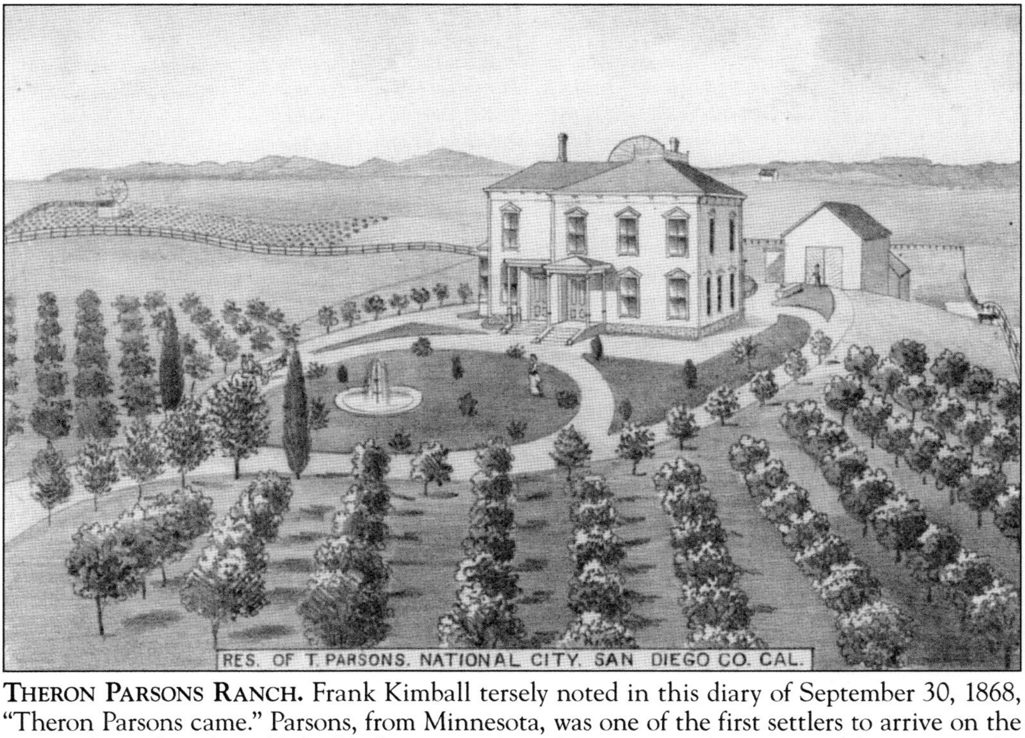

THERON PARSONS RANCH. Frank Kimball tersely noted in this diary of September 30, 1868, "Theron Parsons came." Parsons, from Minnesota, was one of the first settlers to arrive on the National Ranch and quickly build a home. He planted fruit trees and commenced farming. He also bought up land and invested in real estate development. This lithograph of his ranch is from the 1883 publication *History of San Diego County*, by Wallace W. Elliott and Company, Publishers.

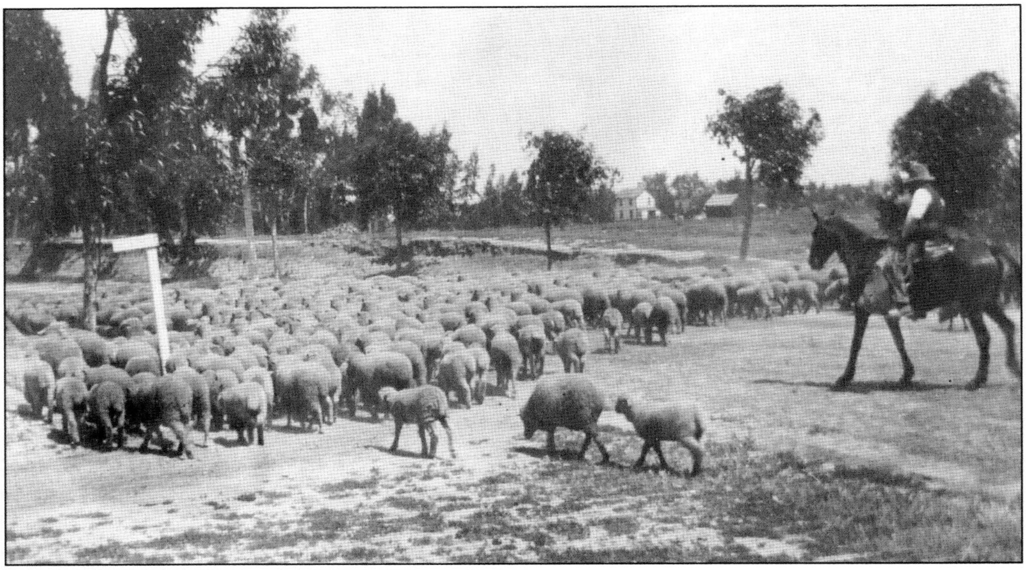

HERDING SHEEP AT NATIONAL CITY BOULEVARD AND FOURTEENTH STREET. In Frank Kimball's diary, December 25, 1873, he writes, "Warren has bought 1300 sheep." One of the Kimballs' earliest enterprises was raising sheep. It entailed long hours under difficult conditions. Frank notes in another diary entry of 1874, "Rained most of the day. Had a terrible time with the sheep and lambs, did not get them corralled till near nine o'clock night."

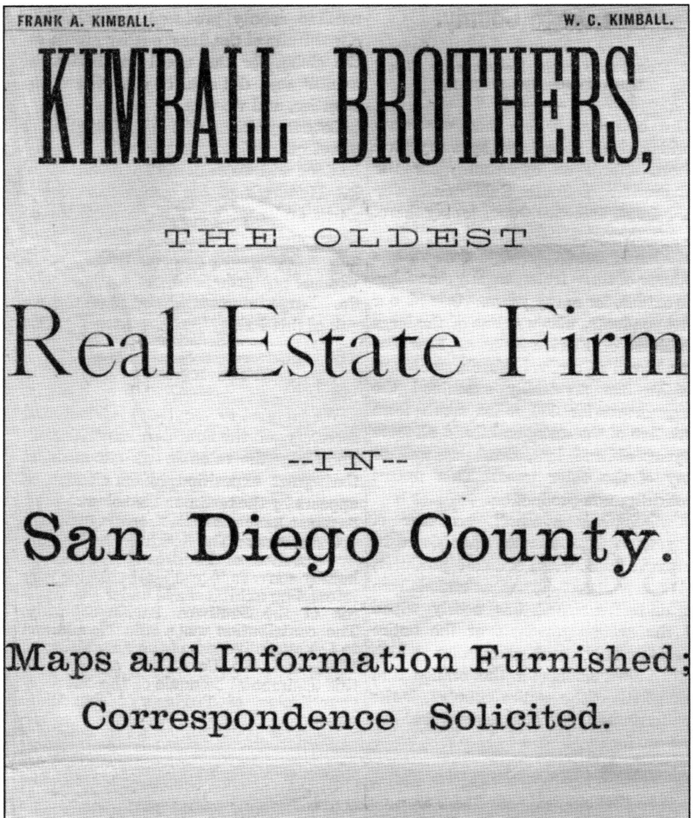

FRANK A. KIMBALL. W. C. KIMBALL.

KIMBALL BROTHERS,

THE OLDEST

Real Estate Firm

--IN--

San Diego County.

Maps and Information Furnished;

Correspondence Solicited.

KIMBALL BROTHERS ADVERTISEMENT, JANUARY 1886. This notice represents many of the advertisements that appeared for years in the local newspapers, offering land for sale in National City and the National Ranch. Frank and Warren Kimball were involved in many business enterprises, but none so long-lived or lucrative as real estate. At the height of his career, January 24, 1889, Frank noted that he had $1,315,341 in assets. By 1897, he had lost all, including his own home.

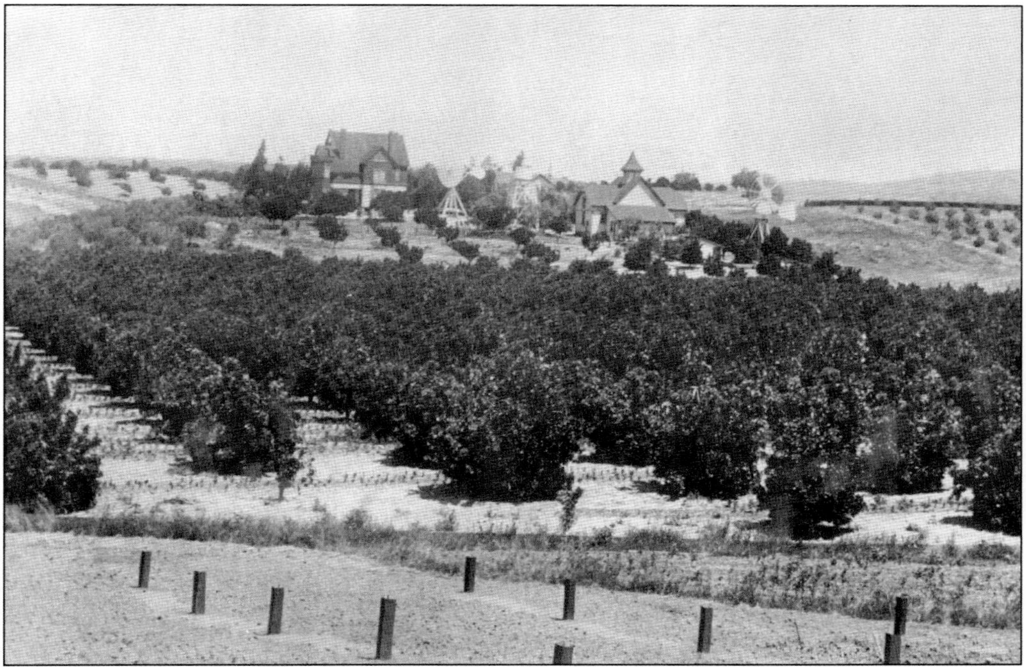

RALPH GRANGER PROPERTY. Although a wealthy man, Ralph Granger continued to be active in business enterprises. He operated a working citrus orchard that surrounded his home in Paradise Valley. A terraced grove of olive trees is planted to the left of the house, while an orange orchard is in the foreground. Windmills and the carriage house are to the right of the house.

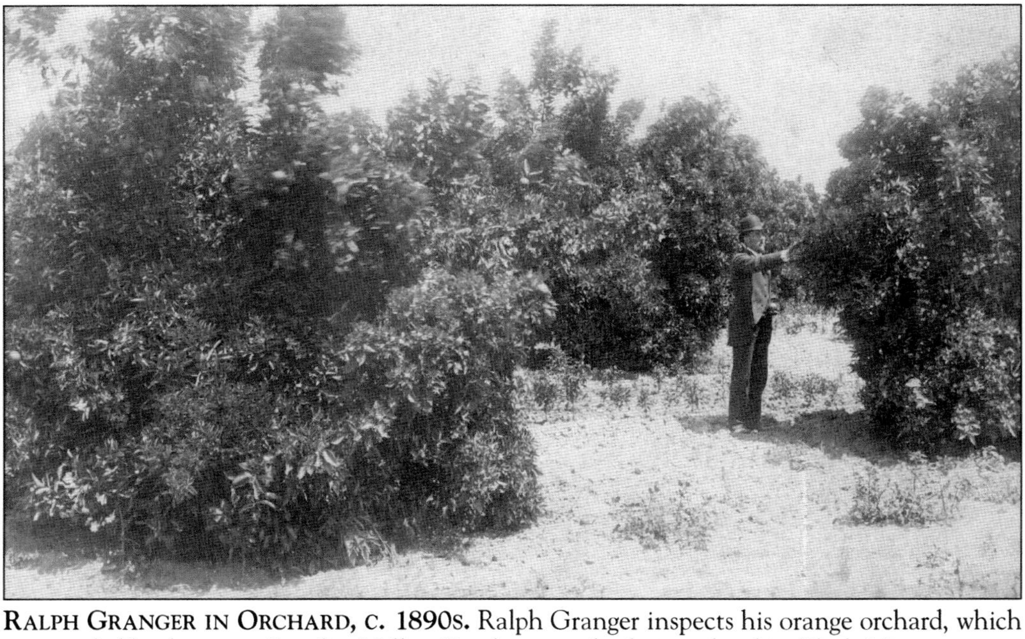

RALPH GRANGER IN ORCHARD, C. 1890S. Ralph Granger inspects his orange orchard, which surrounded his house in Paradise Valley. He also owned a fruit orchard in Chula Vista.

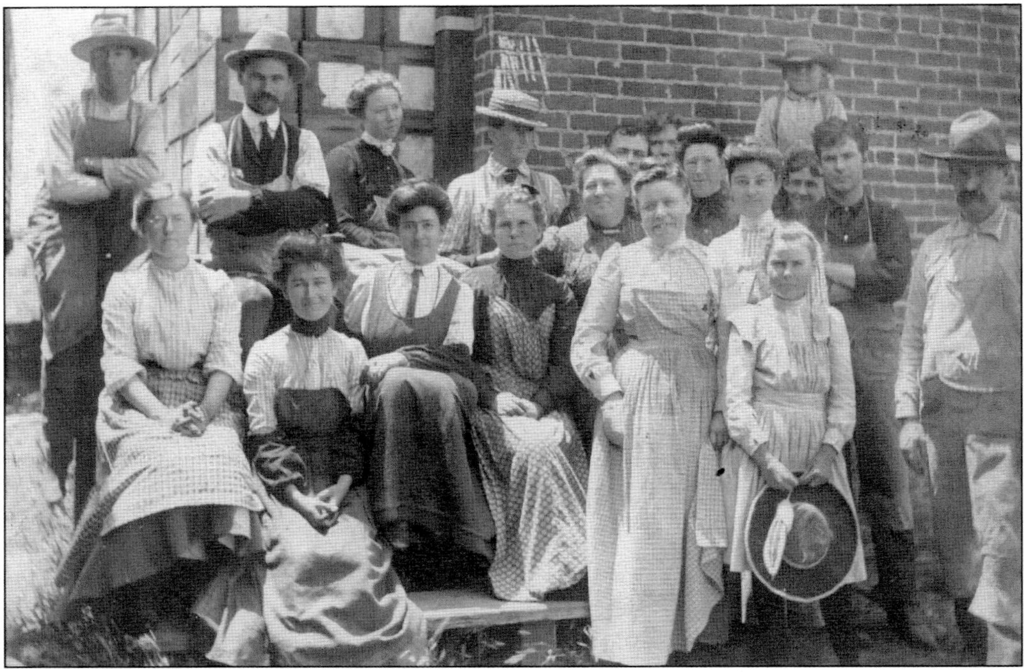

SAN DIEGO FRUIT COMPANY, 1906. A subsidiary of the San Diego Land and Town Company, the San Diego Fruit Company distributed fruit from their many acres of orchards spread throughout National City, Bonita, and Chula Vista. The group of fruit packers includes Edna Patterson, Winnie Eggleston, Lily Padget, Blanche Bragg, and Roy Kincaide.

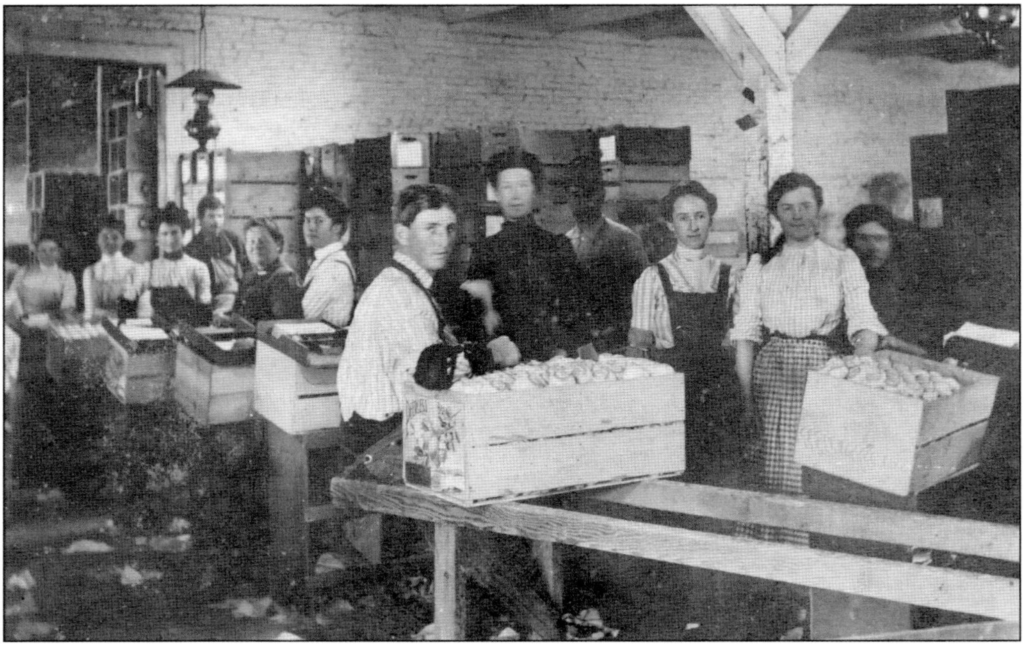

FRUIT PACKINGHOUSE INTERIOR, C. 1906. The San Diego Fruit Company abutted the railroad tracks on the north side of Twenty-third Street, about half a block west of Cleveland Avenue. This subsidiary was a lucrative enterprise for its parent company, the San Diego Land and Town Company.

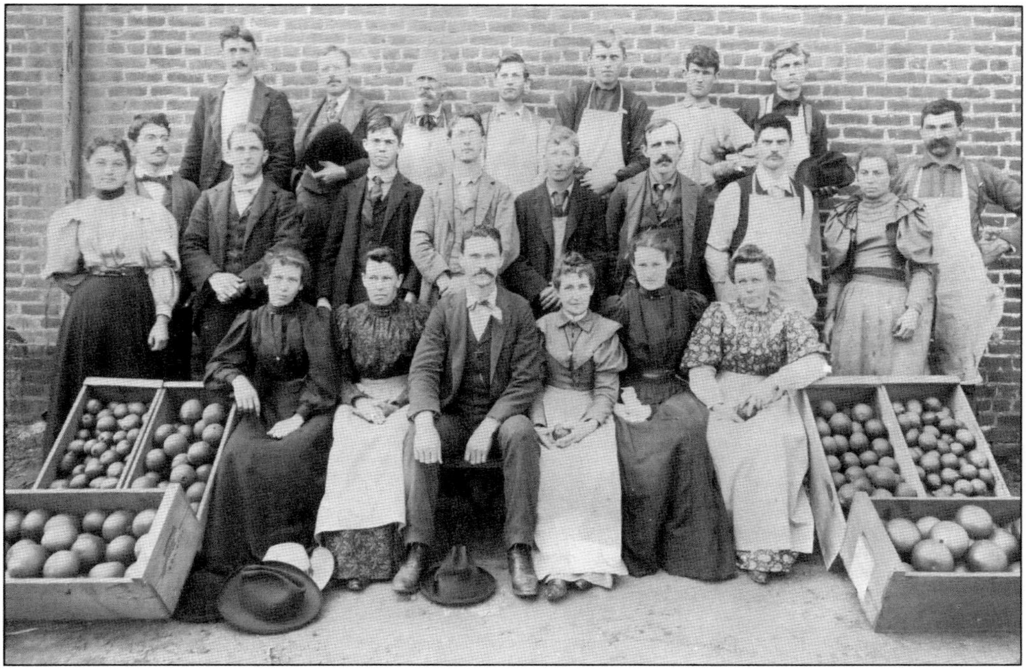

Employees of the San Diego Fruit Company. Working in the fruit packinghouse was a way women could respectably earn money. Frank Kimball notes in his diary of April 10, 1899, that Harriet Johnson packed 26 boxes of lemons in one day and earned $1.30. Seated at the center of his employees is the foreman, L. B. Barnes.

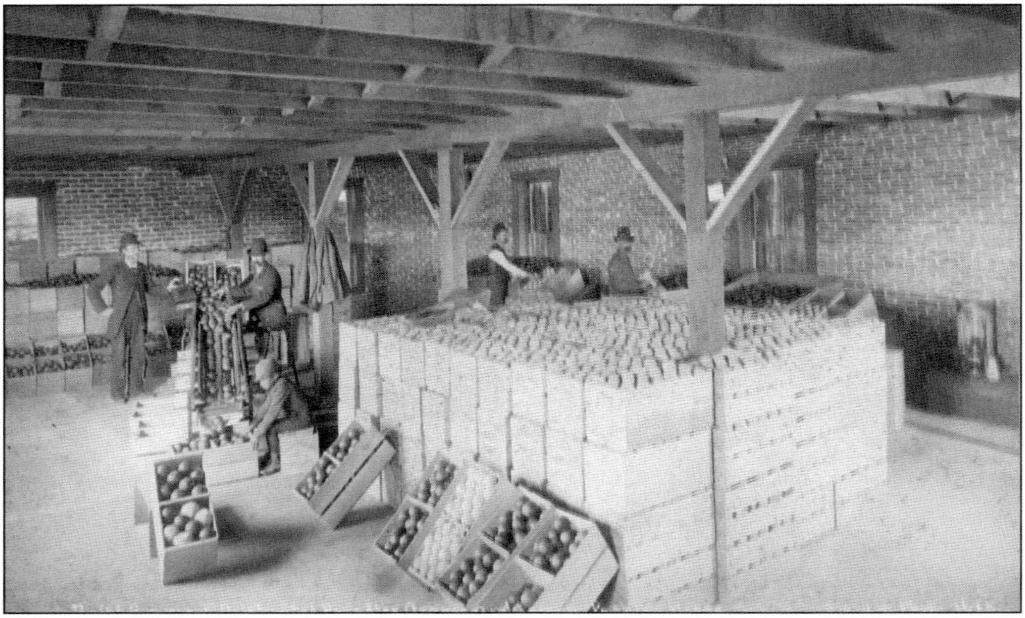

Ralph Granger Citrus Packinghouse. Granger had his oranges and lemons boxed in this brick packinghouse in Paradise Valley in preparation for shipment. Granger stands (left), inspecting his workers. Frank Kimball built the facility and used it for his citrus business until his financial collapse in the mid-1890s. Hard times forced him to sell his beloved orchards and packinghouse to Ralph Granger.

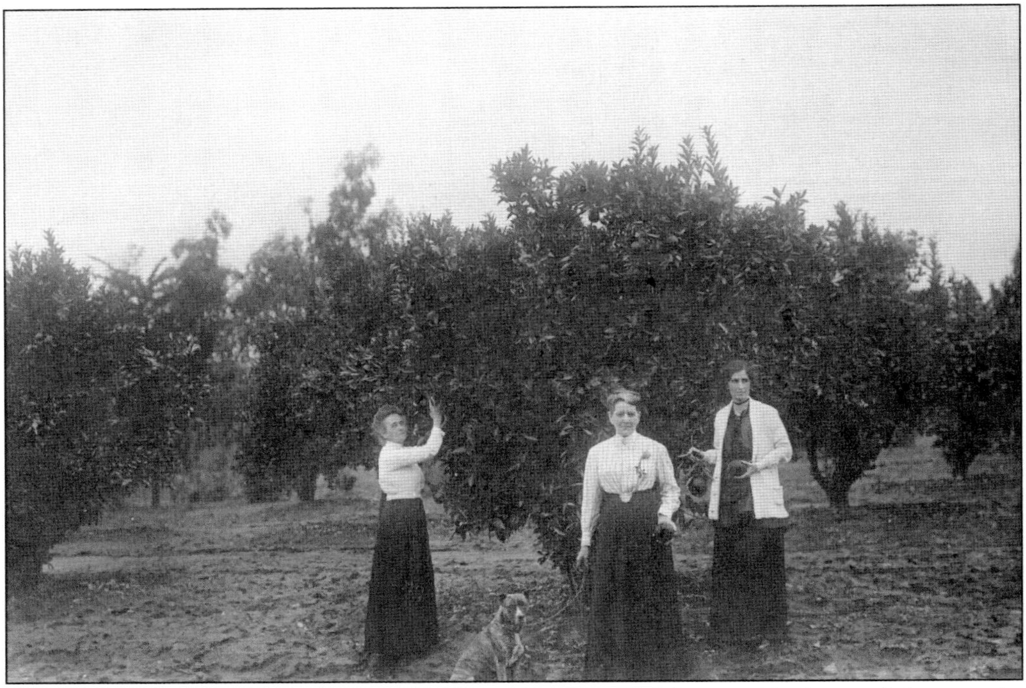

PICKING CITRUS AT OLIVEWOOD, C. 1910. Many Southern Californians liked to send photographs of folks picking oranges to Eastern friends. Receiving a picture such as this, while snow covered the ground, enticed many to move west. In this scene, Vesta Whicker (center) and her daughter Mae Waller Walker (far right) pose with a friend in the orchards of Olivewood, Warren and Flora Kimball's estate. Vesta kept house for Warren after Flora's death.

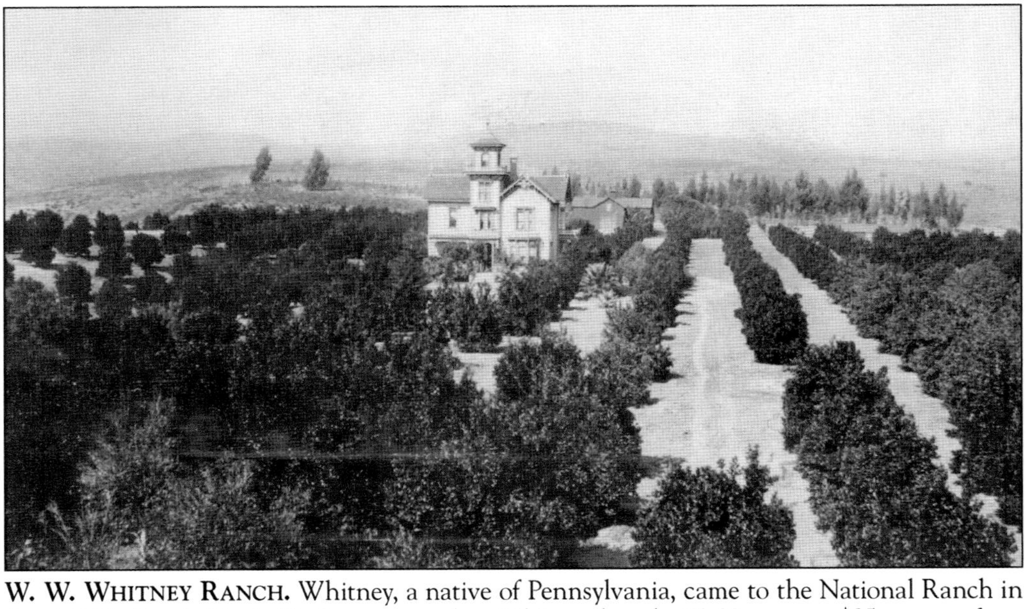

W. W. WHITNEY RANCH. Whitney, a native of Pennsylvania, came to the National Ranch in April 1873. Frank Kimball's diary states that Whitney bought 92.02 acres at $35 an acre from him. In 1886, Whitney's ranch in the Sweetwater River valley, which he named Highlands, supplied 3,000 oranges (at $1.50 per 100) for the Sixth Annual Citrus Fair in National City, held at Horticultural Hall.

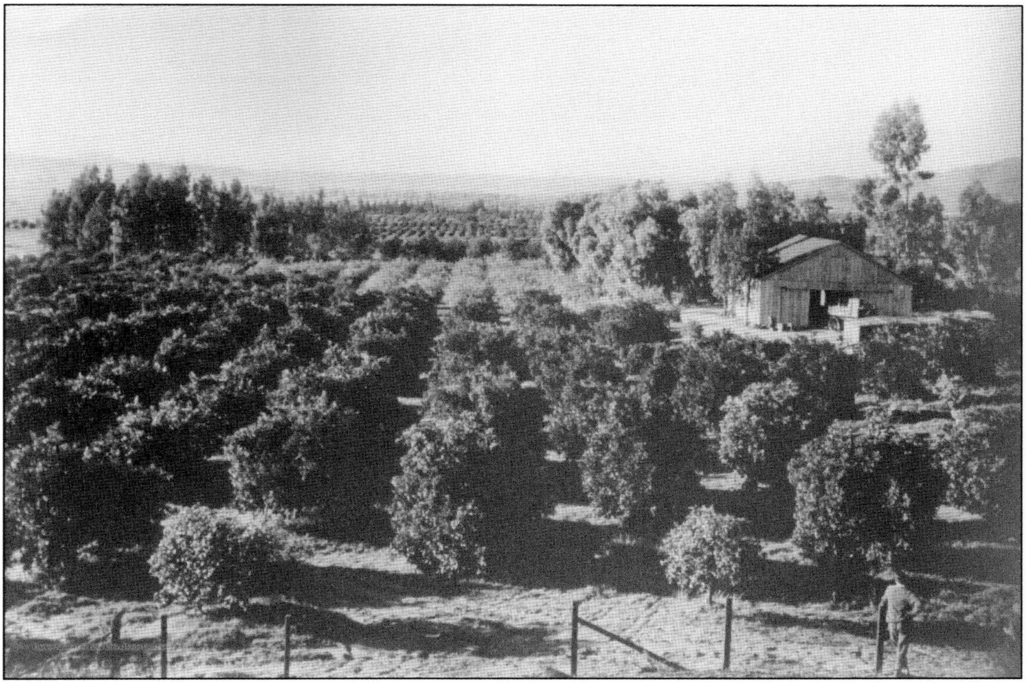

ORCHARD VISTA. Agriculture, first industry of the National Ranch, quickly changed the barren landscape to orchards of olive, lemon, and orange. Fruit farmers planted other fruits as well, such as avocado, pear, and fig. Even apples were grown; Frank Kimball notes in his diary of July 1885 that he brought 135 pounds of apples he had grown to the local grocer, Stevens and Blossom, and sold them for 5¢ per pound.

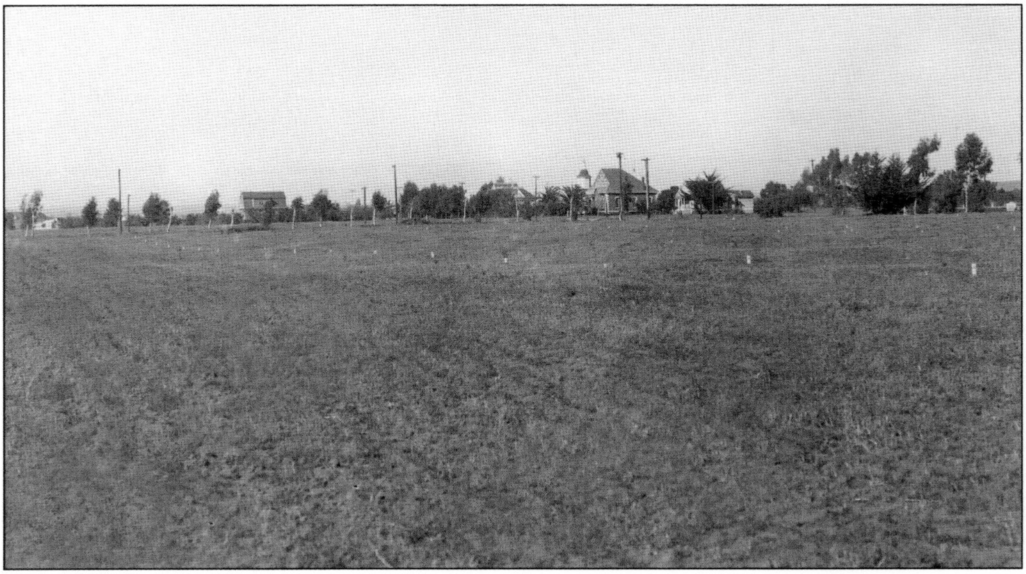

FIELDS WEST OF PALM AVENUE, C. 1912. This photograph looks across the field to Palm Avenue. The brick house with cupola at Seventeenth Street and Palm Avenue is the home of George F. Otto, who ran a nursery. The two-story house on the left is E. A. Wilson's home. Agriculture, the principal industry in National City, shipped in the month of April 1891 alone 101,360 pounds of oranges, 10,490 pounds of lemons, and 62,565 pounds of other fruit and vegetables.

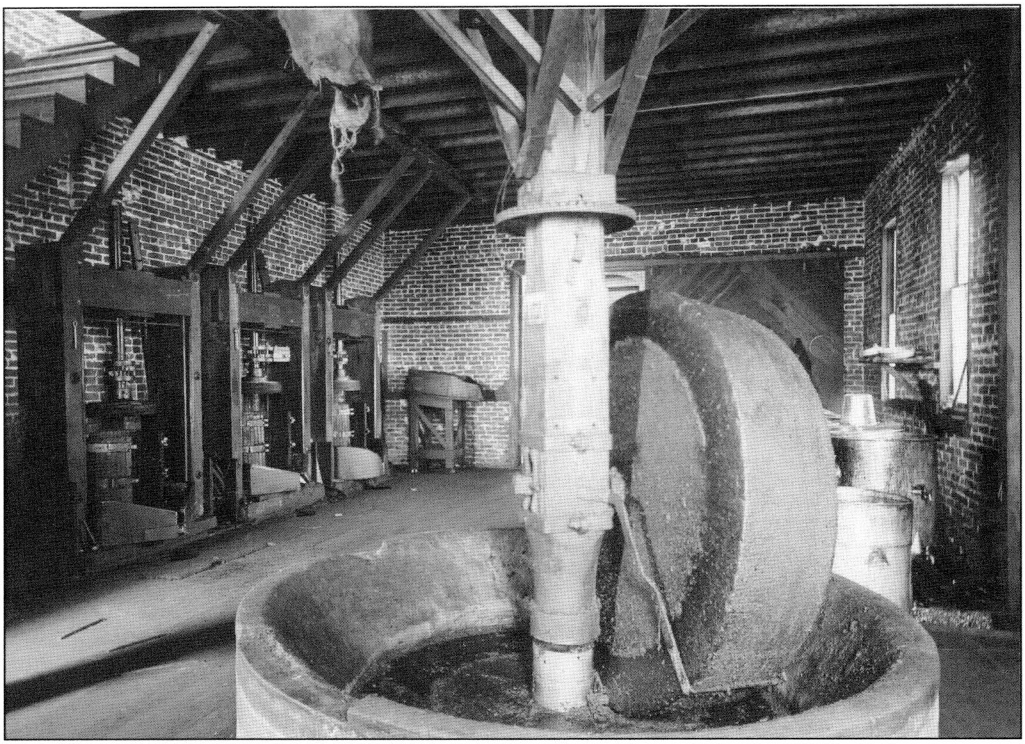

Olive Oil Grinding Stone. On January 4, 1887, Frank Kimball rode to San Diego and ordered the stone for his olive oil mill, located on the west side of Cleveland Avenue between Twenty-third and Twenty-fourth Streets. The magazine *Golden Era* noted in 1888 that the mill could handle 16 tons of olives daily. In 1896, Kimball was awarded the bronze medal from the Columbian Exposition (Chicago) for his olive oil exhibit.

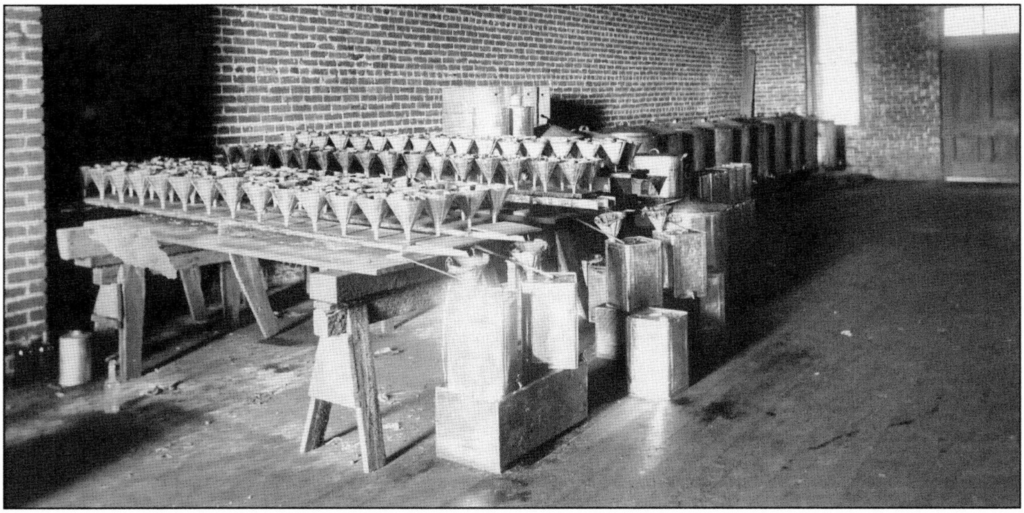

National Olive Oil Works Interior. Crushed fruit was strained through camel hair or vegetable fiber bags to obtain pure olive oil. Of all of Frank Kimball horticultural experiments, olives seem to have been his first love. In an 1872 diary entry, he wrote that he had staked out a lot on which to plant his little trees; the original cuttings had come from the San Diego Mission. At one time, approximately 30,000 olive trees grew on the National Ranch.

Nine

LEISURE ACTIVITIES

THE BEACH, THE MOUNTAINS, AND PLAIN FUN

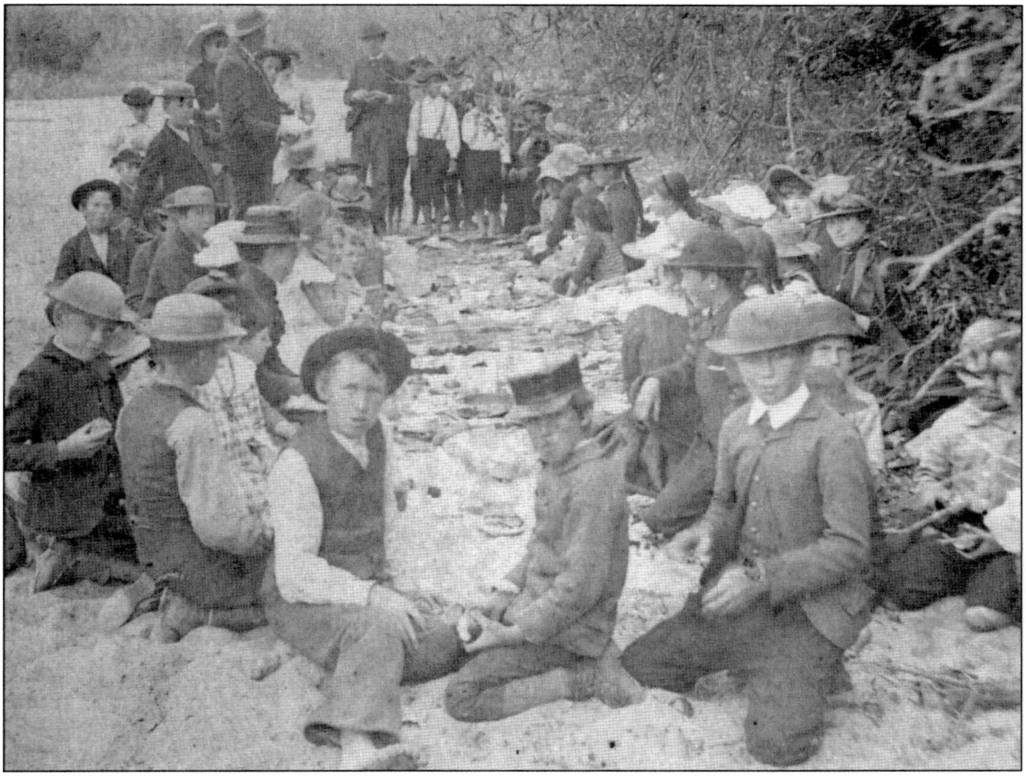

LYNWOOD GROVE, 1895. Soon after Frank Kimball settled on the National Ranch, he set aside 20 acres on the north side of the Sweetwater River, in the Bonita Valley, to be used for community picnics and celebrations. It was known as Lynwood Grove. Throughout the next 25 years, there are frequent mentions in both diaries and the local newspaper of community celebrations held there under the willows. In an era when travel was slow and difficult, and daily chores took up much more time than they do today, it is interesting that folks traveled so frequently on pleasure trips. Besides picnics—always a favorite—people enjoyed hunting trips to the inland hills and mountains, rabbit shooting trips to Coronado, and days spent by the waves at the beach. Boating trips on the bay were also very popular. Folks valued community events and entertainment in this rural community. A large percentage of the new arrivals, like the Kimballs themselves, came from New England, so it is not surprising that a New England Society quickly formed. Numerous other social organizations followed. On a more pragmatic side, the National Grange formed in 1874 to focus on agricultural issues.

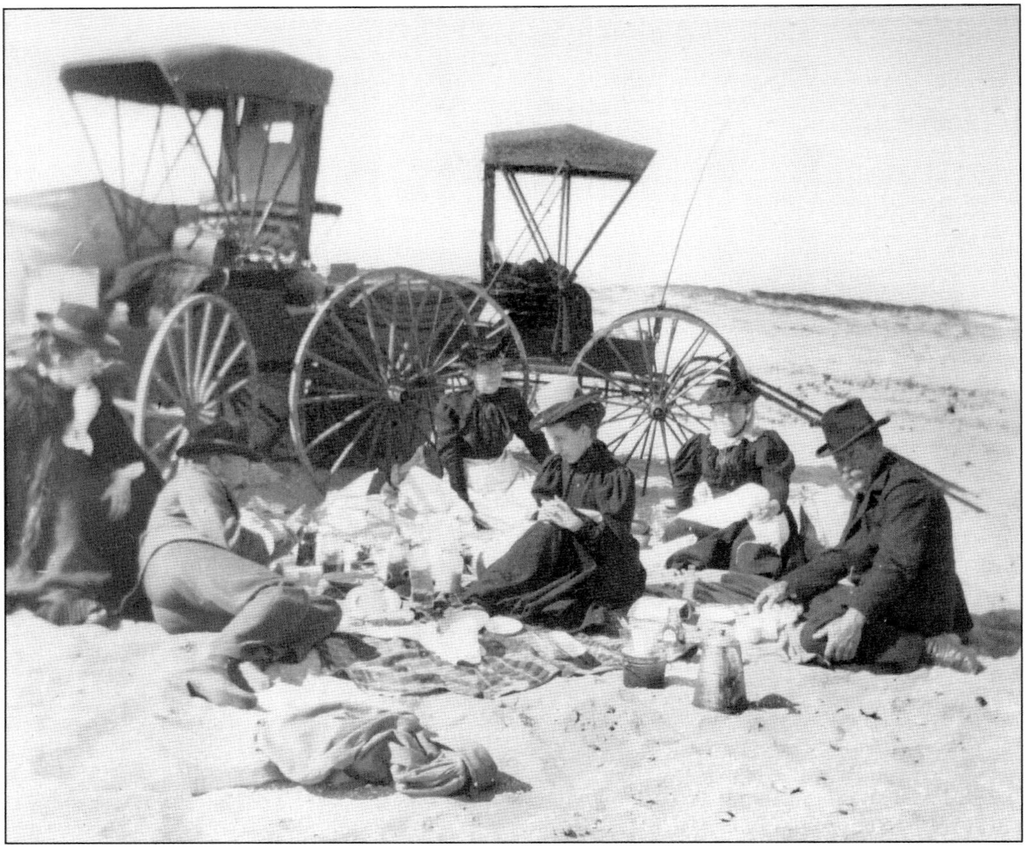

EVANS FAMILY PICNIC. Slow travel over dirt roads did not deter families from sightseeing and enjoying the outdoors. The Cicero Evans family and friends rode to the beach in buggies for a picnic in the fresh sea air. Evans came to National City in 1902 to be principal of National City High School; he purchased a 10.5-acre lemon orchard on which to live.

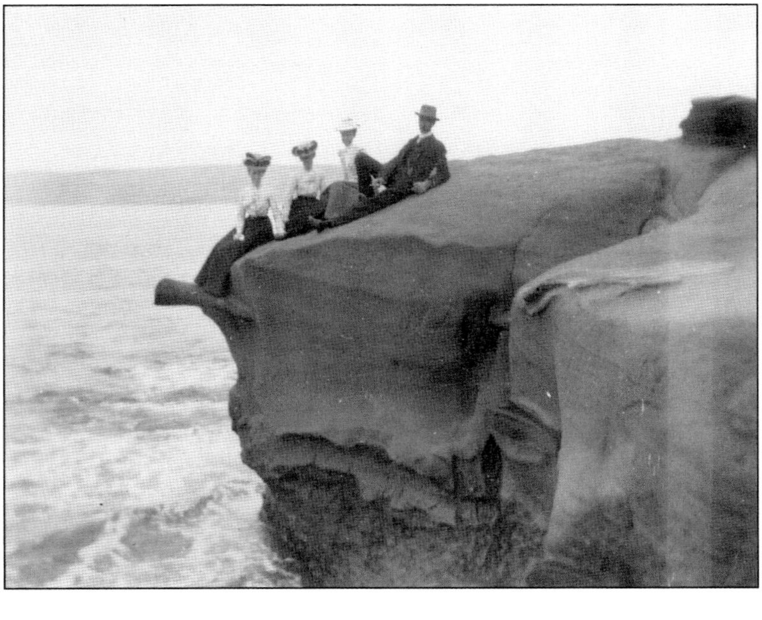

TRIP TO LA JOLLA. The seaside resort of La Jolla proved a popular, scenic destination for a family holiday. Cicero Evans, his wife, Alice, daughter Ava, and a friend chose a risky but picturesque spot for a photograph on the bluffs overlooking the Pacific Ocean.

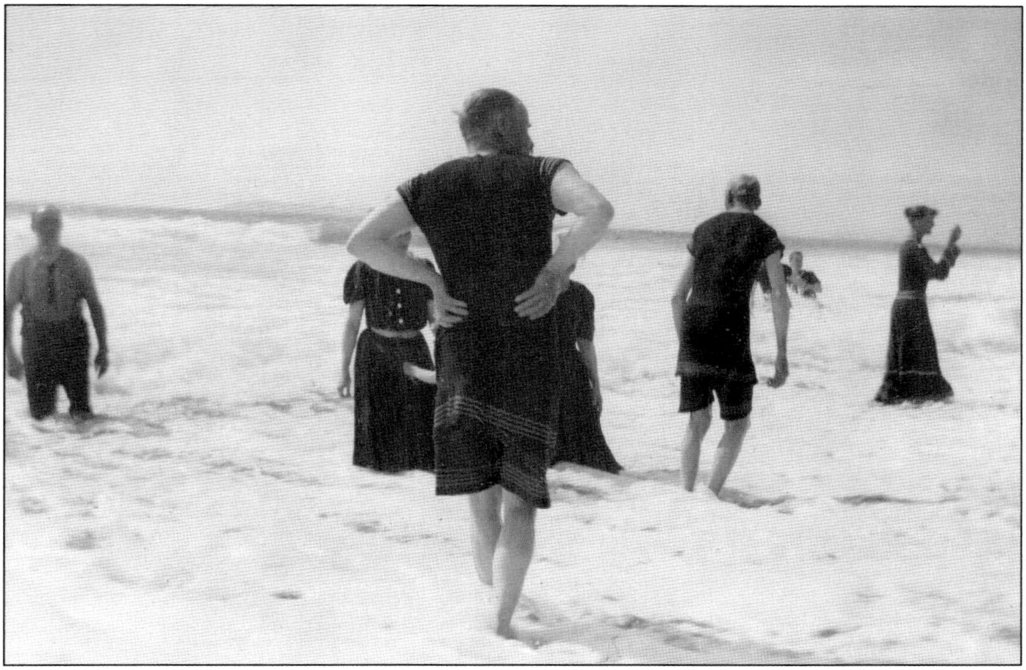

EVANS FAMILY ON THE SILVER STRAND, CORONADO. The Mediterranean climate of National City and the surrounding area made it possible for families like the Evanses to enjoy the water nearly year-round. Women wore modest bathing suits made of dark wool, over bloomers, with matching hats, shoes, and stockings. Frank Kimball noted in his diary of July 4, 1877, "National Independence Day, which I observed by going to the bay to bathe in A.M."

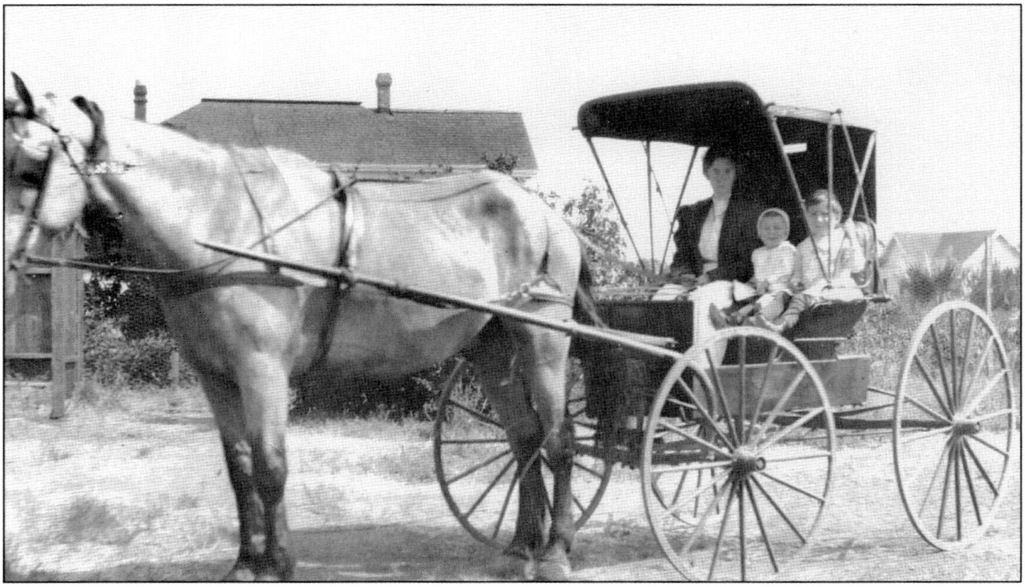

HORSE-AND-BUGGY TRANSPORTATION, 1909. Stopping at Sixteenth Street and K Avenue, M. Grace Mizony and her two young sons, Herbert and Theo, went out for a ride. The National Carriage Manufacturing Company (formerly located at Twenty-third Street and National City Boulevard) built the buggy Grace's parents, James and Mabel O'Connell, purchased in 1889. Streets were still dirt at this time.

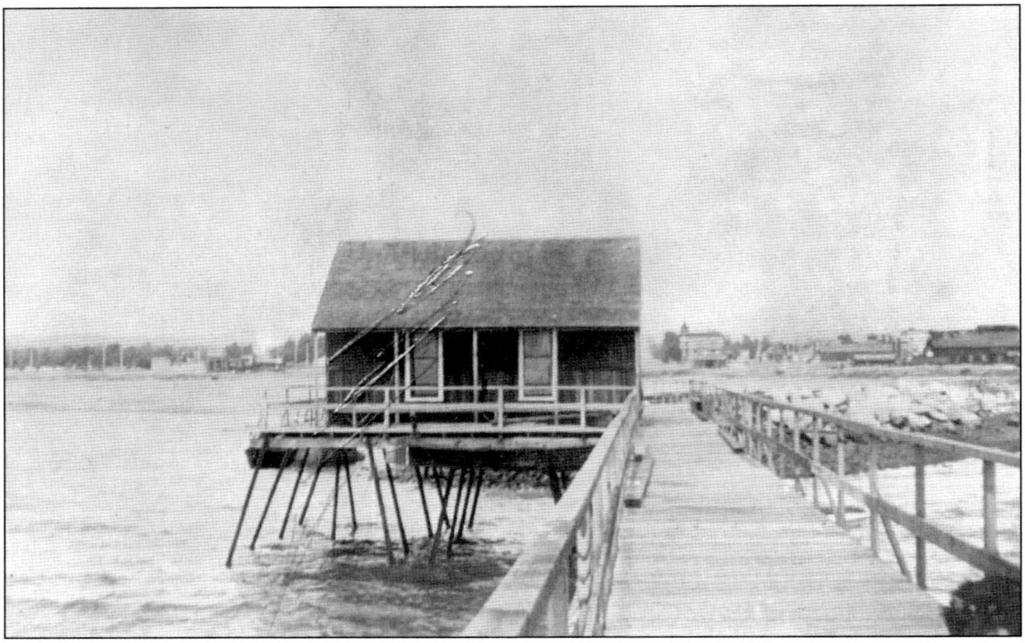

Pleasure Wharf with Bathhouse. When railroad officials heard the plan to build a wharf on the bay, they refused to let any lumber be transported across their tracks to the shore, saying that they would treat this as an act of trespass. The promoters of this idea instead floated the lumber down the bay by raft, which Fred Copeland used to extend the pleasure wharf 400 feet out into the water. Here for the first time on the bay, bathers could enjoy the water without the dangers or discomforts of stingrays and mud.

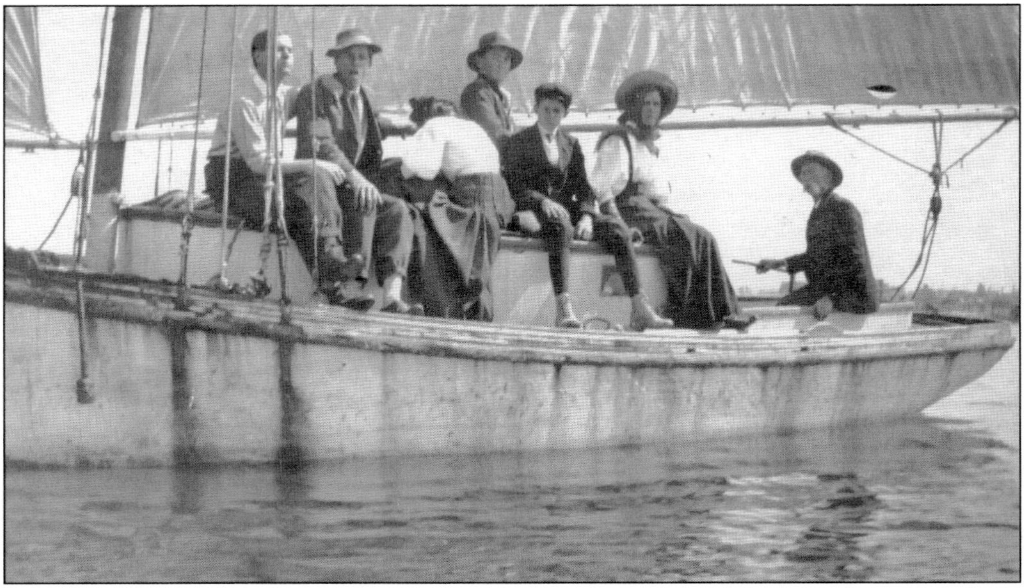

The Yacht *Alpha*, c. 1908. At the tiller sits Jeremiah O'Connell, owner of the *Alpha* and also city marshal. The *National Record* of January 13, 1887, described one such outing as follows: "A party of young folks left San Diego wharf last Saturday evening in the yacht *Nellie*, for a moonlight trip to the Coronado islands. They spent Sunday at the islands and returned home late Sunday evening. All report a very pleasant trip."

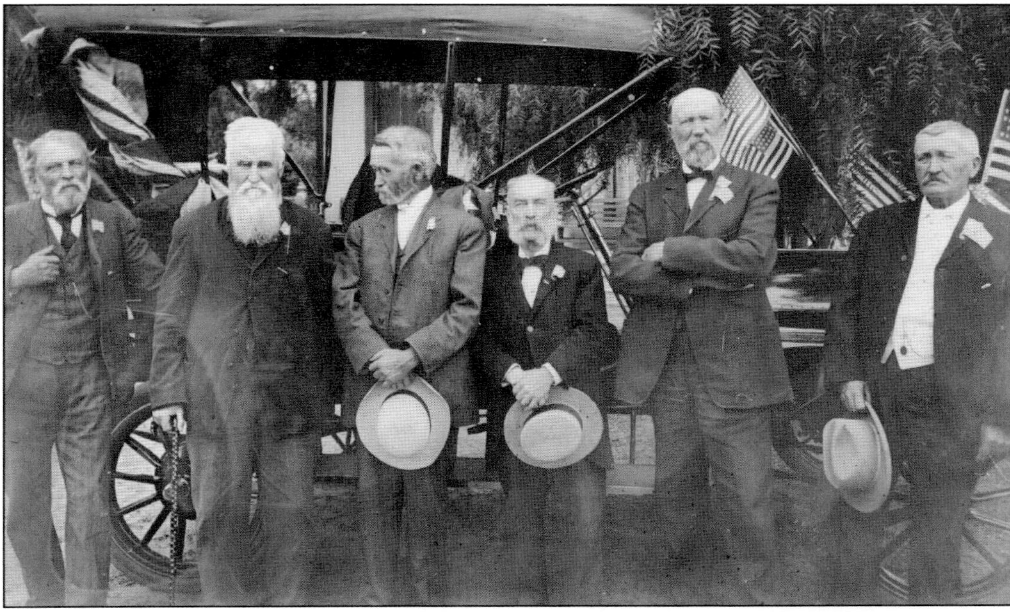

Grand Army of the Republic (GAR), 1910. Veterans of the Civil War organized the GAR in 1866; soon posts grew up in every state of the union. Here the Grand Army of the Republic members pose alongside Warren Kimball (who was in San Francisco during the Civil War). Standing from left to right are Warren C. Kimball, Peleg T. Griffith, Capt. M. J. Hogarty, George W. Grant (city clerk), Gerhard Schutte, and Phil Evans (city marshal).

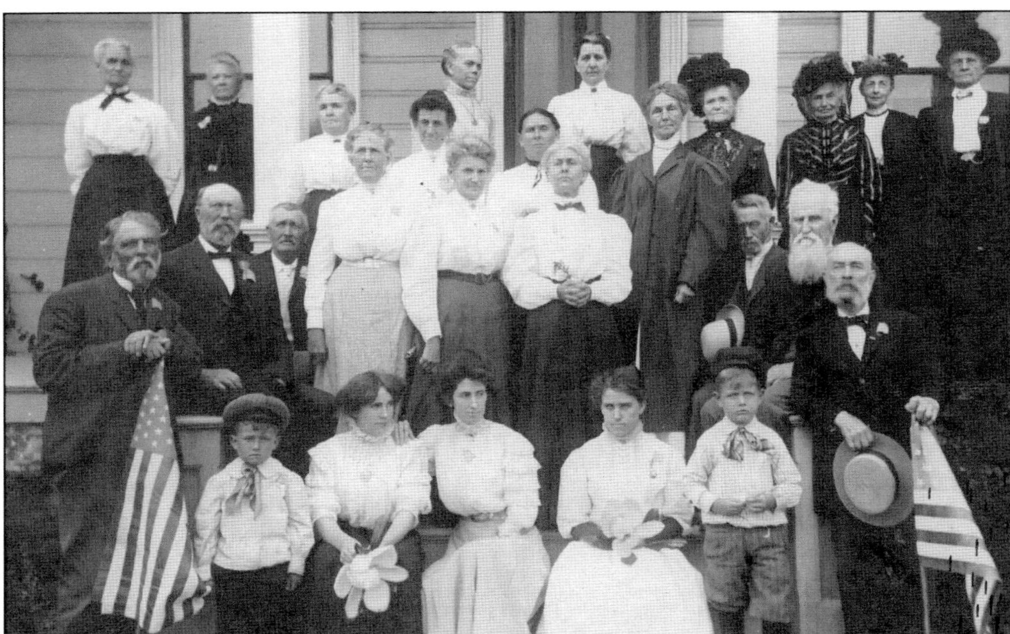

National City Ladies of the Grand Army of the Republic, 1910. Circle No. 48 celebrated Flag Day on the front porch of Warren Kimball's Olivewood. Mae Walker sits third from left. Warren Kimball stands on the left, holding the flag, while his housekeeper, Vesta Whicker, stands in front of the doorway.

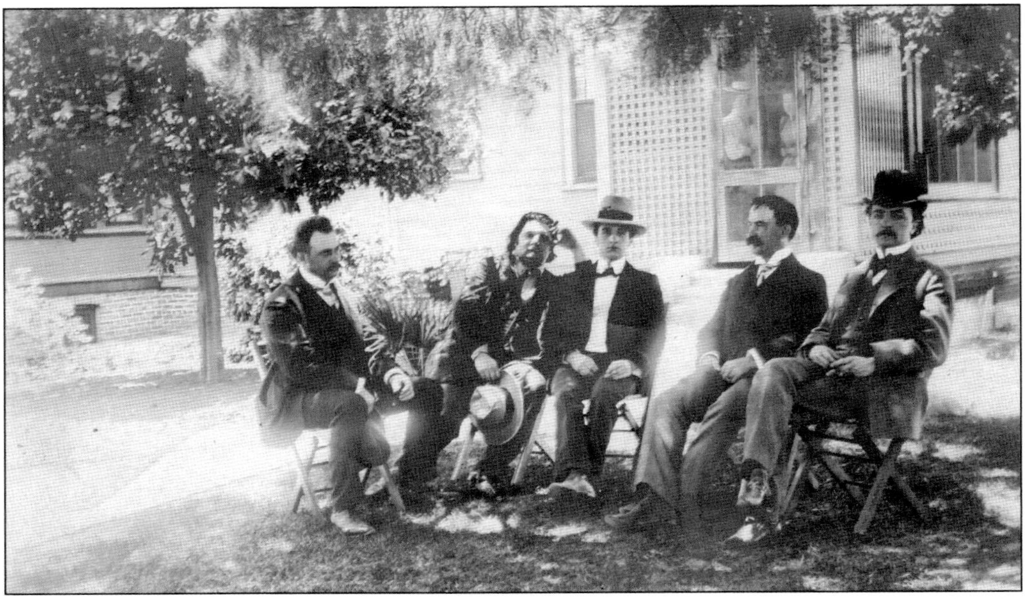

YSAYE CHAMBER MUSIC ENSEMBLE, 1899. Ralph Granger invited many musicians to play for him in his private music hall—and they came, attracted by his collection of Stradivarius and Guarnerius violins. Enjoying the California sunshine are, from left to right, Victor Thrane (tour manager), Eugene Ysaye (violinist), Jean Gérardy (cellist), Henri Marteau (violinist), and Aimé Lachaume (French pianist). Jessie Granger and her sister Medora Hastings peer from behind the kitchen door.

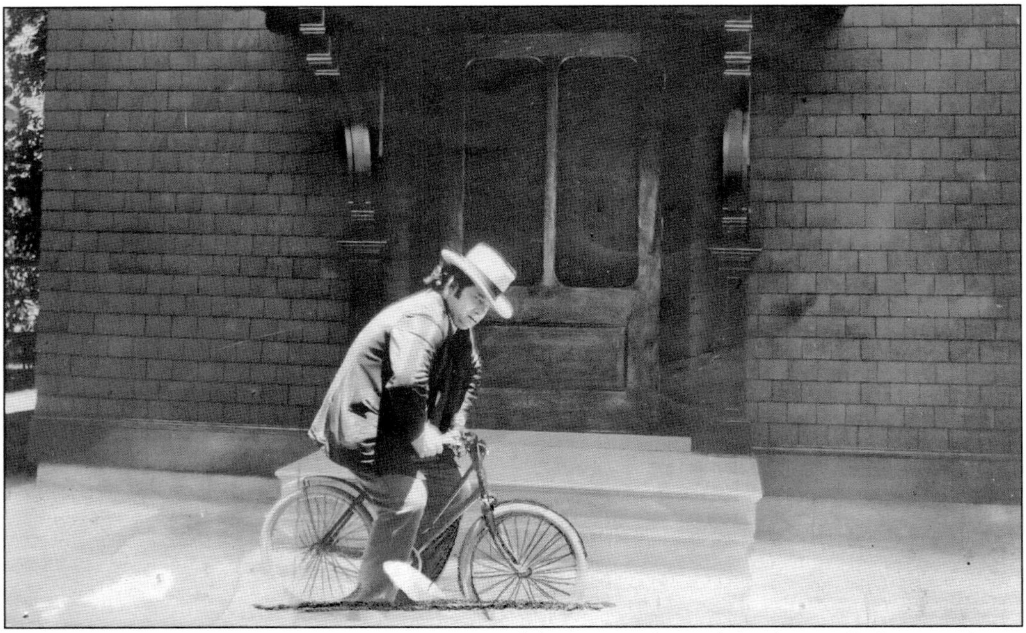

EUGENE YSAYE AT GRANGER'S MUSIC HALL. Ralph Granger hosted the famous Belgian violinist Eugene Ysaye (1858–1931) at his house in Paradise Valley. Ysaye had a sense of humor, as can be seen in this photograph, where he is pictured riding Granger's daughter Rachel's bicycle in front of the music hall. This building, today known as Granger Music Hall, is listed on the National Register of Historic Places.

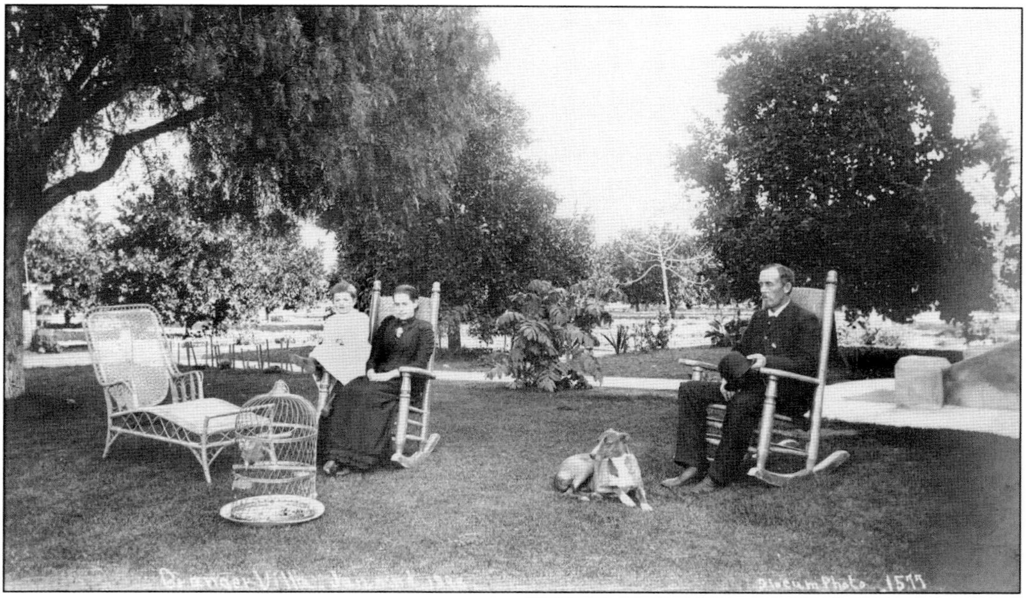

GRANGER VILLA, JANUARY 2, 1898. Relaxing in the backyard are, from left to right, Ruth Baldwin (a young Granger cousin), Madora Hastings (Granger's sister-in-law), and Ralph Granger. In the large birdcage sits a macaw, a Granger pet that was allowed to fly free around the orchards. The Grangers would put a large dish outside the back door to feed their pets. It was said that the macaw would push the dogs and cats out of the way when it wanted to eat.

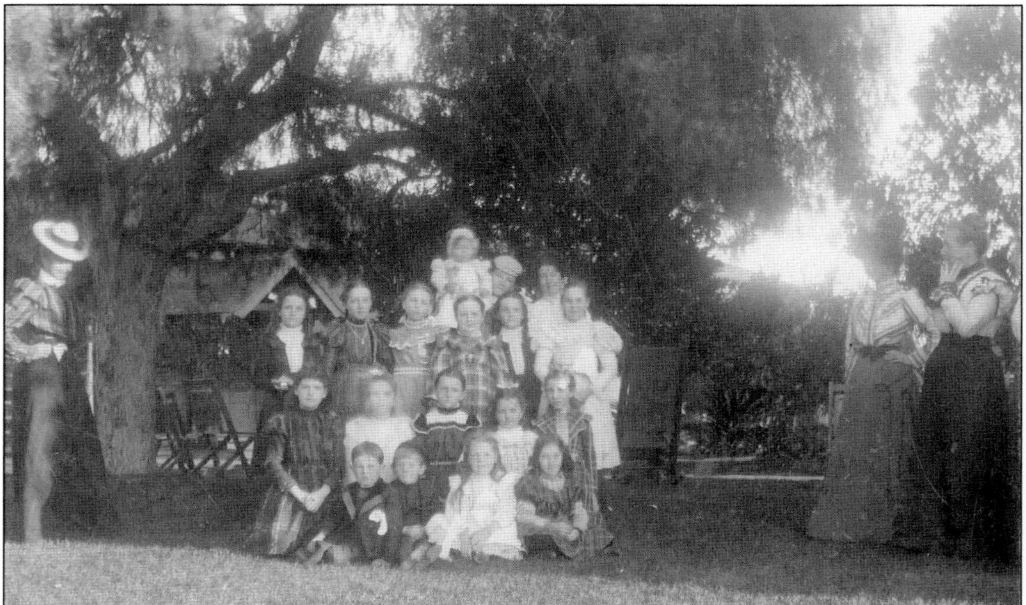

RACHEL GRANGER'S BIRTHDAY PARTY. Posed under a California pepper tree are, from left to right, (first row) Herman Sholl, Paul Granger, Rachel Granger, and unidentified. In the third row, third from left, stands Lilian Rice, who later earned a degree in architecture from the University of California, Berkeley, and designed Rancho Santa Fe. Standing at right are Jessie Granger and Eloise Franklin, the ranch manager's wife. In the background stands Granger's music hall, built in 1896.

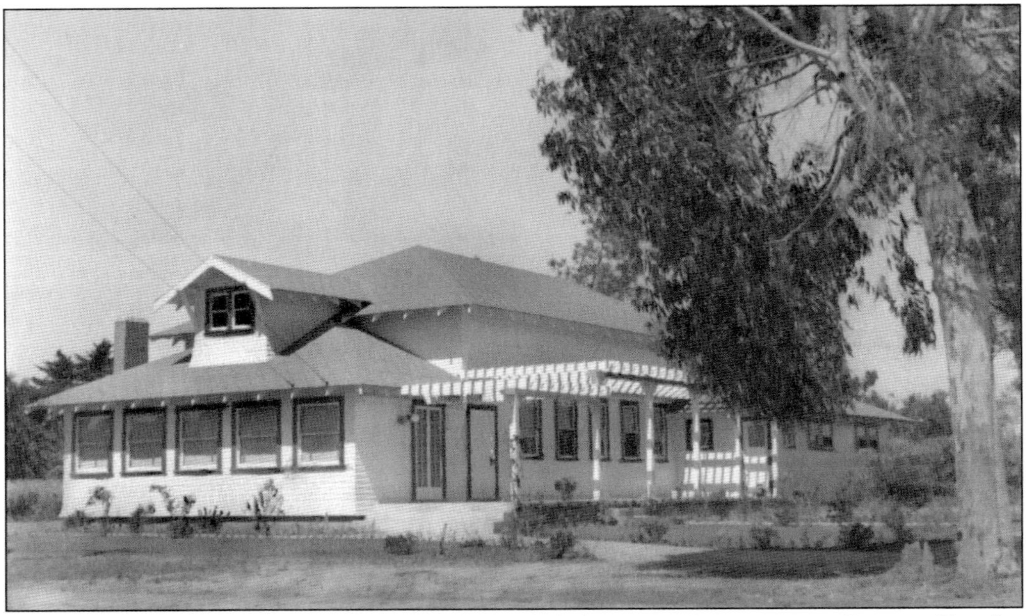

OLIVEWOOD CLUB HOUSE. Flora Kimball founded the Home Improvement Society, Tuesday Club in 1895 for social, literary, and civic endeavors. This group of women was reorganized as the Olivewood Woman's Club in 1908. In 1910, Warren Kimball built a proper meetinghouse for the women, located on a corner of his property at F Avenue and Twenty-fourth Street. He donated it to the club as a memorial to his beloved wife, Flora.

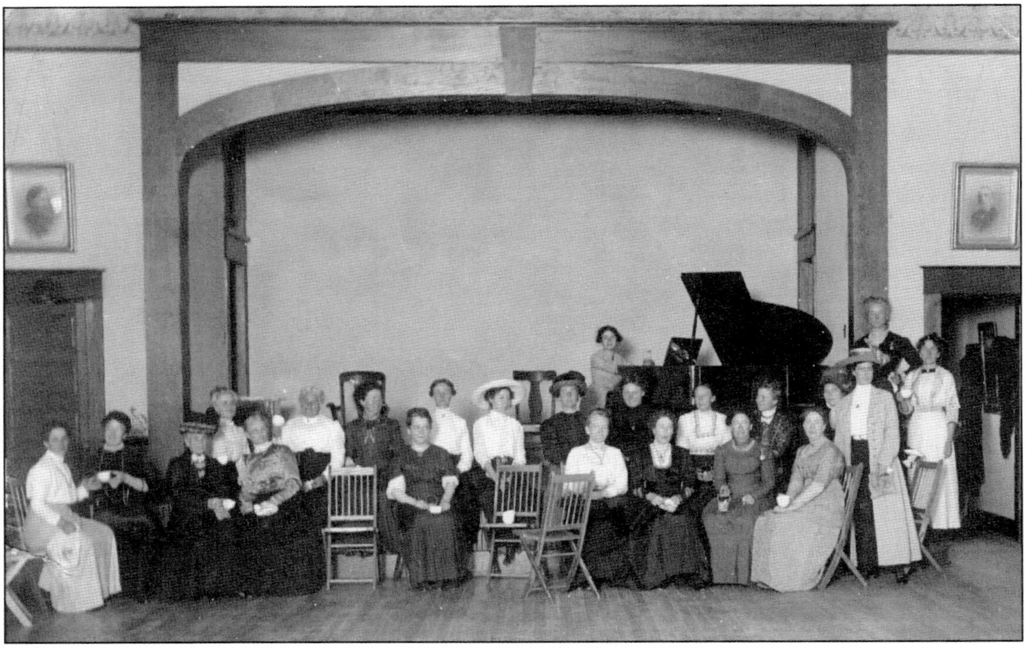

OLIVEWOOD CLUB HOUSE INTERIOR. This photograph was taken soon after the clubhouse was built. A picture of Flora Kimball may be seen on the left, hanging over the door, while Warren Kimball's image hangs to the right. Holding teacups, the women pose around the piano; refreshments followed meetings and entertainment. By 1913, the club had over 100 members, drawn by the social and philanthropic activities of the women.

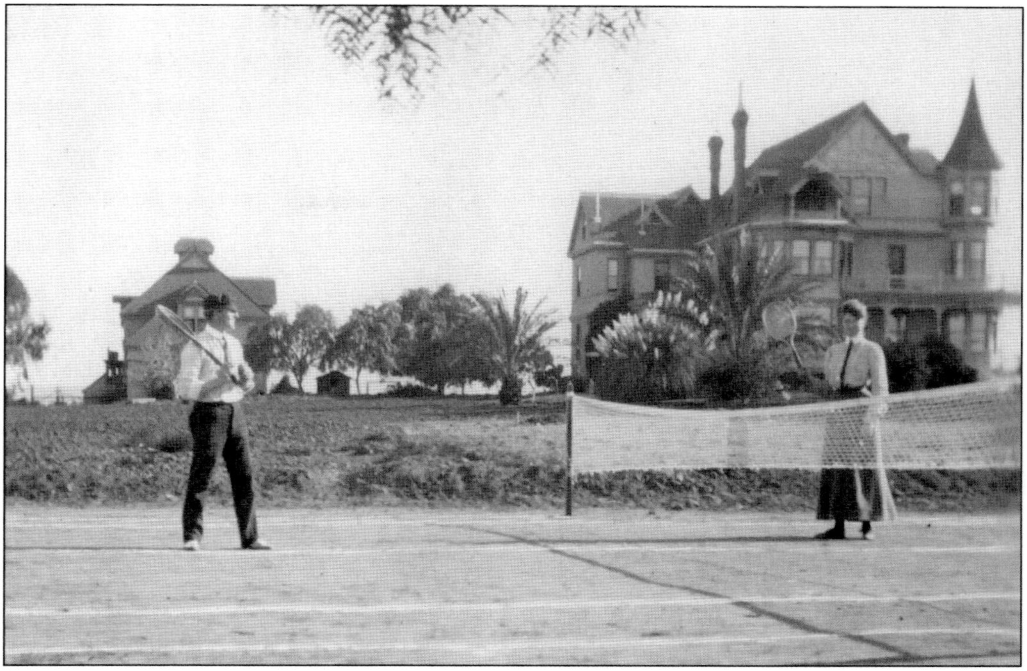

TENNIS COURTS AT DICKINSON-BOAL HOUSE, C. 1900. After the first tennis club was organized at Wimbledon, England, in 1875, the popularity of the game rapidly increased on both sides of the ocean, especially among the upper classes. Tennis courts were a novelty in National City when the Dickinson family had this one built, west of the carriage house (on the left) and the main house. While women did play the game at the turn of the 20th century, they were greatly hampered by long skirts. (Courtesy of Mary Maddox Grandell.)

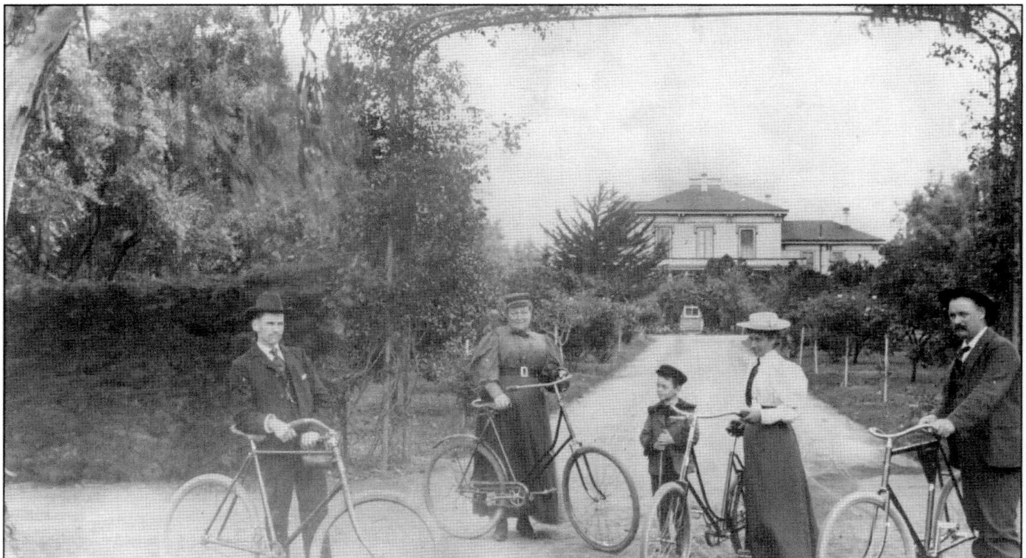

BICYCLING, C. 1895. At the gates to Olivewood on Twenty-fourth Street, stand, from left to right, J. Roscoe Morrill, Clara Morrill, Clarence M. Smith, Alice Morrill Smith, and George B. Smith with their bicycles. They probably are taking a much-needed rest to catch their breath, since the road is on a rather steep incline.

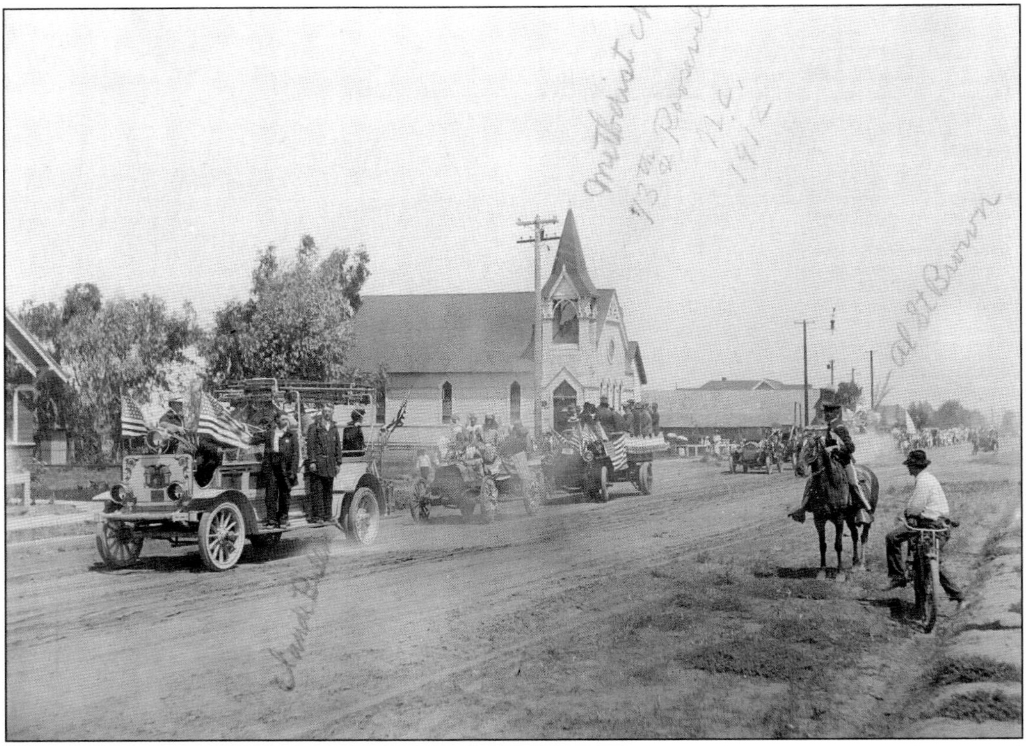

Fourth of July Parade, 1912. The city's new Seagrave fire truck participates in the annual community parade and festivities. The First Methodist Church stands in the center at Thirteenth Street and Roosevelt Avenue. While more and more people relied on automobile power, the horse was still a common sight on the dusty roads of National City.

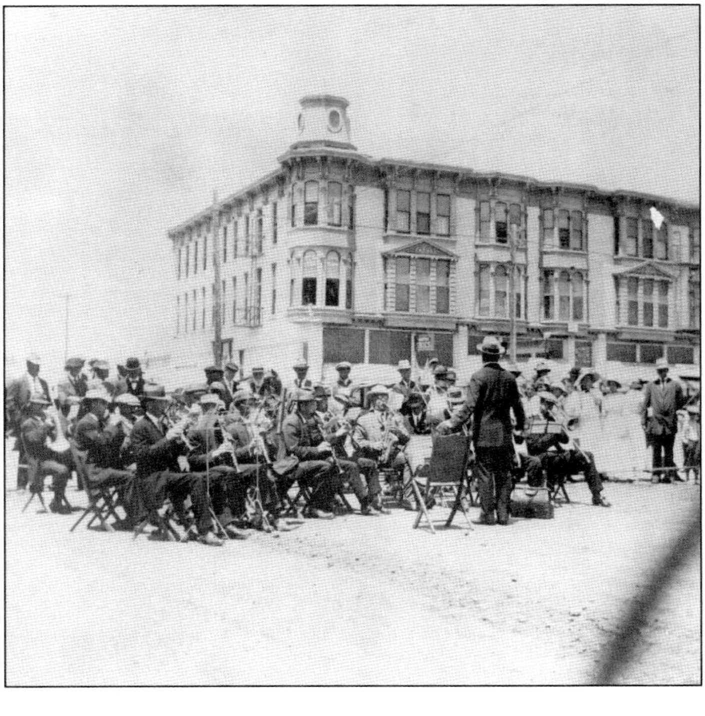

The National City Park Band, July 4, 1913. Their first performance could not have been held at a more visible site than the intersection of Eighth Street and National City Boulevard, with the imposing Steele building in the background. Claus V. S. Wycoff was hired to conduct the group. The band's bylaws proposed that it would become a permanent organization for the enjoyment National City's citizens.

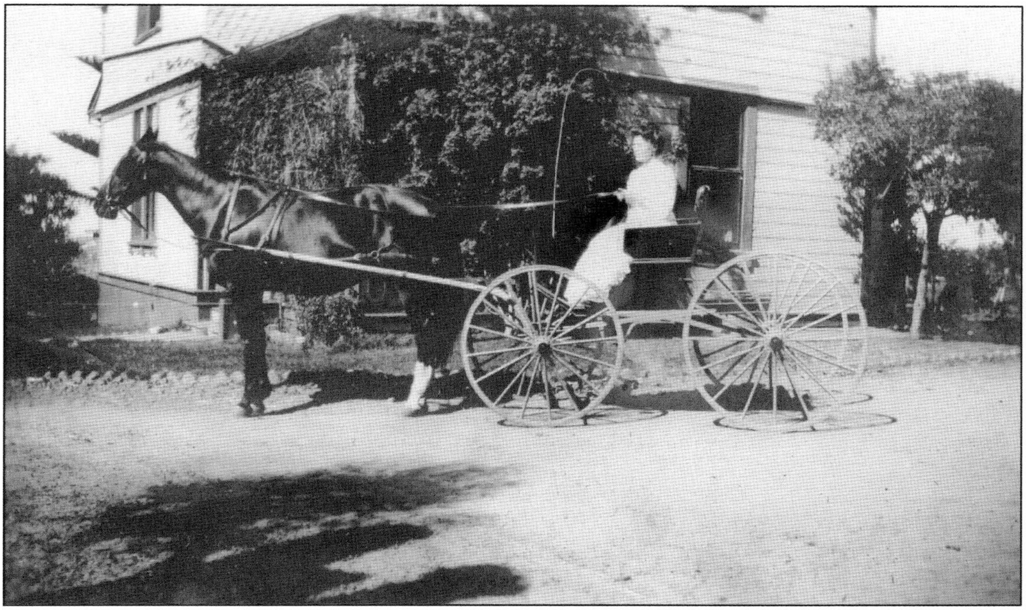

OLD LUCY AND AVA EVANS. Ready for a carriage ride, Ava is pictured in front of her parents' home, that of Cicero and Alice Evans, at 1129 J Avenue. Horses, such as Old Lucy, provided transportation for people well into the second decade of the 20th century; however, the advent of the automobile was on the way.

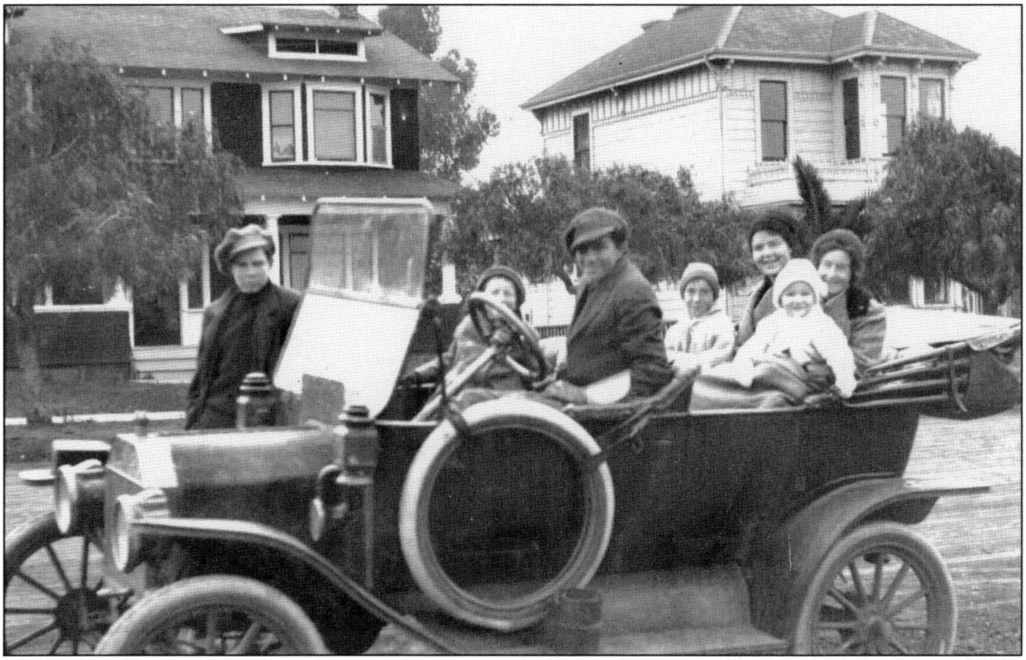

TRIP TO THE CUYAMACA MOUNTAINS, 1915. Touring was always popular in National City, but by the end of the Kimball era, the automobile became increasingly the mode of choice. Shown in front of 614 Highland Avenue, the 1914 Model T holds, from left to right, Paul Colburn, Herbert Mizony, Howard Colburn, Theo Mizony, Marjorie Colburn, M. Grace Mizony, and Edgar Mizony.

ACROSS AMERICA, PEOPLE ARE DISCOVERING SOMETHING WONDERFUL. *THEIR HERITAGE.*

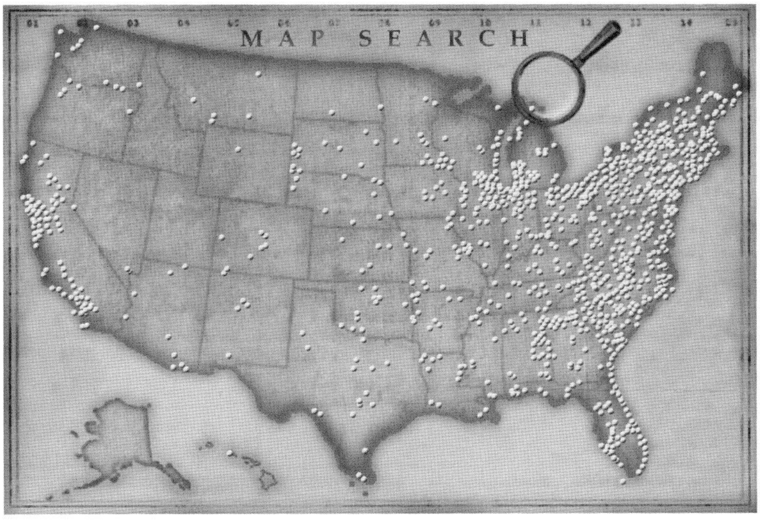